Creating Support for Effective Literacy Education

Creating Support for Effective Literacy Education

WORKSHOP MATERIALS AND HANDOUTS

Constance Weaver
Western Michigan University

Lorraine Gillmeister-Krause
Soulanges Elementary

Grace Vento-Zogby
Sauquoit Valley Elementary

Heinemann

PORTSMOUTH, NH

HEINEMANN
A division of Reed Elsevier Inc.
361 Hanover Street
Portsmouth, NH 03801-3912

Offices and agents throughout the world

The authors and publisher thank those who generously gave permission to reprint borrowed material:

Illustration from *The Bookstore Mouse* by Peggy Christian, illustration copyright © 1995 by Gary A. Lippincott, reproduced by permission of Harcourt Brace & Company.

"Galoshes" from *Stories to Begin On* by Rhoda W. Bacmeister. Copyright 1940 by E. P. Dutton, renewed © 1968 by Rhoda W. Bacmeister. Used by permission of Dutton Children's Books, a division of Penguin Books USA Inc.

Excerpts from *Johnny Tremain* by Esther Forbes. Reprinted by permission of Frances Collin, Literary Agent. Copyright © 1943 by Esther Forbes Hoskins. Copyright © renewed 1971 by Linwood M. Erskine, Jr., Executor of the Estate.

Library of Congress Cataloging-in-Publication Data

Weaver, Constance.
  Creating support for effective literacy education : workshop
materials and handouts / Constance Weaver, Lorraine Gillmeister-
Krause, Grace Vento-Zogby.
    p.   cm.
  Includes bibliographical references.
  ISBN 0-435-08894-7
  1. Reading—Language experience approach.   2. Reading—Aids and
devices.   3. Language arts.   4. Language arts—Audio-visual aids.
  I. Gillmeister-Krause, Lorraine.   II. Vento-Zogby, Grace.
  III. Title.
  LB1050.35.W43   1996
  372.4¢14—dc20   96-33994
                                                              CIP

Editor: Scott Mahler
Production: Melissa L. Inglis
Text design: Jenny Jensen Greenleaf
Text illustrations: Rick F. Racich and Jenny Jensen Greenleaf
Cover design: Michael Leary
Manufacturing: Louise Richardson

Printed in the United States of America on acid-free paper
00 99 98 97 96 DA 1 2 3 4 5 6 7 8 9

This book is dedicated to

Rolland and John

Peter and Dorothy

Eli and Mary Ellen

with gratitude for their inspiration and support

CONTENTS

INTRODUCTION

PART ONE: Workshop and Transparency Materials

Section 1: Learning Theory and the Acquisition of Language and Literacy
Suggestions and background information 3
Learning skills 3
    T1.1   Learning skills naturally
    T1.2   Cartoon of child practicing swimming strokes
    T1.3   What promotes or inhibits learning?
Models of learning 5
    T1.4   Cambourne: Some conditions for language and literacy learning
    T1.5   Holdaway's natural learning model
    T1.6   A constructivist model of learning
    T1.7   Transmission and transactional models
Development of language and literacy 7
    T1.8   Development of language and literacy
Contrasting models for teaching minilessons 8
    T1.9   Behavioral model vs. constructivist model (# 1)
    T1.10 Behavioral model vs. constructivist model (# 2)

Section 2: Language Acquisition: Learning to Talk
Suggestions and background information 21
Introducing language acquisition 21
    T2.1   Learning the language
    T2.2   Past tense rule
More on what children learn 22
    T2.3   First sentences
    T2.4   Patterns of negation
Drawing conclusions 23
    T2.5   How adults facilitate language acquisition
    T2.6   Cartoon of parent and child

Section 3: The Reading Process
Suggestions and background information 31
Anticipation guide on reading

How we transact with texts

Introduction to the reading process 31
    T3.1   Learning to read is like
    T3.2   Discussion questions on reading
    T3.3   Bringing meaning to a text: "Song of the Deranged Sailor"
Sources of information in the reading process 33
    T3.4a "The Animal School"
    T3.4b "The Animal School" (continuation)
    T3.4c "The Animal School" (continuation)
Context and word pronunciation 34
    T3.5   Context and word pronunciation
Context and word meanings 35
    T3.6   Context and word meanings (# 1)
    T3.7   Context and word meanings (# 2)
Getting words and getting meaning 35
    T3.8   Passage to read (on cricket)
    T3.9   Passage from *The Bookstore Mouse*
    T3.10 Words and comprehension (on chlorecyclizine)
Nonsense passages and the reading process 36
    T3.11 "A flannerby barp for Nall"
    T3.12 "The blonke"
Contrasting models of reading 38
    T3.13 Skills model of the reading process
    T3.14 Constructivist model of the reading process
Reading as a dance 39
    T3.15 "Learning to Dance"

Insights from miscues

Good readers' miscues 40
    T3.16 Anne's miscues
    T3.17 First graders' miscues on words in isolation
    T3.18 Good readers' miscues
    T3.19a Jay's miscues
    T3.19b Jay's miscues (continuation)
    T3.20 Questions about strategies
    T3.21 Jay's miscues: Evidence of predicting
    T3.22 Jay's restructuring of text
    T3.23 Characteristics of good readers
    T3.24 Reading levels

Section 4: Teaching and Learning to Read

Suggestions and background information 73
Facilitating reading acquisition 73
    T4.1   How adults facilitate reading acquisition
Stilted versus natural texts 73
    T4.2   Passage to illustrate basalese: "Let's Cook!"
    T4.3   Passage resembling Informal Reading Inventory: "Walk to the Pond"
    T4.4   "Are you sleeping?" (#1) (in English and in French)

T4.5   "Are you sleeping?" (#2) (in German, with another simple text in German)
Shared Book Experience 74
     T4.6   Shared Book Experience: What it typically includes
     T4.7   Shared Book Experience: What can be taught and learned
     T4.8a Shared Book Experience: What can be learned
     T4.8b Shared Book Experience: What can be learned (continuation)
     T4.9   Shared Book Experience: Advantages
A literacy program and literacy events 75
     T4.10 Components of a literacy program
     T4.11 Ways to help children participate in literacy events
Teaching reading/developing reading 79
     T4.12 Comparison between teaching reading and developing reading

Section 5: Phonics and the Teaching of Phonics
Suggestions and background information 94
Poem about letter/sound relations 95
     T5.1   "Phonics Fun"
Spellings and sounds 95
     T5.2   Spelling/sound relationships
     T5.3   Dialect differences
Phonics and words 96
     T5.4   Getting words (# 1)
     T5.5   Getting words (# 2)
Vowel rules 99
     T5.6   Vowel rules (# 1)
     T5.7   Vowel rules (# 2)
     T5.8   Vowel rules (# 3)
     T5.9   Vowel rules (# 4)
Isolated phonics lessons 100
     T5.10 Phonics lessons
Onsets and rimes 100
     T5.11 Some common onsets
     T5.12 Some common rimes
     T5.13 Onsets and rimes (# 1)
     T5.14 Onsets and rimes (# 2)
     T5.15 Onsets and rimes (# 3)
Determining lesson 101
     T5.16a Determining lesson (part 1)
     T5.16b Determining lesson (part 2)
Why not to teach phonics intensively and systematically 102
     T5.17 Why not to teach phonics intensively and systematically
How children learn phonics 106
     T5.18 How children learn phonics
Contrasting models of learning phonics 107
     T5.19 Intensive phonics versus whole language models
     T5.20 Intensive phonics advocates/whole language advocates
Ways of helping children learn phonics 107
     T5.21 Ways of helping children learn phonics

Songs and poems for learning phonics 109
    T5.22 "Cheeky Chipmunk"
    T5.23 "Wet Worm"
    T5.24 "Daisy Dreams"
    T5.25 Rhyming song: "Knick Knack Paddy Wack" (# 1)
    T5.26 Rhyming song: "Knick Knack Paddy Wack" (# 2)
    T5.27 "The Pines"
    T5.28a "Susie Moriar"
    T5.28b "Susie Moriar" (continuation)

Section 6: Strategies and the Teaching of Strategies
Suggestions and background information 145
Reading skills and strategies 145
    T6.1   Reading skills and strategies
Teaching reading skills 145
    T6.2   Comprehension skills: Rosenshine on discrete reading skills
    T6.3   Skills in basal reading programs
Strategies for problem words 146
    T6.4   Strategies for dealing with problem words
    T6.5   Prompts when a child stops and hesitates at a word (# 1)
    T6.6   Prompts when a child stops and hesitates at a word (# 2)
    T6.7   Prompts when a child has made a miscue that doesn't fit the context
    T6.8   Bookmarks (# 1)
    T6.9a Bookmarks (# 2)
    T6.9b Bookmarks (# 3)
Strategies for processing text 147
    T6.10 Proficient reading requires the orchestration of various strategies
    T6.11 Strategies for predicting include
Minilessons for various strategies 148
    T6.12 Word parts and words in context ("fissiparous")
    T6.13 Learning words from context (# 1) (*Johnny Tremain*)
    T6.14 Learning words from context (# 2) (*Johnny Tremain*)
    T6.15 Deciding what to do about unknown words (*Johnny Tremain*)
    T6.16 Where comprehension comes from
Literature discussions 149
    T6.17 "The Moth and the Star"
    T6.18 Questions on "The Moth and the Star"
    T6.19 Literature discussions involve students in . . .
    T6.20 Literature discussions and thinking skills
    T6.21 Benefits of literature discussions

Section 7: Writing and Learning to Write
Suggestions and background information 173
Anticipation guide on writing
Learning to write 173
    T7.1   Learning to write is like (# 1)
    T7.2   Learning to write is like (# 2)
Discussion questions on writing 174

T7.3   Discussion questions on writing
How adults facilitate writing acquisition 174
T7.4   How adults facilitate writing acquisition
Writings from different classrooms 176
T7.5   Phonics and skills classrooms
T7.6   Whole language classroom
Stages in spelling development 176
T7.7   Emergent spelling: Incipient and developing stages (Cory)
T7.8   Emergent spelling: Approximate stage (# 1) (Cory)
T7.9   Emergent spelling: Approximate stage (# 2) (Cory)
T7.10 Emergent spelling: Independent stage (Cory)
Ways of teaching spelling 177
T7.11 Ways of teaching spelling (# 1)
T7.12 Ways of teaching spelling (# 2)
T7.13 Ways of teaching spelling (# 3)
T7.14 Ways of teaching spelling (# 4)
Strategies for correcting spelling 178
T7.15 Strategies for correcting spelling
Errors as signs of progress 179
T7.16 Errors as signs of progress (# 1): Placement of periods (Rachel)
T7.17 Errors as signs of progress (# 2): Overgeneralization of apostrophe (Andrew)
T7.18 Errors as signs of progress (# 3): Placement of commas
From observation to teaching 180
T7.19 From observation to teaching (# 1): No spaces between words (Danielle)
T7.20 From observation to teaching (# 2): Beginning to use spaces (Danielle)
T7.21 From observation to teaching (# 3): Spelling (David)
Examining and guiding progress over time 180
T7.22 Examining and guiding progress over time (# 1):
          Name written backwards (Robbie)
T7.23 Examining and guiding progress over time (# 2):
          Phonemic writing, no spacing (Robbie)
T7.24 Examining and guiding progress over time (# 3):
          Independent writing, first grade (Robbie)
T7.25 Examining and guiding progress over time (# 4):
          Illustration to accompany writing (Robbie)
T7.26a-c Examining and guiding progress over time (#5):
          Second grade writing sample (Robbie)
Stages in the writing process 181
T7.27 Sixth grader's first draft
T7.28 Sixth grader's second draft
T7.29 Sixth grader's third draft
Editing checklist 182
T7.30 Editing checklist

Section 8: Assessment
Suggestions and background information 217
Anticipation guide on assessment
Assessment is/should be like 217

T8.1   Assessment is/should be like

Discussion questions on assessment 217

T8.2   Discussion questions on assessment

Pitfalls of traditional assessment 217

T8.3   Kinds of comprehension questions
T8.4   Why downplay standardized tests

Assessment as collaboration 218

T8.5   Assessment as collaboration among

Questions to guide assessment 219

T8.6   Questions about a child's reading
T8.7   Questions about a child's writing

Kinds of data for assessment 219

T8.8   Kinds of data for assessment

Determining children's spelling and writing growth 222

T8.9   Child's spelling growth (# 1, Cory, dictation)
T8.10 Child's spelling growth (# 2, Cory, dictation)

Documenting stages in spelling and writing development 223

T8.11 Emergent writing: Incipient stage (# 1)
T8.12 Emergent writing: Incipient stage (# 2)
T8.13 Emergent writing: Approximate stage (# 3)
T8.14 Emergent writing: Approximate stage (# 4)
T8.15 Emergent writing: Independent stage (#5)

Writers' hints—children's criteria for good writing 223

T8.16 Writers' hints

PART TWO: Fliers, Letters, Brochures, and Fact Sheets

Introduction 245–246

Section 9: Fliers
Readers' rights
Writers' rights
Hints for getting your child to read
How to help your child learn phonics
Observing and guiding your child's reading growth
How to help your child become a writer

Section 10: Letters
Sample letter on teaching children to read
Sample letter on teaching children to write
Sample letter on spelling for parents of primary children
Sample letter on spelling for parents of intermediate children

Section 11: Brochures
Helping children learn to talk, read, and write
How to help your child become a reader (longer version)
How to help your child become a reader (shorter version)
How to help your child learn phonics (longer version)

How to help your child learn phonics (shorter version)
How will my child learn phonics, spelling, and grammar?
How to help your child become a writer
Why whole language for my child?
Why alternative forms of assessment?
Basal readers and the state of American reading instruction: A call to action
NCTE's position on the teaching of English: Assumptions and practices

Section 12: Fact Sheets
On teaching skills in context
On research on the teaching of phonics
On the teaching of phonics
On the teaching of spelling
On the teaching of grammar
On the nature of whole language education
On myths about whole language education
On phonics in whole language classrooms
On research on whole language education
On standardized tests and assessment alternatives
On student achievement in our public schools
On student achievement in our public schools: SAT scores revisited

INTRODUCTION

"How can I help parents understand why I'm teaching reading and writing this way?" "How can I explain to the principal how and why whole language works?" We hear these and related questions from many teachers, and have asked such questions ourselves. Of course, one of the best solutions is to invite others into our classrooms to see for themselves not only what and how the children are learning, but their enthusiasm for learning. In literacy-rich classrooms, children are not only becoming increasingly proficient readers and writers, but developing a love of reading and writing to last a lifetime.

Yet parents, administrators, and others ask, "What about the basics?" "What about the skills?" They want to know how children are being taught phonics, spelling, and grammar. It is no longer sufficient to teach children effectively; we educators need to be able to explain the rationale for and results of effective literacy practices, integrating research and theory with what we know from our successes as classroom teachers. This book derives, then, from this need to help others understand that children become better readers and writers when skills are taught in the context of their need and use: that is, when children are actually reading and writing texts that are interesting and important to them. Thus this text focuses on effective, research-based ways of helping children develop as readers and writers, along with means of assessment that document such growth.

Part One of the book consists of materials that can be used in workshops with parents, colleagues, administrators, and others. For vari-

ous topics and subtopics relating to the development of reading, writing, and authentic assessment, there are sets of materials that can be copied as transparencies, along with suggestions of how and why you might use them, relevant background information and research, and lists of sources and resources. Many of the transparencies—particularly those on reading—derive from or relate to Constance Weaver's *Reading Process and Practice*, as do many materials in the second part of the book. Therefore, this book could be used as a workshop leader's or teacher educator's companion to that book. However, the present book goes beyond *Reading Process and Practice* in dealing with writing and literacy assessment in greater detail. These sections were drafted by the other two authors, Lorraine Gillmeister-Krause and Grace Vento-Zogby.

Part Two consists of materials that can be photocopied and distributed to others. These materials on reading, writing, and assessment are presented in four different formats: fliers, letters (usually designed to be copied on one side of a sheet), brochures (to copy on both sides of a sheet and make into a trifold), and fact sheets (to copy on two sides of a sheet). There is considerable overlap among the contents, so that you will find, for instance, fliers, a letter, and brochures on helping children become readers; letters, a brochure, and a fact sheet dealing with spelling; and so forth. However, we did not slavishly try to repeat everything in in all four formats.

One important principle that guided us in preparing these materials was choice. With the transparency materials, for instance, we sometimes included two related transparencies, one simpler and another more detailed, or simply two different ones from which a workshop leader could choose. (Translation: There are a lot more "transparencies" than most of us could use, even in one lengthy workshop or a series of workshops. We planned it that way, to offer choices and ownership.) Of course you may also want to use materials from different categories within the same workshop: for example, materials dealing rather directly with phonics, spelling, grammar, and whole language. In short, this book is for the teacher or curriculum specialist who has sufficient background knowledge to make decisions about what to use, to decide how to use the materials, and to add to workshop discussions from their experience and what they already know. As Yetta Goodman has said, "The power of whole language is that you cannot clone the effective whole language teacher. One teacher's greatness cannot be transformed into another teacher." We firmly believe this.

The transparency materials, in particular, have accompanying discussions in which we've shared some of our own experiences in using these materials with others. We decided to personalize these discussions (using "we" or first names rather than "I"), in order to make it clear that these are demonstrations and suggestions, not procedures to follow rigidly. For that reason, we offer here a few comments on where we're at ourselves in our own journeys as teacher/learners.

Connie has authored or edited (or coauthored or coedited) several books that deal with or relate to whole language: *Understanding Whole Language* (1990); *Supporting Whole Language* (1992); *Theme Exploration* (1993); *Reading Process and Practice: From Socio-Psycholinguistics to Whole Language* (2nd ed., 1994); *Success at Last!*, a book on helping children with attention deficit disorders achieve their potential (1994); and a new book, *Teaching Grammar in Context* (1996). Having recently worked with a group of literacy educators in Michigan to convince the State Board of Education that skills

are best taught in the context of their use, Connie originally drafted the fact sheets and some of the brochures in Part Two for the Michigan English Language Arts Framework project. (Some of the fact sheets have also been distributed as SLATE starter sheets by the National Council of Teachers of English.) Working with this project has convinced her of the widespread need for a book like this, and for citizens' advocacy groups like Michigan for Public Education, the group Connie and other educators and librarians have started. Materials like the fact sheets and brochures could be distributed through such groups, and of course you are welcome to copy the materials for this purpose as well as other purposes.

Lorraine is an accomplished teacher. For the past fifteen years, she has been teaching children from kindergarten through grade six in a one-room schoolhouse, Soulanges Elementary, in Quebec. During her twenty-seven years of experience, she has worked with children of all ages and abilities, including adolescents labeled as learning disabled. Never satisfied with the status quo, Lorraine is an avid learner who has developed as a professional over the years by continually challenging herself: by studying, participating in conferences, and involving herself in many conversations about learning. She has taught teachers at McGill University in Montreal and given numerous seminars and workshops to parents and teachers on literacy, learning, and the classroom. As a member of the Board for the Whole Language Umbrella, Lorraine served as membership chair for Canada. Her most recent activities include using the electronic medium in her classroom, thereby expanding its walls and ceiling to include the world in which the children live. She has published an article in the journal *Canadian Children*. For her outstanding teaching, in 1989 Lorraine and her one-room schoolhouse received a National Council of Teachers of English Center of Excellence in the English Language Arts award.

Grace has taught grades four, five, and six and is currently a Title I reading specialist. Considering herself a lifelong learner, she has been involved with various whole language organizations. She is coeditor of the *IRA Whole Language SIG Newsletter*, founder of the Utica (New York) Area T.A.W.L. group, a member of the Catskills Whole Language Council, and an active member of the Whole Language Umbrella, for which she has served as chair of the Electronic Communications Committee. She was a contributor to NCTE's *Ideas and Insights*, edited by Dorothy Watson. Grace has been actively involved in fostering the professional development of other teachers; her teacher development activities include consulting for a migrant program called Eastern Stream, through which she taught other teachers and parents about whole language across the Northeast. She continually presents literacy workshops for teachers. A recent participant in the Reading Recovery program, Grace is currently integrating new techniques with her whole language philosophy of education.

Each section of Part One is paginated separately, and within each section the discussion pages precede and are paginated separately from the transparency pages (the pages that can be copied onto a transparency). At the beginning of the sections on reading, writing, and assessment, there are also anticipation guides that you might use in a workshop setting. The materials in Part Two are not paginated at all, beyond the introduction—which includes a sequential list of the materials in each section of fliers, letters, brochures, and fact sheets.

The transparency materials, fliers, letters, brochures, and fact sheets all include a credit line. Though the materials are copyrighted, you are welcome to copy them for workshop use or distribution. However, we do ask a favor: If you use a number of these items in a workshop for which you receive remuneration, would you donate some portion of that remu-

neration to the Whole Language Umbrella or to the Center for the Expansion of Language and Thinking? You can obtain the current addresses of these organizations from any of the authors, or from Heinemann.

If there is considerable demand, we will probably do another, expanded edition of this book that includes more literacy-related topics and hot topics in education. What about multiculturalism, English as a second language, and bilingualism, for instance? But for topics such as these, we need to draw upon the expertise of others. Therefore, we invite you to send us not only suggestions for revising and adding to the present materials, but materials you have drafted and would be willing to have included in an expanded edition. We and the potential users of this resource book thank you in advance for your help and collaboration.

We especially want to thank Peter Krause for reacting to and helping with some of the materials in this book—and for serving us gourmet meals and putting up with us while we worked! We've all had fun drafting the book together and seeing its potential for making our lives as teachers and workshop leaders easier. We hope you find the book equally helpful in meeting your own needs.

Connie Weaver
Western Michigan University
Kalamazoo, MI 49008

Lorraine Gillmeister-Krause
Soulanges Elementary
St. Telesphore, Quebec
Canada J0P 1Y0

Grace Vento-Zogby
Sauquoit Valley Elementary
Sauquoit, NY 13456

Workshop and Transparency Materials

The materials in this part of the book are designed for use with parents, colleagues, and administrators in a workshop setting. The materials would also be appropriate for use in graduate and undergraduate classes for teachers, particularly if a lot of concepts about literacy development and effective teaching must be introduced in a short time, such as a weekend course. The pages with large print may be copied for use as transparencies (but for transparency use only). Each section begins with suggestions for how you might use the transparencies in that set, along with other comments and resources that may be especially useful.

Each set includes more transparency materials than you are likely to want for any particular occasion. Our idea was to offer choices: sometimes both a simple and a more detailed version of the same thing or on the same topic, and sometimes simply two or more different transparency pages that might suit those with different ideas of how to approach the broader topics and issues in question. We hope that you will find these materials and comments helpful.

Part Two contains fliers, brochures, sample letters, and fact sheets. You may find it useful to copy and distribute one or more of these at your workshop(s).

Additional Resources

There are now many videotapes that would support workshops for parents, including several from Heinemann. Typically, however, the commercially produced materials are quite expensive. Here are two less expensive resources that can be used very effectively with parents and others.

CRAFTON, L., & SILVERS, P. (1993). *A lifetime of success . . . parents, kids and reading.* Deerfield, IL: Center for Learning and Literacy (P.O. Box 133, Deerfield, IL 60015; 708-948-8460). This is a series of four audiotapes, accompanied by a parent handbook. The tapes deal with learning to read easily and naturally; choosing quality children's books and best ways of reading aloud; the place of phonics in reading ("Don't Be Phooled—Phonics Is Not Enough"); and family activities to enhance reading, keeping TV in its place, and what to do if your child hates to read.

PERKINS, P. I. (1994). *What is reading?* Orange, CA: Literacy Possibilities (P.O. Box 220, Orange, CA 92666-0220; 714-538-2990). This videotape (a seventy-five-minute "experience," with nineteen minutes of additional information) is intended to help parents, teachers, and others understand the reading process. To use the video with maximum effectiveness, one needs the accompanying materials and a copy of Leo Lionni's 1969 *Alexander and the wind-up mouse* (New York: Pantheon, a division of Random House; Toronto: Random House). Both the tape and the book can be ordered from Literacy Possibilities.

LEARNING THEORY AND THE ACQUISITION OF LANGUAGE AND LITERACY

The transparency materials in this set are designed to explore the characteristics of "natural" learning: that is, the kind of learning that occurs outside of school. Exploring questions like "How did you learn to ride a bike (or swim, or drive a car)?" can help parents and others understand the kinds of conditions that foster learning, and also the kinds of conditions that tend to inhibit learning (Holdaway, 1986; Cambourne, 1988). One crucial point is that we typically do not practice the parts of these activities before attempting the whole. Rather, we attempt the whole and gradually become more adept at the component parts.

For leading into the way literacy is fostered "naturally," such a discussion can be followed by, or used instead of, a similar discussion about the conditions that foster children's acquisition of language in their earliest years (Section 2).

Learning Skills:
Transparencies 1.1 Through 1.3

You could explore with workshop participants one or more of the questions or sets of questions from **transparency 1.1**. These questions invite participants to explore how they themselves learned to ride a bike, to swim, and to drive a car. Discussion could focus on what others did (particularly adults) that made it possible for you and other workshop participants to learn to do these things. You may also find it helpful to focus on what adults did *not* do, such as yell at you every time you fell off your bike. Given sufficient time, it may be interesting to also (or alternatively) explore how the workshop participants "taught" their own children or perhaps their younger siblings to do these activities. Based on our own experience, here are some points that might emerge from discussion and/or be suggested by the workshop leader. You are welcome to share our examples, too.

1. We don't practice the parts of these activities (such as pedaling a bike, or practicing arm strokes, or practicing steering) before we attempt the whole. (**Transparency 1.2** shows a cartoonlike drawing that should help convey the ridiculousness of having children practice stroking and kicking before they're allowed to paddle around in the water—at least shallow water.) Typically, we attempt the whole of an activity like riding a bike, swimming, or driving a car, then gradually refine the parts. Implication: this is the way we develop language as young children, and this is the way parents naturally foster the development of literacy in the home. Effective teachers draw upon this natural progression in helping children become literate.

For example, Connie taught herself to swim at about age eight by getting into water that was up to her neck, practicing floating (first by holding on to the side of the pool), then gradually trying to imitate the kicking and arm movements of other swimmers. The edge of the pool provided scaffolding (Ninio & Bruner, 1978), and the skill of others provided demonstrations of the desired behavior (Holdaway, 1986). However, this more purposive learning behavior on Connie's part occurred only after she had spent days and weeks in the shallow end just playing in the water and trying to dogpaddle. And only after she had become an emergent swimmer was she ready and willing to take swimming lessons to refine her swimming technique and learn some specific strokes.

When Lorraine was learning French as a second language, she was immersed in the language and culture of Quebec City with other adult second-language learners. They were requested not to speak any other language but French for two weeks. As Lorraine lived with a Quebec City resident and studied, she did not practice parts of the language (such as *le*, *la*, vocabulary, verb conjugations, spelling rules and exceptions, etc.) before she attempted the whole. She attempted the whole and gradually refined the parts. She imitated the speaking of French during class and all day, including evenings in the city. As she became more and more proficient in the language, she was able to use French for very practical assignments such as buying a watchband, ordering a beer, and requesting tourist information. Implication: immersion is perhaps the best way to develop fluency in a second language (Krashen, 1981), and immersion in books and print is the most common way children develop literacy in the home—though in both situations, there is feedback and guidance from those already proficient in the skill. Effective teachers draw upon this natural whole-to-part progression in helping children become literate.

2. We find it easy to learn when we receive encouragement and support for our efforts.

For example, Grace learned how to spin wool from a friend who took the time to demonstrate the techniques involved in carding and spinning within a nonthreatening environment. Sitting next to her, offering positive feedback, allowing Grace to take the time to practice controlling the wool as it was being spun, and offering words of encouragement when she "overspun" the yarn, Grace's friend

enabled her to become a spinner. Spinning wool is something Grace continues to do when she has time.

Connie's father supported her in learning to ride a bike by grasping the handlebars with one hand and the back of the seat with the other, helping Connie get up speed while holding the bike upright and running alongside, and letting go only when the bike was moving fast enough to remain upright, thus providing scaffolding that enabled Connie to engage in the whole of the process while beginning to master the parts. Connie's son had the support of a smaller bike and training wheels, which similarly enabled him to learn the skills involved in bike riding while having needed support.

3. We become discouraged and may quit trying when our efforts are repeatedly criticized or viewed as unsuccessful.

For example, Connie quit trying to play golf, even after taking a class in golfing, because her golfing companion made her feel incompetent, which not only spoiled her enjoyment of golf but made her so nervous that she did worse than if he had not "helped" her with advice. Similarly, Connie's mother learned to drive as a teenager but actually quit driving after she got married in her early twenties, because her husband was always treating her as incompetent by telling her what to do and what not to do.

In contrast to Connie, Grace is a nonswimmer. In an attempt to learn, she signed up for lessons. Although it was expected that she learn how to swim, she needed many more demonstrations and time to practice without critical supervision in order to develop coordination and control in swimming. She only began to feel secure in the shallow end of the pool and was not ready to move to the deeper end with the rest of the class. She needed to decide for herself when she would "go off the deep end." Instead, she was forced to jump into the twelve-foot end to practice what was taught. Fortunately, she did rise to the surface—with the assistance of a lifesaving pole!

Needless to say, she did not return to class and now avoids swimming at all costs.

In addition or as an alternative to transparency 1.1 and the cartoon in transparency 1.2, you might use **transparency 1.3**, with these questions:

"Think of something you're good at doing. How did you learn to do it?"

"Think of something you've tried but are *not* good at. Why do you think you didn't learn to do it well?"

Similar points can emerge from discussing the responses to these questions.

Models of Learning: Transparencies 1.4 Through 1.7

You could show **transparency 1.4** and/or **1.5**, on conditions for learning and on the phases that seem to characterize "natural" learning.

The first of these transparencies includes three key conditions for learning from Cambourne (1988), slightly rephrased. (He focuses on language and literacy learning, but clearly these conditions are relevant to learning in general.) According to Cambourne's model, people try hard to learn something new and freely engage in it *if and only if*: (1) they *want* to do it; (2) they are convinced they *can* learn to do it; and (3) they can attempt and practice it without someone criticizing or punishing their efforts or making them feel incompetent.

Transparency 1.5 includes the four phases in Holdaway's natural learning model (1986). First is the *observation of demonstrations*: for example, we watch other children ride a bike or swim, and we watch our parents drive. Second is *guided participation*: we learn to ride a bike with the assistance of training wheels; we learn to swim while being held up in the water and perhaps using water wings; we drive a car with an experienced driver to guide us—and dual controls to use if necessary. Third is *unsupervised role-playing practice*: we practice riding the bike, first with the training wheels; we practice swimming, first in water that is not

over our heads; we get our driver's license and practice driving without the watchful eye of the teacher or our parents. At this point we are ready to refine the parts of the activity, to learn through risk-taking, mistake-making, and more and more practice. Finally comes *performance*, when we are ready to share our skills and have our accomplishments celebrated: we ask for the training wheels to be removed and we demonstrate that we can now ride a bike; we demonstrate that we can swim across the pool at the deep end; we drive the family car on vacation. We have learned these skills naturally, refining their parts as we engaged in the whole of the activity.

Of course, the purpose here is to lead into a demonstration and discussion of how reading and writing can be acquired in much the same way.

Transparency 1.6 is our constructivist model of learning, which draws upon all the previously cited references and more (e.g., Smith, 1975, 1990). The jagged lightning bolts are meant to suggest that input from the environment (people, things, circumstances) is made comprehensible through cues and indicators in the environment itself, through the action of the mind upon that input, and with the potential assistance of varying amounts of *directive*, facilitative instruction, with one possibility being no directive instruction at all. The constructivist model derives from cognitive psychology, with studies in language acquisition contributing significantly to the insight that humans learn concepts and processes by continually formulating and reformulating hypotheses about their world. Usually directive instruction is not included in a constructivist model of learning at all, but we wanted to suggest that some learners need or benefit from targeted help with things like reading strategies, while others develop such strategies more intuitively and without direct help. As for the difference between direct and directive instruction, we think of the former as instruction more likely offered according to the plan of some textbook or curriculum guide, while *directive* instruction would be relevant instruction offered at the point of need. Clearly directive instruction is likely to facilitate learning more often and for more people, so that's what we have included in our model.

In sharing transparency 1.6 in a workshop setting, you might just explain key points related to the model, allowing for questions and comments from participants. Here are additional points related to the visual model, as well as more elaboration on some of the points just made:

Learning is primarily constructive in nature. While we humans may learn some things through repetition, rehearsal, and/or practice, the learning of concepts and complex processes is fundamentally an active mental process, not a passive process of habit formation or of merely absorbing information from the environment. Both adults and children construct meanings and knowledge by transacting (interacting) with the environment. They actively form, test, and revise hypotheses; develop, refine, and modify concepts; develop, refine, and orchestrate skills and strategies. As expressed in the visual model, humans apply hypothesis-forming and concept-forming capacities in their continual quest to learn from the external environment (people, experiences, texts, and so forth).

For us to learn, input from the environment needs to be comprehensible. This does not mean that every aspect of incoming data needs to be comprehensible for us to make sense from it. For example, when we adults talk to babies they obviously have not come into the world already comprehending what we are saying. Although they come mentally equipped to learn any language, they do not know any one language specifically. However, we make our utterances at least partially comprehensible through pointing, emphasizing, and through the situational context: the situation in which we are engaged (the act of covering, changing, or feeding the baby, and so forth). An important point is that in any given situation where learning might take place, different people will learn different things from the same situation,

and some may learn little or nothing (or something radically different from what a teacher or parent intended), depending—in part—upon their interest in learning from the situation and their comfortableness with the learning situation. Their prior experiences, concepts, and beliefs are important too; these typically facilitate, limit, or otherwise affect what is learned.

Thus, input from the environment is made comprehensible in two basic, complementary, and interactive ways. That is, the environment itself partially determines the comprehensibility of the input. Second, the mind acts upon the input to make sense of and from it. Both processes are critical and operate more or less simultaneously and complementarily when we are attending to and trying to make sense of external input.

Directive instruction may be one way that the environment makes input comprehensible. Some important points to be made with this aspect of this model are:

- that directive instruction can, in fact, include direct instruction, but we have chosen the term "directive" so that individuals looking at the transparency will not confuse it with direct instruction of the DISTAR variety
- that the term "directive" instruction is meant to imply guidance and support, or scaffolding, not merely the transmission of information
- that learners do not necessarily need directive instruction to learn something (language and reading being two good examples)
- that different learners need varying amounts of directive instruction
- that learners may benefit from directive instruction at different points in their learning
- that learners will not all find the same kinds of directive instruction meaningful or relevant, particularly if they see no reason to learn what is being taught or if they are afraid of being criticized or found wanting in their efforts to learn

What may emerge from discussion is the observation that a great deal of the direct instruction that occurs in schools may have little lasting value because basic conditions for learning are not met (Cambourne, 1988, and transparencies 1.1 through 1.5).

As indicated, we consider it important to include directive instruction in a constructivist model of learning because it does seem to us that while some children need little or no directive instruction in learning, for example, to read and write or to swim or drive a car, other children benefit from or really need more directive instruction. The directive instruction that takes place in whole language classrooms is not isolated skill and drill, but rather direct help with something the children are trying to do—help offered at the point of need, and help that builds upon what the children already know. Such help may be offered spontaneously or soon thereafter in planned minilessons—which then are applied with teacher and/or peer assistance, as needed.

Transmission and Transactional: Transparency 1.7

This transparency contrasts a transmission model of learning, derived from behavioral psychology, with a transactional model of learning, based on cognitive psychology. The contrasting points are either self-evident (we hope) or ones we have previously discussed. For an expanded set of contrasts between the transmission and transactional models, see Weaver (1994), Chapter 8.

The Development of Language and Literacy: Transparency 1.8

Transparency 1.8 might be conceptualized as a constructivist description of language and literacy development. We have tried to condense into four sets of patterns some of the phases that children go through in learning the vocabulary and especially the structure of their native language, and also in learning to read and write—when literacy development is fostered in ways akin to how we adults foster the learning of language with young children. (Note, of course, that the earliest evidence of language development and the earliest evidence of reading and writing development do not all occur at the same time, though there are parallels between learning to speak and learning to read and write.)

Reading and writing development are likely to be familiar to anyone using this book as a workshop resource, but the stages of language acquisition ("speaking") perhaps require more comment. (And see the separate bibliography on literacy development references for parents, after the description of the other transparencies in this section.)

Research has demonstrated that at about six months of age, children begin babbling selectively, making only the kinds of sounds heard in the speech of those around them. Their cries and wails, especially, begin very early to suggest the ups and downs (intonation patterns) of the speech they hear. Their first "sentences" are single words that stand for the whole of what they are trying to say; of course, they rely upon the situation, gestures, and objects to help convey their meaning. One-word sentences give way to two-word sentences, which in turn are expanded into longer sentences that eventually include function words (like *a, an, the; in, on, at; and, but; because*) and grammatical endings (like plural and past tense). By the time they enter first grade, children are typically using all of the basic patterns (like subject–verb–direct object) and most of the grammatical structures (like gerunds and participial phrases and subordinate clauses) found in adult speech, though in their simpler and least elaborated forms and positions (O'Donnell, Griffin, & Norris, 1967). Though from one perspective it looks as if children are learning language from part to whole, we suggest the opposite interpretation: that children begin with the whole of what they want to communicate, but only gradually master the parts for communicating as adults do. Similarly, most children seem to find learning to read and write easiest and most natural when they begin with the whole (such as trying to retell a familiar story from memory and the pictures, or to scribble a message) and gradually master the parts of the task (such as sight words, phonics, conventions of print, and spelling).

We have collapsed some of the stages found in other sources and given our stages new names: *incipient, developing, approximate,* and *independent.* In much of the professional literature, the term "emergent" is used to include at least the first three of these sets of patterns, if not all four. It is important to view these common patterns as increasingly sophisticated aspects of development, not as stages that any particular child will necessarily go through.

Incidentally, you might share with workshop participants the children's book *Least of All,* by Carol Purdy (Macmillan, 1987). It's about a child who teaches herself to read by reading and rereading familiar Bible verses, thereby making the connection between spoken and written words.

As a follow-up to transparency 1.8 comparing the acquisition of language with the acquisition of reading and writing, you might also share **transparency 4.1** on facilitating reading acquisition and **transparency 7.4** on facilitating writing acquisition. You might also consider using transparencies from Section 4, "Teaching and Learning to Read."

Contrasting Models for Teaching Minilessons: Transparencies 1.9 and 1.10

To some degree, transparencies 1.9 and 1.10 are the flip side of 1.6 and 1.7. The earlier ones focused on learning, while 1.9 and 1.10 focus on teaching that facilitates relatively natural learning, particularly the development of reading and writing (transparency 1.8).

The two transparencies on teaching are slightly different versions of the same thing. Both compare the typical lesson in a transmission-oriented classroom with the minilessons in a transactional-oriented classroom. In **trans-**parency 1.9, the characterization of transmission-oriented teaching of minilessons is based loosely on Madeline Hunter's Instructional Theory Into Practice (ITIP) sequence (1982), while the characterization of transactional teaching is based on the concept of minilessons as articulated by Nancie Atwell (1987) and Lucy Calkins (1986/1994). In the typical transmission model, the teacher prepares the learners for what they are about to be taught by stating objectives and doing anything else needed to orient them to the learning task. For step 1, the major difference between the models is that in a transmission classroom, what's being taught is likely to be determined by curriculum objectives or a scope and sequence plan in a textbook, whereas in a transactional classroom the teacher is more likely to teach skills and strategies when the students are observed to need them, in order to accomplish, for example, their reading and writing more effectively. The other major difference is that in the transmission model, students are likely to be assigned practice on skills in isolation, then tested to see whether they can demonstrate these skills—again in isolation from the task for which the skills may have been intended. In contrast, a teacher in a transactional classroom may explain something during a minilesson, then help students apply it in their reading or writing when the occasion next arises. Usually a transactional teacher assesses not through tests, but by observing individual students to see whether or not they are applying what has been taught—and if not, the teacher will give the students further help. There is growing evidence that the skills of reading and writing are best learned in transactional or "whole language" classrooms, with their emphasis on application rather than on isolated mastery and testing (see, for example, ch. 7 of Weaver, 1994, and ch. 6 of Weaver, 1996).

Transparency 1.10 makes the same contrast, but with an expanded version of the transactional model: a version that includes "collaborative practice to develop understanding" and "checking understanding" as a follow-up to the collaborative practice. This reflects the conviction that even in transactional classrooms, it *can* be useful for students to work together to understand and/or apply some skills and strategies, before independent application is expected (Wilde, 1992; Weaver, 1996). In her 1996 book, Connie calls such lessons "expanded minilessons."

More on Minilessons

We have found that the following explanation regarding our use of minilessons often leads to thoughtful discussions. Your own experiences regarding the use of minilessons will add further insights when discussing this topic in a workshop.

In planning our minilessons, we think about the message we want to share with our students as well as the materials we use to teach the brief lesson. Our lessons tend to last ten to twenty minutes, so we want to share the best examples, using the best of children's literature when appropriate. One goal is that the minilesson should have an effect on the children's reading and/or writing. But of course we realize that there is much more to helping children understand what good writing is all about than a minilesson can provide. Connections and demonstrations take place throughout the day during literature circles, read-alouds, conferences, and so forth.

The following are examples of minilessons we have used. Keep in mind that no two classes are alike; each group of students is unique, and we need to consider their needs when formulating our lessons. We need to listen to their conversations, read their pieces, and be good kidwatchers.

One purpose of a minilesson might be to expose children to a particular genre, such as letter-writing. *The Jolly Postman* has become a well-known book among teachers. Written by Janet and Allan Ahlberg, it is a series of letters written to various fairy-tale characters. Each letter may be removed from its own envelope. During a minilesson, this book may be read to the students, with the teacher taking the time to discuss the form and intended audience of each letter. Students may be encouraged to bring in samples of various letters, such as junk mail, invitations, and thank-you notes.

A follow-up minilesson might be the study of the genre of greeting cards. Children can be encouraged to bring various cards to school to study the illustrations and the text: how they complement each other, the mood they create, and so forth.

An example of another minilesson involving *The Jolly Postman*, a lesson that focuses on mechanics as well as content, could involve the creation of a rubric, or set of standards for letter writing. Students and the teacher could study the proper format in developing a letter (date, greeting, body, closing, along with conventional punctuation). The chart may be referred to by students when writing letters.

Many teachers Grace works with write a daily morning message on the chalkboard to their students. They sometimes intentionally make errors in mechanics, grammar, spelling, and so forth. When discussing the message with the class, the teacher and students point out errors and correct them, thus engaging in other minilessons.

Sources and Resources

Ahlberg, J., & Ahlberg, A. (1986). *The jolly postman, or other people's letters*. Boston: Little, Brown.

Atwell, N. (1987). *In the middle: Writing, reading, and learning with adolescents*. Portsmouth, NH: Boynton/Cook.

Calkins, L. M. (1986/1994). *The art of teaching writing*. Portsmouth, NH: Heinemann.

Cambourne, B. (1988). *The whole story: Natural learning and the acquisition of literacy in the classroom*. New York: Scholastic. See p. 33 for the complete model, which is discussed in his Chapter 4.

Holdaway, D. (1986). The structure of natural learning as a basis for literacy instruction. In M. R. Sampson (Ed.), *The pursuit of literacy: Early reading and writing* (pp. 56–72). Dubuque, IA: Kendall / Hunt.

HUNTER, M. (1982). *Mastery teaching*. El Segundo, CA: TIP Publications.

KRASHEN, S. D. (1981). *Second language acquisition and second language learning*. Oxford: Pergamon Press.

NINIO, A., & BRUNER, J. (1978). The achievement and antecedents of labeling. *Journal of Child Language, 5*, 1–15.

O'DONNELL, R. C., GRIFFIN, W. J., & NORRIS, R. C. (1967). *Syntax of kindergarten and elementary school children: A transformational analysis* (Research Report No. 8). Urbana, IL: National Council of Teachers of English.

PURDY, C. (1987). *Least of all*. New York: Macmillan.

SMITH, F. (1975). *Comprehension and learning: A conceptual framework for teachers*. Katonah, NY: Richard C. Owen.

SMITH, F. (1990). *To think*. New York: Teachers College Press.

WEAVER, C. (1994). *Reading process and practice: From socio-psycholinguistics to whole language* (2nd ed.). Portsmouth, NH: Heinemann.

WEAVER, C. (1996). *Teaching grammar in context*. Portsmouth, NH: Boynton/Cook.

WILDE, S. (1992). *You kan red this! Spelling and punctuation for whole language classrooms, K–6*. Portsmouth, NH: Heinemann.

Books on Literacy Development

The following books are appropriate for parents as well as teachers. The asterisked books are especially easy and delightful reading:

*Barron, M. (1990). *I learn to read and write the way I learn to talk: A very first book about whole language*. Katonah, NY: Richard C. Owen. Available in both an English version and a Spanish version.

CLAY, M. M. (1987). *Writing begins at home*. Portsmouth, NH: Heinemann.

DOAKE, D. (1991). *Reading begins at birth*. Richmond Hill, Ontario: Scholastic.

*LAMINACK, L. L. (1991). *Learning with Zachary*. Richmond Hill, Ontario: Scholastic.

NEWMAN, J. M. (1984). *The craft of children's writing*. Richmond Hill, Ontario: Scholastic. (Available in the U.S. from Heinemann.)

VILLIERS, U. (1990). *Luk Mume luk Dade I kan rit*. New York: Scholastic. Consists of young children's writing samples, with explanations of their writing development.

Learning Skills Naturally

How did you learn to

ride a bike?

swim?

drive a car?

How did you teach your child or children to

ride a bike?

swim?

drive a car?

What Promotes or Inhibits Learning?

Think of something you're good at doing.

How did you learn to do it?

Think of something you've tried but are NOT good at.

Why do you think you didn't learn to do it well?

Cambourne: Some Conditions for Language and Literacy Learning

Child believes:

1. This is something I <u>want</u> to do.

2. This is something I <u>can</u> learn to do.

3. This is something I <u>can risk trying</u> without fear of being criticized or punished.

Holdaway's Natural Learning Model

1. Observation of demonstrations

2. Guided participation

3. Unsupervised role-playing practice

4. Performance: sharing and celebration of accomplishment

Based on Don Holdaway, The stages of natural learning model. In M. R. Sampson (Ed.), *The pursuit of literacy: Early reading and writing.* Dubuque, IA: Kendall / Hunt, 1986.

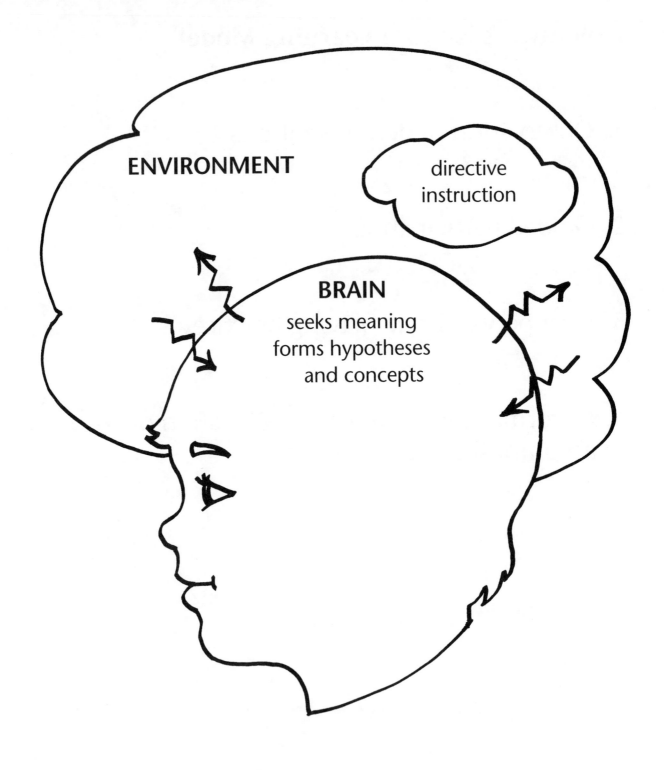

ENVIRONMENT

directive
instruction

BRAIN
seeks meaning
forms hypotheses
and concepts

Transmission	**Transactional**
behavioral, reductionistic	constructivist, holistic
habit formation, simple association	hypothesis formation, developing cognitive structures (schemas)
practice one thing at a time, progress step by step	attempt the "whole"; gradually refine the parts
teach; practice/memorize; test	demonstrate, assist; apply; observe, record
part + part + part = whole	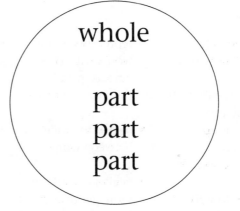

T1.7   *Transmission and Transactional Models*   *Creating Support for Effective Literacy Education*
by C. Weaver, L. Gillmeister-Krause, & G. Vento-Zogby, © 1996. Portsmouth, NH: Heinemann. May be copied for transparency use only.

INCIPIENT	DEVELOPING	APPROXIMATE	INDEPENDENT
Speaking			
• babbling & cooing	• single word sentences ("mama")	• longer sentences	• uses mostly conventional grammar
• intonation patterns	• two-word sentences ("Me go?")	• some function words and grammatical endings	• uses most of the grammatical structures in adult speech
• sounds represent words ("wa"=water)	• uses words and context to convey meaning	• approximated grammar ("Me go play?" "I gots a ball" "Me no want milk")	• increasing sophistication within patterns
Reading			
• enjoys listening to stories	• retells familiar text from pictures & memory	• begins to coordinate meaning and letters/sounds to get words	• coordinates meaning and letters/sounds to get meaning
• enjoys looking at books	• reads familiar patterned stories	• uses increasing stock of sight words and letter/ sound patterns	• reading begins to sound like talking
• gets meaning from illustrations	• matches some spoken and written words	• reads pattern, predictable, and other familiar books	• reads familiar and some new books independently
Writing			
• scribbles, makes letter-like forms	• represents whole words with one letter, typically the first consonant	• represents first and last sounds; also vowel & consonant combinations	• continues using some approximate spellings
• writes words with little if any relationship between letters & sounds	• begins to space between words	• overgeneralizes spelling patterns but also spells some words correctly	• begins to build repertoire of spelling patterns, sight words, & spelling strategies
• begins to write about self and family, e.g., names, captions under pictures	• begins to write in more genres: e.g. lists, notes, signs, letters, cards	• begins to write to record and share information on impersonal topics	• stories resemble narratives, with familiar beginnings & endings

T1.8 *Development of Language and Literacy*   *Creating Support for Effective Literacy Education* by
C. Weaver, L. Gillmeister-Krause, & G. Vento-Zogby, © 1996. Portsmouth, NH: Heinemann. May be copied for
transparency use only.

Behavioral	Constructivist (#1)
1. Anticipatory set and statement of objectives	1. Objectives phrased in terms of sharing helpful hints or ideas
Objectives are usually determined by curriculum guides or textbooks.	Usually the teacher has determined the need by observing students' work: their processes and products.
2. Instruction and modeling	2. Demonstration and explanation
3. Checking understanding	
4. Guided practice	
5. Independent practice	
6. Assessment	
	3. Guided application
	4. Assessment through observation
	5. Independent application
	6. Assessment through further observation

T1.9 *Behavioral Model vs. Constructivist Model (#1)*   *Creating Support for Effective Literacy Education* by C. Weaver, L. Gillmeister-Krause, & G. Vento-Zogby, © 1996. Portsmouth, NH: Heinemann. May be copied for transparency use only.
From *Teaching grammar in context* by Constance Weaver. Portsmouth, NH: Boynton/Cook, 1996.

Behavioral   Constructivist   (#2)

Behavioral	Constructivist
1. Anticipatory set and statement of objectives	1. Objectives phrased in terms of sharing helpful hints or ideas
Objectives are usually determined by curriculum guides or textbooks.	Usually the teacher has determined the need by observing students' work: their processes and products.
2. Instruction and modeling	2. Demonstration and explanation
	3. Collaborative practice to develop understanding
3. Checking understanding	4. Checking understanding
4. Guided practice	
5. Independent practice	
6. Assessment	
	5. Guided application
	6. Assessment through observation
	7. Independent application
	8. Assessment through further observation

T1.10 *Behavioral Model vs. Constructivist Model (#2)*   *Creating Support for Effective Literacy Education* by C. Weaver, L. Gillmeister-Krause, & G. Vento-Zogby, © 1996. Portsmouth, NH: Heinemann. May be copied for transparency use only.

LANGUAGE ACQUISITION
Learning to Talk

One of the cornerstones of a constructivist model of learning is the evidence that children construct increasingly sophisticated hypotheses about the structure of their native language in the process of learning it. Often, parents and others can better appreciate the "natural" development of literacy if they first explore children's language acquisition and consider what they have and haven't done to "teach" their children the structure of their native language. Some or all of these transparencies could be used to facilitate such discussion.

Introducing Language Acquisition: Transparencies 2.1 and 2.2

The first transparency in this set is related to transparencies in Section 1, which invite workshop participants to explore how they learned to ride a bike, swim, and drive, and from their experiences to draw tentative conclusions about what does and doesn't facilitate learning. **Transparency 2.1** asks, "As parents and caretakers, how do we teach babies and toddlers to talk?" and "How do we teach them the grammatical patterns and 'rules' of the language?"

One of the points commonly made is that we point to objects and name them, and children imitate us. While this is obviously true, you may want to lead participants to consider why, for example, a young child who used to say "We went" may begin to say "We goed," or why a child who used to say "Mommy bought it" may begin to say "Mommy buyed it." Researchers have concluded that children first learn irregular past tense verbs as inseparable words, then begin adding a past tense ending when they've internalized the rule for past tense. Time permitting, it may be useful at this point to turn to **transparency 2.2** on making regular verbs past tense. If you ask participants to make the verbs in the first column past tense and to speak them aloud, you will find that they add a /t/. If you do the same with the verbs in the second column, you'll notice that people add a /d/. For the verbs in the last column, a schwa-like vowel and /d/ are added. What's the rule? When making a regular verb past tense, add /t/ if the verb ends in an unvoiced consonant sound; add a /d/ if the verb ends in a voiced consonant sound or a vowel (vowels too are voiced); add a schwa-like vowel (sort of a cross between "uh" and "ih") plus /d/ if the verb already ends in /t/ or /d/.

This is an elegant rule, and children's overgeneralization of the rule shows that they are learning it. But is this a rule that adults teach to children? Hardly. Most adults don't even know the rule, and young children couldn't learn it—much less apply it—if parents did try to teach them the rule directly. What children do is reconstruct the rule, given their inherent language-learning and concept-forming abilities.

Often, this demonstration helps parents and others understand that we do not have to directly teach everything that children need to learn—not in learning their native language, and not in learning to read or write, either.

More on What Children Learn: Transparencies 2.3 and 2.4

One or both of these transparencies may be useful to further emphasize the point that preschool children learn a marvelously complex language system, with almost no direct instruction whatsoever.

Transparency 2.3 shows some of the first two-word sentences found in the literature on child language acquisition (unfortunately we have lost track of the references, most from the 1970s). These sentences illustrate quite a range of semantic relationships:

Agent/action:	Mommy read.
	Doggie bite.
Action/object:	Pick flower.
	Eat cookie.
Agent/object:	Snoopy bone.
	[watching Snoopy bury it]
	Daddy TV.
	[watching Daddy move the TV]
Attribution:	Dirty pillow.
	Spoon sticky.
Entity/location:	Cookie here.
	Sweater chair.
Action/location:	Sit chair.
	Play outside.
Recurrence:	More milk.
Nonexistence:	No money.
Rejection:	No wash.
	[to mean "Don't wash me."]

Though these examples do not illustrate all of the semantic relationships evidenced in children's two-word utterances, they do illustrate most of these relationships. You may want to point out that children typically go through a phase of being able to utter sentences of only one word, then sentences of no more than two words. So for instance if a child wanted to convey the proposition that "Daddy is moving the TV," she might say "Daddy move" (agent/action), "Move TV" (action/object), "Daddy TV" (agent/object), or perhaps two of these in sequence: "Daddy move, move TV." But the child just beginning to put two words together would not yet be able to put three words together in a single utterance (Brown, 1973). This, in fact, seems to be a universal fact of language acquisition: no matter what language is being acquired, children typically go through a state wherein they can put two words together to form a sentence, but not three or more (Slobin, 1972).

Obviously transparency 2.3 demonstrates very little about children's learning of the grammar of their language, except for the fact that they don't use function words or grammatical markers in two-word sentences, while they *do* normally preserve the word order of adult sentences. Note, for instance, that an adult model for "Big dog" might be "It's a big dog," while an adult model for "Spoon sticky" might be "The spoon is sticky." In other words, adult language includes instances in which an adjective precedes a noun, but also instances in which the adjective follows the noun and a linking verb. Thus the differing patterns confirm rather than contradict the generalization that children's early utterances follow the word order of adult sentences. This is the beginning of children's acquisition of grammar.

Transparency 2.4 shows commonly occurring stages in children's acquisition of the adult rule for making sentences negative. You could invite workshop participants to formulate a rule for making negative sentences from underlying affirmatives, taking one set at a time. For the first set, an appropriate rule is rather obvious: put "no" before the entire utterance. Usually people have much more trouble formulating a rule for the second set, wherein "no" or "not" is simply added between the subject and the predicate part of the sentence. In the third set, "didn't" is added to a nonnegative ("I did it," "You caught me," "I caught it"). Since the affirmative sentence is already past tense, adding "didn't" produces a double past: "didn't did," "didn't caught." Later, the child will learn to remove the tense marker from the main verb when adding "didn't."

An interesting example of the force of children's own developmental language patterns comes from Marie Linvill's son, who was 21 months old at the time of this incident.

Ryan was reading *The Fuzzy Kitten*, which contained the following text: "Here's your ball . . . Here's your mouse . . . Here's your tree—please don't fall!" In reading the text aloud to himself, Ryan said "Here a mouse, here a ball. Here a tree, no fall please!" Two aspects of language acquisition are particularly noteworthy: the omission of the contraction of *is*, and the negative, in which the negative word precedes the main part of the sentence (as in the first set of examples on T2.4). In fact, Ryan's own pattern for forming the negative overrode the force of the rhyme pattern!

The question to be posed, of course, is "How do children learn these rules?" Clearly it's not by direct teaching. Furthermore, children who are not in contact with peers speaking the same way will still go through stages of negation like these, or very similar to these. Again, we see the child's hypothesis-forming and rule-forming capacity at work. Child after child reinvents such rules and applies them, in the process of learning to negate sentences the way adults do. The process is gradual and does not require direct instruction.

Cross Reference to Transparencies 1.4 Through 1.7

As a follow-up to this discussion of children's language acquisition, you might want to use one or more of transparencies 1.4 through 1.7. Transparency 1.4 includes three key conditions for learning from Cambourne (1988); transparency 1.5 includes Holdaway's natural learning model (1986); transparency 1.6 includes our constructivist model of learning; and transparency 1.7 includes a comparison of transmission and transactional models of teaching and learning.

Drawing Conclusions: Transparencies 2.5 and 2.6

Transparency 2.5 summarizes some of the things adults do and don't do in helping their children acquire their native language.

Some people may comment that indeed they do correct children's pronunciation and grammar. However, neither is usually corrected until after the child has begun school. If grammar is corrected before then, it's usually for social acceptability ("Don't say 'aint,' say 'isn't'"). For the most part, pronunciation and grammar are both taught through modeling. The child may say "hickpopple" imploringly, and the parent, knowing the meaning of the word, may reply to the child's utterance and model the correct pronunciation by saying "You want a Popsicle? Okay, honey" (example from Connie's son, years ago). Sometimes, adults provide modeling by simply affirming and expanding upon a child's utterance. The child may say "red truck" and the parent may reply, "Yes, that's a red fire truck." Transparency 2.6 suggests the expansion and modeling that parents naturally do in helping their children learn their native language.

What we adults do *not* do is explicitly teach grammatical rules for children to apply as they're learning to talk. This point is especially important when applied by analogy to the teaching of phonics or spelling. Direct teaching of rules is not necessary and indeed may make learning to read and write unnecessarily difficult. On the other hand, helping children notice letter/sound and spelling patterns may be beneficial, particularly when done in the context of children's actual reading and writing (see Section 4, "Teaching and Learning to Read," and Section 5, "Phonics and the Teaching of Phonics").

The sixth point, that adults support language acquisition by *expecting* that children will learn to talk, is also especially important when applied by analogy to learning to read and write. All too often, school personnel have taken it for granted that a sizeable proportion of children will not learn to read and write well. This assumption of possible failure may, of course, all too readily become a self-fulfilling prophecy.

Transparency 2.6 is a cartoon drawing of a father responding to his child. The child says "Wa wa wa wa" and holds out his cup, apparently in a request for water. The father doesn't chide the child for not saying "water" distinctly; rather, he replies, "Yes, water!" He responds positively to the content of the child's utterance and expands it, instead of responding negatively to the immaturity of the child's speech. In a workshop setting you can lead participants to understand that we can encourage emergent reading and writing in similar ways.

Sources and Resources

BROWN, R. W. (1973). *A first language: The early stages*. Cambridge: Harvard University Press.

DEVILLIERS, J., & DEVILLIERS, P. (1979). *Early language*. Cambridge: Harvard University Press. This is an interesting and readable introduction to various aspects of child language acquisition.

LINDFORS, J. W. (1987). *Children's language and learning* (2nd ed.). Englewood Cliffs, NJ: Prentice Hall.

SLOBIN, D. I. (1972). They learn the same way all around the world. *Psychology Today, 6,* 72–74, 82. An intriguing article on language acquisition.

Learning the Language

As parents and caretakers, how do we teach babies and toddlers to talk?

How do we teach them the grammatical patterns and "rules" of the language?

Past Tense Rule

stop   stab   wait

lick   plug   wade

laugh   love

unearth   writhe

kiss   fizz

lurch   judge

wish

T2.2 *Past Tense Rule*   *Creating Support for Effective Literacy Education* by C. Weaver,
L. Gillmeister-Krause, & G. Vento-Zogby, © 1996. Portsmouth, NH: Heinemann. May be copied for
transparency use only.

First Sentences

Mommy read.
Doggie bite.

Pick flower.
Eat cookie.

Snoopy bone.   [Snoopy is burying the bone]
Daddy TV.   [Daddy is moving the TV]

Dirty pillow.
Spoon sticky.

My ball.
Ursula nose.   [puts her finger on her nose]

Cookie here.
Sweater chair.

Sit chair.
Play outside.

More milk.

No money.
No wash.

Patterns of Negation

1. No a boy bed.
    No the sun shining.
    No sit there.

2. He no bite you.   They not hot.
    There no squirrels.   Paul not tired.
    I no want envelope.   He not taking the
                                 walls down.

3. I didn't did it.
    You didn't caught me.
    I didn't caught it.

How Adults Facilitate Language Acquisition

1. By immersing the child in oral language.

2. By modeling adult language, not merely baby talk.

3. By responding positively to children's attempts to communicate.

4. By providing an emotionally safe environment for risk-taking.

5. By supporting children in their efforts to communicate.

6. By expecting children to eventually learn to talk like an adult.

THE READING PROCESS

This section on reading and learning to read includes two subsections, "How We Transact with Texts" and "Insights from Miscues."

Most of the concepts touched upon in this section are explained more fully in Connie's book on the reading process: Constance Weaver, *Reading Process and Practice: From Socio-Psycholinguistics to Whole Language*, 2nd edition (1994); however, the majority of the specific examples in the transparency materials are new. Other helpful references are Kenneth Goodman's *On Reading* (1996) and Frank Smith's *Reading Without Nonsense* (1979). References will be included in full at the end of each subsection.

Before the transparencies is an anticipation guide. If your workshop or series of workshops will touch upon most of the points in the anticipation guide, you might find it valuable to photocopy this guide and invite participants to respond to it at the outset—and perhaps again, as you are concluding your workshop(s).

How We Transact with Texts

One of the challenges effective teachers face is that of helping others understand why intensive, systematic phonics is not the best way to teach children to read, even though in becoming independent as readers, children clearly do need to develop at least an intuitive awareness of letter/sound patterns and the ability to use that knowledge together with other kinds of knowledge in processing texts.

Our aim here has been to include materials you can use to help parents and others understand that reading is not merely a matter of pronouncing words or of getting words and their meanings and then combining them. Rather, reading effectively requires that we read with the *intent* of constructing meaning, and that we draw upon our prior knowledge and the context together with knowledge of words and letter/sound patterns as we strive to construct meaning. It requires constantly thinking about what we are reading, monitoring our comprehension, and using fix-it strategies when meaning has gone awry or we seem unable to construct meaning (see Section 6, "Strategies and the Teaching of Strategies"). Reading requires us to use our schemas (organized chunks of knowledge) and everything we can glean from the text, in order to make sense of the text. That is, effective reading is a transaction between the reader and the text, not a matter of absorbing meaning from the page (Rosenblatt, 1964, 1978; Weaver, 1994, ch. 2).

Introduction to the Reading Process: Transparencies 3.1 and 3.2

Either transparency 3.1 or 3.2 could be used to introduce a workshop on the reading process, or both could be used in sequence.

Transparency 3.1 invites workshop participants to discuss what reading is like, or most like: making a cake? building a tower of blocks? learning to ride a bike? dancing? Connie first used this transparency when she wanted to end a workshop with the concept of reading as a dance (transparency 3.15), but of course many other responses make good sense, too. For example, though Connie originally thought of building a tower as a hierarchical process starting with the foundation up, and thus a part-to-whole concept different from the way we conceptualize learning to read, she has found that workshop participants sometimes make excellent analogies: they talk about starting with an overall blueprint, the whole, and gradually assembling the parts; or they talk about scaffolding that may give temporary support to the builder, then later be removed. Both are excellent analogies, we think. In any case, you will probably want to accept all offerings and suggest that the group reconsider possible analogies after they have engaged in further investigation and discussion.

Transparency 3.2 includes some discussion questions that may be useful in helping participants think about themselves as readers. In preparation for whole-group discussion of responses to these questions, you might use the "think/pair/share" procedure. That is, invite participants to think about their responses and jot some of them down, then turn to a partner nearby and share reflections. Surely some participants will have learned to read before starting school, so you can ask what their parent(s) and/or older brothers and sisters did that enabled them to learn to read. With participants who say they were taught by phonics, you might ask whether someone was also reading to them at home and, if yes, point out that it may have been the interactive one-on-one reading experiences that facilitated their learning to read, as much or more than the phonics instruction.

The third question, "What kinds of things do you NOT read, and why?" may elicit from some people the confession that they never liked reading and don't read anything they don't have to read. Why? Often, the explanation may be that they never liked reading in school, or never got to read for pleasure in school. Exploration of such responses (and comparison with the responses of others) may

enable you to convince people that reading *in* school needs to be enjoyable if we want students to become willing and avid readers outside of and beyond school. Such a discussion may tie in with people's responses to questions 4 and 5 as well.

Bringing Meaning to a Text: Transparency 3.3

Transparency 3.3 can be used to quickly introduce the idea that readers necessarily construct meaning by transacting with a text, instead of merely absorbing meaning from it. The process is two-directional (really, multidirectional) rather than unidirectional, from text to reader. Transparency 3.3 is a poem Connie once wrote. If you ask workshop participants what the poem "says," surely you and various participants will find differing meanings in this poem, even though you have all read the same words. We all construct partially different meanings from texts. (In case you're interested, Connie borrowed an assignment from a poet in her department—an assignment to write a poem about a body part. This was the result when Connie tried the assignment herself.)

The transparency includes only the first two stanzas of the poem. The last two stanzas read as follows:

> What's a Naval good for, you ask?
> Well, to get rid of things, obviously:
>   rust, seeds, people.
> But yours and mine—Navals, that is?
> Well, they're different.
> Mine forms a tiny pool
> to catch the raindrops
> of your tears
> While yours, tongue-kissed
> is my passport to Beyond,
> the hole where Alice disappeared,
> an airdrop to a wonder crazy world
> where navals don't matter anymore.
>
> Or is it people?

Sources of Information in the Reading Process: Transparencies 3.4a Through 3.4d

Transparencies 3.4a through 3.4d are intended to generate some of the same insights as related activities in Connie's *Reading Process and Practice*, Chapter 5 (pp. 175–77 and 212–15). If you have participants try to read "The Animal School" in chorus and discuss their problems and strategies and processes, here are some of the conclusions that may emerge:

1. Prior knowledge is very important in constructing meaning from a text.

2. We naturally use context, as well as prior knowledge, to predict what is coming next. In fact, as proficient readers we are so accustomed to using context that the force of context tends to override our inclination to look at the number of hyphens (part of the visual details in paragraphs 2, 3, and 4) to work out the word. Thus, the strategy of predicting leads us to make miscues—just as it does in reading normal, unmutilated texts.

3. We have the most difficulty when (1) the text contains a relatively unusual word that isn't very predictable (at least not in this context); or (2) the prior context allows for more than one reasonable prediction. (For example, the word "gl-nts" (*glints*) may not be immediately identifiable because it's not a word we encounter every day, or the word "dr--m-r" may not be readily identified because we don't usually think of deer as being dreamers. In the latter case, using everything we know may foil us, at first, in our efforts to identify the word.)

4. When prior knowledge, context, and limited visual information have led us to mispredict a word, we are sometimes able to correct by using the following context. (For example, some readers are able to get the word "f--l-d" after, but only after, reading the following context and realizing that a fish wouldn't be very

good at running, climbing, singing, and night defense: hence the word must be "failed.")

5. We can usually get the meaning without getting all the words. (See particularly the section where every fifth word is blacked out.)

6. We don't always bother to correct out loud or even silently, when we have been able to get meaning without identifying the exact word.

7. Within a meaningful text that we have sufficient prior knowledge to understand, vowels are relatively unimportant. In fact, we can predict many (perhaps most) of the words from prior knowledge, context, and consonants alone. (This, in turn, can lead to the observation that teaching rules for pronouncing vowels is unnecessary. For related transparencies, see Section 5, "Phonics and Teaching Phonics.")

Of course all of these observations hold true for proficient readers when reading potentially comprehensible and "normal" text. The purpose for doing the activities is to help others realize the complexity of what is involved in reading. This may help in explaining why phonics instruction need not and should not be a prerequisite to reading texts with oral support, and why teaching phonics intensively and systematically, in isolation, is not the best way to teach phonics.

Note on Particular Sections of "The Animal School"

The section with just the vowels looks impossible to read, and may indeed be so. However, Connie has found with the comparable "Lobo" passage in *Reading Process and Practice* (1994, p. 176) that people can usually read it *if* she supplies the word when it is especially unpredictable *and* if she supplies the word when participants suggest a word that's a good prediction, but not the exact word of the text (this happens particularly with function words, in instances where two or more of them would be logical predictions from the preceding context).

You may find that similar help can enable workshop participants to read the consonant-less passage in "The Animal School," too—though in our experience, this passage is harder to read, even with help.

We have attempted to write the very last section in Pitman's Initial Teaching Alphabet, using the symbols and rules from Pitman & St. John (1969). You may find it useful to first write the following symbols on a blank transparency (ω ŋ ʄh ∫ æ), ask participants what sounds these symbols probably represent, have participants read "The Animal School," and then point out that they could read the ending without knowing all the sound/symbol relations. However, this particular passage does not contain as many of the unusual symbols as the ITA passage in Connie's *Reading Process and Practice* (1994, pp. 212–13), so the activity may not be as convincing with the new text. (You may put the "Lobo" story on transparencies, if you like.)

"The Animal School" in Its Entirety

For your clarification, here is "The Animal School" as originally drafted. It is based on but not taken directly from the animal school parable in a 1972 book by Leo Buscaglia (who has indicated that it is a widely known story):

> Once upon a time there was a school for animals in the forest. The curriculum consisted of swimming, running, jumping, climbing, singing, and night defense.
>
> The fish, of course, could swim beautifully, darting between the rocks and reflecting glints of light from the morning sun. He could hunt for bugs, too, provided he didn't have to leap too high out of the water. But of course the fish failed at running, jumping, climbing, singing, and night defense.
>
> The deer excelled at running; she could run faster than any of the other animals, and she could jump across creeks and climb hills with ease. Her singing sounded more like snorting, though, and she preferred wading to swimming. Night defense wasn't her specialty either, because she was a dreamer and liked to go roaming in the moonlight.

> The bear was a snorter, too, not a singer. But he could lumber along at a rapid pace, swim when necessary, and climb trees. Tree climbing was, in fact, the one area in which he was superior to all the other animals in the school.
>
> Sure, the bird could climb the side of a tree a little bit, but she wasn't nearly as good as the bear at climbing. Her greatest strength lay in singing: she could sing several songs that delighted the other forest animals. However, the bird failed at swimming, running, and jumping, and her idea of night defense was simply to wrap her claws around a branch, close her eyes, and sleep. The bat, on the other hand, was terrific at night defense. He could detect danger by screeching and using his sonar. However, the bat fell asleep every day during school, when all the other classes were held. The teachers could never even determine whether the bat could or couldn't swim, run, jump, or climb. As for singing, the bat only succeeded at screeching all night, when all the other animals were trying to sleep.
>
> The other member of the class was a mongrel dog that had wandered into the forest and joined their school. He could swim across a stream, though he hated to get wet; he could run a little, even though he limped; he could jump a little, though not as far as the deer; he could climb hills and leap at trees in a pretense at climbing; he could sing a little, though his singing sounded more like howling; and he could defend himself and his friends at night by barking and raising an alarm. Even though the dog couldn't do anything really well, he was the class valedictorian because he could do everything a little and didn't fail anything.

Context and Word Pronunciation: Transparency 3.5

This transparency is based on pp. 129–30 of Connie's *Reading Process and Practice* (1994). To help others realize that even pronunciation sometimes depends upon context, you can first cover the sentences and ask participants to read the six words at the top of the transparency. Of course people will surely realize that the words can be pronounced in more than one way, depending on the meaning. (However, many people may not realize that "minute" can be pronounced with the accent on either the first or the second syllable, depending on whether the word refers to a measure of time or whether it indicates something tiny.)

If you then have participants read the eight sentences below the words, they will either read these six words correctly or correct their pronunciation after they process the following part of the sentence. (Again, "minute" in #7 might be an exception.) You may be able to lead participants to observe that they could read most of these sentences without even thinking about the pronunciation of the words, and from this you can point out that we just naturally use prior knowledge and context along with words and letter/sound knowledge as we read. (For example, did you yourself hesitate over the mental pronunciation of "lead" in the previous sentence, or over the pronunciations of the two instances of "read"?)

Context and Word Meanings: Transparencies 3.6 and 3.7

The materials for these transparencies and most of the following comments are taken from or based on Connie's *Reading Process and Practice* (1994, pp. 16–17 and 35 respectively). These transparencies can be used to help people understand that reading is not a matter of identifying words and combining their meanings, but rather a matter of using everything we know to construct meaning—and in the process, *imposing meanings on words*, based on the context and our prior knowledge. More generally, these transparencies can be used to help participants understand the transactional nature of the reading process, including the fact that we must bring meaning *to* a text in order to get meaning from it.

With **transparency 3.6**, you can ask workshop participants what the word "run" means in each sentence, and how they know. In the first five sentences, "run" occurs in a context that signals its use as a verb, while in the last five it occurs in a context that signals

its use as a noun; these contexts partially delimit the meaning of the word "run."

In "run the store," we know that "run" means something like 'manage'; in "run the word processor," we know that "run" means something like 'operate'; in "his milk run," we know that "run" means something like 'route'; and so forth. Interestingly, in the sentences where "run" is a verb, the precise meaning is determined by a noun that comes after it, rather than before. The semantic context of the surrounding words clarifies the meaning of "run" in any particular sentence.

With "It was a long run," we need the situational context or more verbal context beyond the sentence to clarify the meaning of "run." In the context of stockings, "run" would refer to a tear (pronounced to rhyme with "bear"). In the context of a dog kennel, "run" would mean an enclosure. In the context of fishing, "run" would mean migrating fish. In the context of skiing, "run" would mean a downhill path or route. In the context of theater, "It was a long run" would mean that the play was performed for a long period of time. And so forth.

A large dictionary will include numerous meanings for basic prepositions like "by," in **transparency 3.7**. However, we do not know the relevant meaning(s) of such a word until we see it in context. In the first sentence, "by" indicates the agent, Dr. Lucy. In the second sentence, "by" probably means 'next to' or 'close to.' In the third sentence, "by" indicates the *means* of transportation used. In the fourth sentence, "by" means 'according to.' And what does "by" mean in the fifth sentence? It's almost impossible to say.

Getting Words and Getting Meaning: Transparencies 3.8 Through 3.10

Transparency 3.8 is a passage you can use to demonstrate to people that it is possible to "get" (identify, pronounce) all or almost all the words in a selection, without "getting" much meaning. This happens, of course, when we have insufficient background knowledge. The passage is from Brian Cambourne's *The Whole Story* (1988, p. 161), and Connie was so unable to construct meaning from it that without reconsulting Cambourne's book, she requested permission to use his passage about "rugby." Wrong, Connie: it's about cricket! (She should have known better, having briefly observed a rugby game from a distance while in Australia. Or was it a cricket game instead?)

Cambourne discusses in some detail (pp. 161–62) the questions he uses to get people to realize that they can pronounce all or almost all of the words except the proper nouns (specific names), and can supply at least one possible meaning for most of them—without necessarily constructing much meaning from this passage, other than that a sporting event is being described and one team (perhaps the local favorite?) is being soundly defeated by the other.

Transparency 3.9 is taken from a children's story, *The Bookstore Mouse*, by Peggy Christian (1995). A reading specialist, Peggy claims that Connie's *Reading Process and Practice* (1994) taught her how to read, and that this professional book served as the inspiration for *The Bookstore Mouse*. The plot is complex, but one major strand involves the way Cervantes, the bookstore mouse, learns to construct meaning from texts, not just read the words. The book delightfully presents many research-based observations about proficient reading, including the observation that readers can supply about every fifth word in a passage for which they have adequate background knowledge (as in the traditional cloze procedure). Transparency 3.9 is such a passage, though in this message there usually are somewhat longer intervals between missing words.

Cervantes the mouse has fallen into a book and its story; more precisely, he has fallen into a "scriptorium" where a young man, Sigfried, labors as a scribe copying manuscripts for the monk overseeing his work, the armarius. Left alone while the monks are at mass, Sigfried and Cervantes hear a knock at the door and admit a rain-soaked messenger with a crumpled, muddy piece of parchment for the armarius. Finally Cervantes convinces Sigfried that they must try to read the message, since the messenger seemed so urgent. The rain-spattered message is reproduced as transparency 3.9.

In a workshop setting, you can share the preceding explanation with participants, then lead them to try to read the message, putting in *something* whenever appropriate. Can participants make good guesses at what some of the blurred words might be? You can then discuss what seems to be the essence of this message, and point out how they as readers—like Cervantes and Sigfried—could decipher enough of the message to take informed action, even with several of the words missing.

Transparency 3.10 allows for almost the opposite point to be made. That is, on the one hand, readers may have difficulty pronouncing some of the words, and unless they're pharmacists or chemists (or have a good memory for high school or college chemistry), they may be unable to supply any meaning or definition for some of the words. But if you tell them that this is a description accompanying a medication (as it was presented in Dundas & Strong, 1991), they probably can tell you whether the medication would help an allergy ("it . . . antagonizes allergic manifestation") and whether it will relieve pain ("it anesthetizes . . . pain"). Thus, an examination of this passage can demonstrate how we often can and do read for and obtain the information we want, without "getting" all the words.

Nonsense Passages and the Reading Process: Transparencies 3.11 and 3.12

Transparency 3.11 includes a short nonsense passage, "A Flannerby Barp for Nall," accompanied by so-called comprehension questions. **Transparency 3.12** is "The Blonke," from Connie's *Reading Process and Practice* (1994, p. 40; see also p. 41 and p. 47).

You might cover the questions about the

first passage and have workshop participants read the passage aloud, in chorus. Then have them answer the questions. The answer to the first question is, obviously, the characters are Nall and Charkle. The answers to 2a and 2b can be taken directly from the text, without understanding anything: (a) They were larping to the flannerby; (b) She wanted to grunk a flannerby barp so she could crooch out carples. The best answer for the third question is less certain: response (a) seems least appropriate, since it focuses just on the characters and not on what they did; however, an argument could be made for each of the other options.

Here is the passage as Grace originally drafted it:

> Nall was so excited. She was going to the library with Charkle. She would get a library card so she could take out books. Charkle helped her fill out the form.
> "Thanks, Charkle," said Nall excitedly.
> "Now we can take out books together!" laughed Charkle happily.

And here are some points that can be elicited or supplied during discussion:

1. Most people can read such a passage without having any significant trouble with the words. They don't apply phonics rules but instead read the nonsense words by analogy with familiar words and word parts. For example, "crooch" will probably be pronounced with the same vowel sound as "pooch" or "boot," though it could alternatively be pronounced with the vowel sound of "hook" or "book." In either case, our pronunciation is likely to be guided by analogy with known words, even if we aren't conscious of drawing such analogies. This is the way both children and adults commonly use phonics in reading: they read unfamiliar words, or sound out the parts of these words, by analogy with existing words and word parts (see, for instance, the transparencies on onsets and rimes in Section 5 on phonics). Like some of the preceding transparencies, numbers 3.11 and 3.12 can be used to help

clarify why teaching phonics *rules* is not particularly helpful.

2. We can get some meaning from the nonsense passage (perhaps even more than from Cambourne's passage on cricket, which uses real words in a way that is meaningful—but only to those who have the background knowledge). We can probably tell that Nall and Charkle are engaging in some activity that pleases them and that will enable them to do something pleasurable in the future.

3. Even if we didn't get any meaning, though, we could answer the "comprehension" questions intelligently. Or in other words, questions like this, which have traditionally permeated the basal reading programs, don't require much genuine understanding of what has been read. Many such questions can be answered just by manipulating the language of the text.

The same points and more can be made by reading and discussing "The Blonke," which incorporates words that were once meaningful in English (Susan Kelz Sperling, *Poplollies and Bellibones: A Celebration of Lost Words*, 1977). Here are some "comprehension" questions you might ask:

1. Where was the small wam?
2. What is "drumly"?
3. Why weren't the other blonkes drumly?
4. In what way(s) was the drumly blonke like/unlike all the others?
5. If bellytimber is venenated, is it wise to givel it in the flosh? Why or why not?

When Connie has used this passage in a workshop, she has typically found that people *do* get some meaning on a first or second reading of the passage. They commonly get the impression that the blonke is an animal of some sort, one who is obviously different from the others of his kind. Often, people comment that something seems to be wrong with this particular blonke. Then, Connie sometimes supplies the meanings of just two words: A "blonke" is a large, powerful horse; the word "drumly" means something like 'sluggish.' Rereading the passage with just these two words supplied may give some hint as to what is wrong with the blonke, what has made him so sluggish (see especially the last paragraph). When time is at a premium, Connie may supply not only the meanings of "blonke" and "drumly" but also the meanings of two other words: "bellytimber," which means 'food,' and "venenated," which means 'poisoned.' With this much information, people can usually explain, in general terms and in ordinary words, what's being recommended in the last two sentences: put the poisoned food somewhere where the blonkes that aren't already poisoned can't get to it. (This explains *why* it's indeed wise to givel venenated bellytimber in the flosh.)

As with some of the earlier transparencies, one of the most important points to be made with this passage is the observation that we can often get the essential meaning of a text without identifying or knowing all the words. Even in situations where comprehension would seem to require knowing all the words, this is rarely so. Perhaps discussing "The Blonke" will help parents realize that it's not usually a problem if their child does not read all the words or identify *every* word while reading. In fact, many readers who make a lot of miscues on words are able to get considerable meaning from what they read—even when many of the miscues suggest a loss of meaning. Prior knowledge and redundancy within the text come to their aid.

For the curious, here is a list of the "lost" words in the passage about the blonke:

Bellytimber—Food, provisions

Blonke—A large, powerful horse

Blore—To cry out or bleat and bray like an animal

Crinet—A hair

Drumly—Cloudy, sluggish

Fairney cloots—Small, horny substances above the hoofs of horses, sheep, and goats

Flosh—A swamp or stagnant pool overgrown with weeds

Givel—To heap up

Icchen—To move, stir

Kexy—Dry, juiceless

Lennow—Flappy, limp

Maily—Speckled

Quetch—To moan and twitch in pain, shake

Samded—Half-dead

Shawk—Smell

Sparple—To scatter, spread about

Spiss—Thick, dense

Venenate—To poison

Wam—A scar, cicatrix

Wong—Meadowlands, commons

Yerd—To beat with a rod

Contrasting Models of Reading: Transparencies 3.13 and 3.14

Transparency 3.13 is in effect a "skills" model of reading. It suggests that reading is a combination of skills (phonics skills, word analysis skills, comprehension skills, and critical thinking skills) and a collection of verbal units (sight words; vocabulary, including word pronunciations and meanings; and texts, including various story and text structures). Probably it would be more accurate to say that this model reflects not so much anyone's concept of reading itself, but a model of learning to read that can be inferred from traditional practice that teaches these skills and aspects of language apart from actual reading. This is the kind of model rejected by those who understand reading to be a transactional, meaning-constructing process.

In contrast is **transparency 3.14**, which is based on Connie's model in Chapter 5 of *Reading Process and Practice* (1994, p. 213). Without going into detail about the supporting research, suffice it to say that this "constructive" or "redundancy" model of the reading process itself indicates that when we construct meanings from text, we are simultaneously using all kinds of visual and nonvisual information, which complement and reinforce each other. For example, words are easier to identify when we are using prior knowledge and context; letters are easier to identify when we know the word in which they occur; word meanings depend upon context; comprehension is made easier when we can readily identify most of the words and simultaneously bring prior knowledge to the task; and so forth. This model suggests the need for reading instruction that helps children learn sight words and vocabulary, develop letter/sound knowledge and word analysis skills, and hone their critical thinking skills *in the context of also using prior knowledge and context to construct meaning from texts.* (We might also have included metacognition in the middle of the model, to indicate that readers make conscious use of various kinds of strategies. However, years of analyzing readers' miscues and comparing the strategies readers use with the strategies they *say* they use have led us to the conclusion that proficient readers are not *necessarily* conscious of the productive strategies that they do, in fact, use.)

Reading as a Dance: Transparency 3.15

Transparency 3.15, "Learning to Dance," is meant to summarize in poetic form the transactional nature of the reading process. In sharing and perhaps discussing it with workshop participants, you may want to refer back to transparency 3.1, which invites people to consider analogies for reading.

Sources and Resources (Professional)

CAMBOURNE, B. (1988). *The whole story: Natural learning and the acquisition of literacy in the classroom.* Auckland, New Zealand: Ashton Scholastic.

DUNDAS, V., & STRONG, G. (1991). *Readers, writers, and parents learning together.* Katonah, NY: Richard C. Owen.

GOODMAN, K. S. (1996). *On reading.* Portsmouth, NH: Heinemann.

PITMAN, SIR J., & ST. JOHN, J. (1969). *Alphabets and reading: The initial teaching alphabet.* New York: Pitman Publishing Corporation.

ROSENBLATT, L. (1964). The poem as event. *College English, 26,* 123–128.

ROSENBLATT, L. (1978). *The reader, the text, the poem: The transactional theory of the literary work.* Carbondale, IL: Southern Illinois University Press.

SMITH, F. (1979). *Reading without nonsense.* New York: Teachers College Press.

WEAVER, C. (1994). *Reading process and practice: From socio-psycholinguistics to whole language* (2nd ed.). Portsmouth, NH: Heinemann.

Other Credits

BUSCAGLIA, L. (1972). *Love.* New York: Fawcett Crest.

CHRISTIAN, PEGGY. (1995). *The bookstore mouse.* San Diego: Harcourt Brace Jovanovich (Jane Yolen Books).

SPERLING, S. K. (1977). *Poplollies and bellibones: A celebration of lost words.* New York: Clarkson N. Potter.

Insights from Miscues

As readers and users of this book are likely to know, Kenneth Goodman coined the term "miscue" to describe any departure from the text that a reader makes in reading aloud, or silently—an unexpected response (K. Goodman, 1965). Goodman pointed out that miscues provide us with a window to the reading process. That is, research into the nature of proficient readers' miscues gives us insight into the nature of reading itself.

Most of the transparencies from 3.16 through 3.24 show examples of miscues, while the others relate to these. This set of transparencies could be used in a separate workshop introducing the concept of miscue, or interspersed with previous ones to help clarify the nature of the reading process itself. The following conventional miscue markings are used:

SUBSTITUTION

After a hearty supper Hayes joined the other

around

smokers about the fire.

(A word written over another word indicates a substitution.)

OMISSION

. . . she always stays (at) home . . .

(A circle around a word or group of words indicates an omission.)

INSERTION

at all

His appearance did not ⋀ settle all the questions. . . .

(A caret points to whatever is inserted.)

REVERSAL

They saw ⌐simply a loose, lank youth. . . .

(The typical editor's symbol is used to indicate a reversal.)

CORRECTION

©*young*

They saw simply a loose, lank ⌐youth⌐ with tow-colored sunburned hair. . . .

(The © indicates that the miscue was corrected, and the underlining indicates what portion of the text was repeated as the reader made the correction.)

Good Readers' Miscues: Transparencies 3.16 Through 3.23

The examples of miscues in most of the transparencies from 3.16 through 3.23 are taken from Connie's *Reading Process and Practice* (1994).

Transparency 3.16 shows the miscues of Anne, a first grader. If you read the passage aloud the way Anne read it, people will usually realize that the essential meaning is not changed by her miscues, even though she identified only 92 percent of the words exactly. The miscues in the following transparencies can be used similarly, as explained below.

Transparency 3.17 shows some examples of good readers' typical insertions, omissions, and substitutions. They come from K. Goodman (1973, passim), but are included also in Weaver (1994). An important point from the research is that good readers actually make more miscues on function words and pronouns (as illustrated here) than poorer readers (K. Goodman, 1973). This is because good readers are constantly predicting what might logically come next, using context and everything they know.

Transparency 3.18 shows words on which various first graders miscued in isolation, along with sentences or parts of sentences wherein the children identified the words correctly. You might use this transparency to help explain how readers develop the ability to recognize words gradually, by seeing them again and again in familiar or at least meaningful contexts. For example, when Lester Laminack's son Zachary could identify the name "McDonald's" on the golden arches, he at first could identify it only in that context. When Lester pointed to the name on a cup, Zachary read it as "orange drink," while on the bag of fries he read the same logo as "french fries." It was only gradually that he learned to identify the word in other familiar contexts, and then in any context or situation whatsoever (Laminack, 1991).

It's important for parents of emergent readers to understand that word recognition develops gradually, and therefore not to be overly concerned when a child can identify a word in a familiar context but not yet in isolation. Some researchers make the point that really good readers can automatically read most of the words they encounter (Adams, 1990). However, what they don't also point out is that children acquire this ability partly if not mainly by seeing words again and again in their reading, particularly in contexts that make the words understandable and somewhat predictable. Children thereby learn not only some particular words, but the letter/sound patterns that are repeated over and over again in many words. (See also the fact sheet on Research on the Teaching of Phonics, in Part Two.) You might share with participants the picture book *Least of All*, by Carol Purdy, in which a young girl teachers herself to read by going over familiar biblical passages again and again. Or you might compare the gradual learning of words with children gradually learning to ride a bike or swim, or with young adults gradually learning to drive a car in traffic. Adult-level mastery doesn't come all at once.

Transparencies 3.19a and 3.19b can be used in a way similar to transparency 3.16, but this extended example allows for more points to be derived from it. Most of the discussion below is taken from an article of Connie's (Weaver, 1996).

In order to help others understand that proficient reading is characterized more by a drive to construct meaning than by accurate word identification (even with readers who identify almost all the words accurately), Connie has sometimes read aloud the passage with Jay's miscues (transparencies 3.19a and b) and invited listeners to be alert for miscues—that is, for departures from what the original probably said. If you try the same procedure, you might tell workshop participants that in this excerpt from "Jimmy Hayes and Muriel" the author, O. Henry, has sometimes represented features of southwestern dialect (Porter, 1936). The passage below recapitulates the way the original was read by Jay, a sixth grader who was considered to be the best reader in his class. (Jay's self-corrections are not included here.) In first reading this passage, you as well as your workshop participants might be alert for probable miscues:

> After a hearty supper Hayes joined the smokers around the fire. His appearance did not at all settle all the questions in the minds of his brother rangers. They simply saw a loose, lank young with tow-colored sunburned hair and a berry-brown, ingenious face that wore a quizzical, good-natured smile.
>
> "Fellows," said the new ranger, "I'm goin' to interduce you to a lady friend of mine. Ain't heard much about her beauty, but you'll all admit she's got a fine points about her. Come along, Muriel!"
>
> He held open the front of his blue flannel shirt. Out crawled a horned toad. A bright red ribbon was tied jauntily around its spiky neck. It crawled to its owner's knee and it sat there motionless.
>
> "This here's Muriel," said Hayes, with an oratorical wave of his hand. "She's got qualities. She never talks back, she always stays home, and she's satisfied with one red dress for everyday and Sunday, too."
>
> "Look at that blamed insect!" said one of the rangers with a grin. "I've seen plenty of them horny toads, but I never knew anybody to have one for a partner. Does the blame thing know you from anybody else?"
>
> "Take her over there and see," said Hayes.

Listeners will surely notice "young" for *youth*, in the phrase *a loose, lank youth*. The word "young" was a reasonable prediction, based on prior context and sampling of the letter/sound cues, but it did not fit with the following grammar; not surprisingly, Jay corrected it. The word "a" was also a logical prediction, in the context *you'll all admit she's got. . . .* However, the following phrase was actually *fine points*, so the singular "a" didn't quite fit with the grammar of the following context. This miscue Jay didn't correct. Nor did he correct the other miscue that some listeners will have noticed, namely "ingenious" for *ingenuous*. Probably Jay didn't know the word *ingenuous*. It is very difficult to sound out words correctly when they aren't part of at least our aural vocabulary, the words we know upon hearing them.

These, however, are only three of the twenty-three miscues Jay made (Weaver, 1994, pp. 259–61; the discussion is from Weaver, 1996). The other twenty miscues do not reflect a significant difference in meaning, nor do they disrupt the flow of the text.

Questions About Strategies: Transparency 3.20

Transparency 3.20 includes questions to ask about readers' use of effective reading strategies (see Section 6 for more information on strategies). These relate to transparency 3.23, "Characteristics of Good Readers." Asking such questions of a reader's miscues enables us to determine whether a reader is using crucial reading strategies with reasonable effectiveness.

Jay's Predicting and Restructuring: Transparencies 3.21 and 3.22

In a workshop setting, you could return to transparencies 3.19a and 3.19b to demonstrate Jay's effective use of reading strategies: he predicts, monitors comprehension, makes appropriate use of grapho/phonemic cues along with prior knowledge and context, and orchestrates various sources of information to construct meaning from text. Alternatively, you might use **transparency 3.21** to demonstrate how Jay uses prior knowledge and context to predict, and/or use **transparency 3.22** to demonstrate how he restructures text to maintain grammar and meaning while producing a fluent rendition of the text. When we look at strategies for processing text instead of simplistically looking at word identification alone, we can see that Jay is a superb reader. This conclusion is reinforced by Jay's ability to retell and discuss what he has read.

Characteristics of Good Readers: Transparency 3.23

From analyzing the miscues of many other good readers too, researchers have found (e.g., K. Goodman, 1973) that good readers exhibit such characteristics as the following:

1. They concentrate more upon constructing meaning from texts than upon identifying all the words correctly (as Jay obviously did).

2. They are constantly monitoring comprehension (which Jay did), noticing when meaning has gone awry, and when necessary, doing whatever they can to restore meaningfulness (which Jay didn't need to do).

3. They use prior knowledge and context to predict (perhaps unconsciously) what's coming next. Sometimes this *causes* miscues (as it often did with Jay). At other times, this strategy prevents miscues or simply enables readers to identify words by just sampling the visual information. We see this combined use of prior knowledge, context, and minimal visual information most clearly when it doesn't quite work, as when Jay first read "young" for *youth*, only to find that the next word needed to be a noun.

4. While good readers may indeed "see" most of the visual information in most of the words in a text (Adams, 1990), this doesn't mean that they normally or necessarily use all the available visual information to identify words. Miscue analysis suggests, instead, that when reading whole and coherent texts, good readers normally take advantage of the redundancy of the language, orchestrating prior knowledge and context to predict, and thereby to reduce their reliance on visual information from the words they are about to encounter.

5. Most of the miscues made by proficient readers are both grammatical and meaning-preserving in context, or else corrected (as Jay's were).

All of these observations about good miscues demonstrate, in effect, the nature of the reading process itself. It is not a precise process of identifying every word, but an ongoing construction of meaning from the text.

Reading Levels: Transparency 3.24

Transparency 3.24 on reading levels (from Weaver, 1994, p. 226, but based on other sources) may be used to suggest the inappropriateness of using the percentage of words identified correctly as a measure of a child's reading ability. For both Anne in transparency 3.16 and Jay in transparencies 3.19a and 3.19b, the selections would be deemed at their instructional level if word accuracy were the criterion—despite the fact that most of their miscues preserved the essential meaning and flow of the text. Of course the quantity of words identified correctly would not be so inappropriate if, before the count, the teacher/researcher were to eliminate self-corrections, repetitions of the same miscue, and miscues that aren't corrected but that preserve grammar and meaning. Even so, however, the quantity of miscues or of words identified accurately is not as good a criterion as the reader's ability to retell and discuss a reading selection—and this is not the same as answering the usual kinds of questions found in a basal reading program or an Informal Reading Inventory manual. See, for example, the Reading Miscue Inventory manual (Y. Goodman, Watson, & Burke, 1987).

Sources and Resources

ADAMS, M. J. (1990). *Beginning to read: Thinking and learning about print.* Cambridge: Harvard University Press.

GOODMAN, K. S. (1965). A linguistic study of cues and miscues in reading. *Elementary English, 42,* 639–643.

GOODMAN, K. S. (1973). *Theoretically based studies of patterns of miscues in oral reading performance.* Detroit: Wayne State University. (ERIC: ED 079 708).

GOODMAN, Y. M., WATSON, D. J., & BURKE, C. L. (1987). *Reading miscue inventory: Alternative procedures.* Katonah, NY: Richard C. Owen.

LAMINACK, L. L. (1991). *Learning with Zachary.* Richmond Hill, Ontario: Scholastic.

WEAVER, C. (1994). *Reading process and practice: From socio-psycholinguistics to whole language* (2nd ed.). Portsmouth, NH: Heinemann.

WEAVER, C. (forthcoming). Understanding and helping Jaime with reading and with language: A psycholinguistic and constructivist perspective. In E. R. Silliman, L. C. Wilkinson, & L. P. Hoffman, *Children's journeys through school: Assessing and building competence in language and literacy.* San Diego: Singular Publishing Group.

Other Credits

BARR, J. (1949). *Little circus dog.* Chicago: Albert Whitman.

CHRISTIAN, P. (1995). *The bookstore mouse.* San Diego: Harcourt Brace Jovanovich (Jane Yolen Books).

PORTER, W. S. (1936). *The complete works of O. Henry.* Garden City, NY: Doubleday.

PURDY, C. (1987). *Least of all.* Illus. T. Arnold. New York: Macmillan, Aladdin Books.

The following anticipation guide is designed to raise questions. Please begin by indicating your response in the "Before" column. You may use the following key: SA for "strongly agree"; A for "agree"; U for "uncertain"; D for "disagree"; and SD for "strongly disagree."

When you have finished, please circle three or four items you particularly want to have clarified by today's workshop, and/or list some other questions that you have generated.

Before	After	
_____	_____	1. It's important to identify all the words when you're reading.
_____	_____	2. Words are easier to identify in context than in isolation.
_____	_____	3. By informally discussing literary works, children refine their ability to comprehend texts and think critically.
_____	_____	4. Phonics should be taught intensively and systematically.
_____	_____	5. Good readers make more miscues ("errors") involving basic sight words (like *a, the, in, and, that*) than less proficient readers.
_____	_____	6. It's more important to give a child a strategy than to give a child a word.
_____	_____	7. Using non-visual cues (prior knowledge and context) enables readers to construct meaning without overattending to visual cues.
_____	_____	8. Some miscues are actually an improvement upon the author's text.
_____	_____	9. We should be selective in helping children notice common onsets of words (e.g. *fl-, pr-, st-*) and common rimes (e.g. *-an -ent, -ook*).
_____	_____	10. We need to teach the reading comprehension skills in basal reading programs, rather than leave comprehension to chance.
_____	_____	11. One important way to teach phonics is by encouraging approximated spelling.
_____	_____	12. We should correct readers when they make miscues ("errors").
_____	_____	13. Constructing meaning from text is more important than identifying all the words.
_____	_____	14. Readers who might otherwise be considered nonproficient can often demonstrate excellent understanding during literature discussions.
_____	_____	15. Correcting readers' miscues helps convince them that they cannot read independently, without someone to help them with words.
_____	_____	16. We cannot read something for which we lack prior knowledge.

My questions:

Learning to Read Is Like

- making a cake

- building a tower of blocks

- learning to ride a bike

- dancing

Discussion Questions on Reading

1. How did you learn to read?

2. What kinds of things do you read?

3. What kinds of things do you NOT read, and why?

4. Have your reading habits changed over the years? If so, how and why?

5. How do you feel about yourself as a reader? Why do you feel that way?

T3.2 *Discussion Questions on Reading*   *Creating Support for Effective Literacy Education* by C. Weaver, L. Gillmeister-Krause, & G. Vento-Zogby, © 1996. Portsmouth, NH: Heinemann. May be copied for transparency use only.

"Song of the Deranged Sailor"

Have you contemplated your ??? today?
Let's see, what was it—
Tongue, toenails, tummy (wrong letter)
Yes, noggin, nose, nellie, belly—
Ah, belly button, known to sophisticates
    as the Naval.

Have you contemplated your Naval today?
Let's see, we have naval oranges, naval
    battles, naval jelly.
If naval jelly takes the rust off metal,
naval oranges *ought* to take the seeds
    out of the orange.
Yes, it makes sense.
But what of naval battles?
Ah, yes, of course—they take *people*
    off the earth.

"The Animal School"

Once upon a time there was a school for animals in the forest. The curriculum consisted of swimming, running, jumping, climbing, singing, and night defense.

Th- f-sh, -f c--rs-, c--ld sw-m b---t-f-lly, d-rt-ng b-tw--n th- r-cks -nd r-fl-ct-ng gl-nts -f l-ght fr-m th- m-rn-ng s-n. H- c--ld h-nt f-r b-gs, t--, pr-v-d-d h- d-dn't h-v- t- l--p t-- h-gh --t -f th- w-t-r. B-t -f c--rs- th- f-sh f--l-d -t r-nn-ng, cl-mb-ng, s-ng-ng, -nd n-ght d-f-ns-.

Th- d--r -xc-ll-d -t r-nn-ng; sh- c--ld r-n f-st-r th-n -ny -f th- -th-r -n-m-ls, -nd sh- c--ld j-mp -cr-ss cr--ks -nd cl-mb h-lls w-th --s-. H-r s-ng-ng s--nd-d m-r- l-k- sn-rt-ng, th--gh, -nd sh- pr-f-rr-d w-d-ing t- sw-mm-ng. N-ght d-f-ns- w-sn't h-r sp-c--lty, --th-r, b-c--s- sh- w-s - dr--m-r -nd l-k-d t- g- r--m-ng -n th- m--nl-ght.

--e -ea- -a- a --o--e-, -oo, -o- a -i--e-.
-u- -e -ou-- -u--e- a-o-- a- a -a-i- -a-e, --i-
--e- -e-e--a--, a-- --i-- --ee-. --ee --i--i--
-a-, i- -a--, --e o-e a-ea i- --i-- -e -a-
-u-e-io- -o a-- --e o--e- a-i-a-- i- --e ---oo-.

Sure, ■■ bird ■■■■ climb ■■ side ■■ tree ■
little bit, ■■ she wasn't nearly ■ good ■ ■ bear ■
climbing. Her greatest strength lay ■■ singing: she
■■■■ sing several songs ■■■ delighted ■■ other forest
animals. However, ■■ bird failed ■ swimming,
running, ■■■ jumping, ■■■ her idea ■ night defense
was simply ■■ wrap her claws ■■■■ ■■ branch, close
her eyes, ■■ sleep. ■■■ bat, ■■ ■ other hand, was
terrific ■ night defense. He ■■■ detect danger ■
screeching ■■■ using his sonar. However, ■■■ bat fell
asleep every day ■■■■ school, when all ■■ other
classes ■■■■ held. The t------- could never even
determine w------ the bat could or c------- swim, run,
jump, or c----. As for singing, the b-- only succeeded at
screeching a-- night, when the other a------ were trying
to sleep.

T3.4b   *"The Animal School" (continuation)*   *Creating Support for Effective Literacy Education* by
C. Weaver, L. Gillmeister-Krause, & G. Vento-Zogby, © 1996. Portsmouth, NH: Heinemann. May be copied for
transparency use only.

T-- other member of the c---- was a mongrel dog
t--- had wandered into the f----- and joined their school.
H- could swim across a s-----, though he hated
to g-- wet; hee cwd run a littl, eeven
thœ hee limpt; hee cwd jump a
littl, thœ not as far as the deer;
hee cwd cliem hills and leep at
trees in a preetens at climiŋ;
hee cwd siŋ a littl, thœ his
siŋiŋ sounded mor liek houliŋ;
and hee cwd deefend himself and
his frends at niet by barkiŋ and
ræsiŋ an alarm. Eeven thœ the
dog cwdn't dœ enythiŋ reely well,
he was the class valedictoreean
beecas hee cwd dœ everythiŋ
a little and didn't fœl enythiŋ.

T3.4c   *"The Animal School"* (continuation)   *Creating Support for Effective Literacy Education* by
C. Weaver, L. Gillmeister-Krause, & G. Vento-Zogby, © 1996. Portsmouth, NH: Heinemann. May be copied for
transparency use only.

Context and Word Pronunciation

read   tear

wind   minute

wound   bow

1. Can you read rapidly?

2. There was a strong wind blowing.

3. She wound the string up tightly.

4. I looked up and read the sign.

5. Her dress had a tear in it.

6. I saw a tear in her eye.

7. She looked at the minute printing on the label.

8. He made her a bow and arrow.

T3.5 *Context and Word Pronunciation*   *Creating Support for Effective Literacy Education* by C. Weaver, L. Gillmeister-Krause, & G. Vento-Zogby, © 1996. Portsmouth, NH: Heinemann. May be copied for transparency use only.
From *Reading process and practice* (2nd ed.) by Constance Weaver. Portsmouth, NH: Heinemann, 1994.

Context and Word Meanings (#1)

1. Can you <u>run</u> the store for an hour?

2. Can you <u>run</u> the word processor?

3. Can you <u>run</u> the 500-yard dash?

4. Can you <u>run</u> in the next election?

5. Can you <u>run</u> next year's marathon?

6. I helped Samuel with his milk <u>run</u>.

7. They'll print 3,000 copies in the first <u>run</u>.

8. Sherry has a <u>run</u> in her hose.

9. There was a <u>run</u> on snow shovels yesterday.

10. It was a long <u>run</u>.

T3.6   *Context and Word Meanings (#1)*   *Creating Support for Effective Literacy Education* by
C. Weaver, L. Gillmeister-Krause, & G. Vento-Zogby, © 1996. Portsmouth, NH: Heinemann. May be copied for
transparency use only.
From *Reading process and practice* (2nd ed.) by Constance Weaver. Portsmouth, NH: Heinemann, 1994.

Context and Word Meanings (#2)

1. That was prescribed <u>by</u> Dr. Lucy.

2. Charlie sat down <u>by</u> Dr. Lucy.

3. Woodstock went <u>by</u> plane.

4. <u>By</u> Snoopy's calculations, it ought to work.

5. <u>By</u> the way, how old do you think Snoopy is?

T3.7   *Context and Word Meanings (#2)*   *Creating Support for Effective Literacy Education* by
C. Weaver, L. Gillmeister-Krause, & G. Vento-Zogby, © 1996. Portsmouth, NH: Heinemann. May be copied for
transparency use only.
From *Reading process and practice* (2nd ed.) by Constance Weaver. Portsmouth, NH: Heinemann, 1994.

Passage to Read

Richmond was in dire straits against St. Kilda. The opening pair who had been stroking the ball with beautiful fluency on past occasions were both out for ducks. Once again the new ball pair had broken through. Then Smith turned on surprising pace and, moving the ball off the seam, beat Mazaz twice in one over. Inverarity viciously pulled Brown into the gully but was sent retiring to the pavilion by a shooter from Cox.

Jones in slips and Chappell at silly mid on were superb, and Daniel bowled a maiden over in his first spell. Yallop took his toll with three towering sixes but Thompson had little to do in the covers.

Grant was dismissed with a beautiful yorker and Jones went from a brute of a ball. Wood was disappointing. The way he hung his bat out to the lean-gutted Croft was a nasty shock. The rout ended when McArdle dived at silly leg and the cry of "How's that!" echoed across the pitch.

T3.8 *Passage to Read*   *Creating Support for Effective Literacy Education* by C. Weaver,
L. Gillmeister-Krause, & G. Vento-Zogby, © 1996. Portsmouth, NH: Heinemann. May be copied for transparency use only.

From Brian Cambourne, *The whole story: Natural learning and the acquisition of literacy in the classroom.* Auckland, New Zealand: Scholastic, 1988, p. 161. Reprinted with permission.

Words and Comprehension

Chlorecyclizine hydrochloride is an antihistamine which is related structurally to cyclizine and meclizine. A combination with hydrocortisone acetate provides anti-inflammatory, antipruritic, and anesthetic properties. It blocks the actions of histamine, antagonizes allergic manifestation, and anesthetizes free nerve endings that mediate pain. The combination provides dual and additive effects to combat antigen-antibody reaction.

T3.10   *Words and Comprehension*   *Creating Support for Effective Literacy Education* by C. Weaver, L. Gillmeister-Krause, & G. Vento-Zogby, © 1996. Portsmouth, NH: Heinemann. May be copied for transparency use only.

Reprinted with permission from Vince Dundas and George Strong, *Readers, writers, and parents learning together.* Katonah, NY: Richard C. Owen Publishers, Inc., 1991, overhead 2.7.

"A Flannerby Barp for Nall"

Nall was so plamper. She was larping to the flannerby with Charkle. She would grunk a flannerby barp so she could crooch out carples. Charkle lanted her gib out the nep.

"Parps, Charkle," jibbed Nall plamperly.

"Now we can crooch out carples together!" pifed Charkle trigly.

1. Who are the characters in the story?

2. Answer the following questions by writing a complete sentence:
    a) Where were they larping?
    b) Why did she want to grunk a flannerby barp?

3. A good title for this story would be:
    a) "Nall and Charkle Together"
    b) "Larping to the Flannerby"
    c) "Lanting Nall Grunk a Flannerby Barp"
    d) "Grunking a Flannerby Barp"

"The Blonke"

The blonke was maily, like all the others. Unlike the other blonkes, however, it had spiss crinet completely covering its fairney cloots and concealing, just below one of them, a small wam.

This particular blonke was quite drumly—lennow, in fact, and almost samded. When yerden, it did not quetch like the other blonkes, or even blore. The others blored very readily.

It was probably his bellytimber that had made the one blonke so drumly. The bellytimber was quite kexy, had a strong shawk, and was apparently venenated. There was only one thing to do with the venenated bellytimber: givel it in the flosh. This would be much better than to sparple it in the wong, since the blonkes that were not drumly could icchen in the wong, but not in the flosh.

Skills Model of the Reading Process

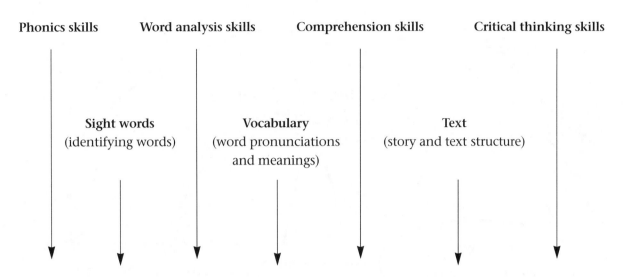

Phonics skills   Word analysis skills   Comprehension skills   Critical thinking skills

Sight words
(identifying words)

Vocabulary
(word pronunciations
and meanings)

Text
(story and text structure)

READING

THE WRITTEN TEXT

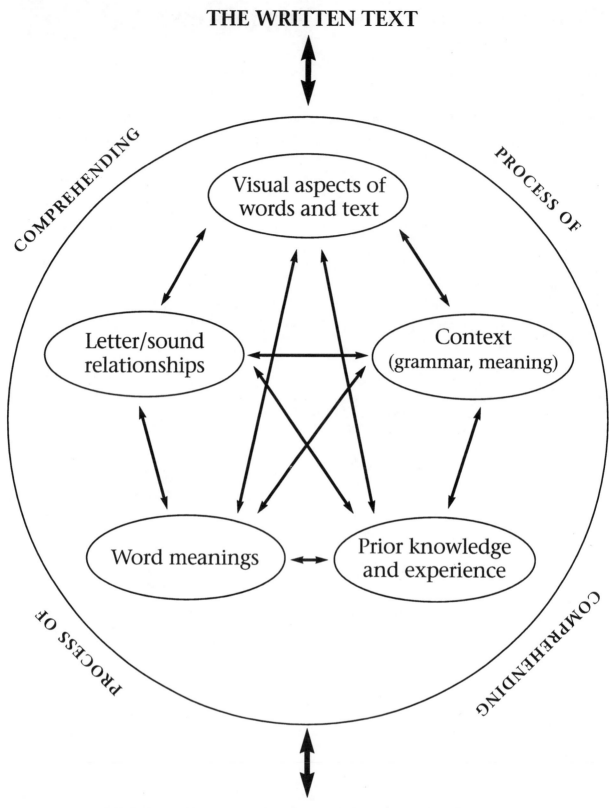

COMPREHENDING

PROCESS OF

Visual aspects of
words and text

Letter/sound
relationships

Context
(grammar, meaning)

Word meanings

Prior knowledge
and experience

PROCESS OF

COMPREHENDING

READER'S ONGOING COMPREHENSION

T3.14 *Constructivist Model of the Reading Process*   *Creating Support for Effective Literacy Education* by C. Weaver, L. Gillmeister-Krause, & G. Vento-Zogby, © 1996. Portsmouth, NH: Heinemann. May be copied for transparency use only.

Adapted from *Reading process and practice* (2nd ed.) by Constance Weaver. Portsmouth, NH: Heinemann, 1994.

"Learning to Dance"

"Let Text lead,"
they insisted.
"Your task is to passively follow."

And so
eyes shuffling listlessly
we intoned
word after word
across the page

docile women,
limp in Text's embrace

our minds waiting
numbly
for Text to reveal
his meaning.

He rarely did.

But that was before
"Reader's liberation,"
before we clasped
Text eagerly, first
leading, then
following,
synchronizing

Text and Reader,
equal partners
in the reading dance.

—Connie Weaver

Anne's Miscues

Now the band began to play. Then the lions roared.

① *about*

Peter the pony ran around the ring. Bill the circus boy

②ⓒ /et

③ *Everyone*

led Penny the elephant into the circus ring. Everybody

forgot to eat popcorn. They forgot to drink soda pop.

④ *A*

They forgot to wave balloons. The circus man made a bow.

Trixie ran into the middle of the ring. She sat and

⑤ *went*

waited. Carlo the clown ran up to Trixie. Trixie jumped

⑥ *on*

⑦ *the*

up and sat in his hand. Carlo put Trixie on a box. Trixie

stood on her hind legs. Then she jumped onto Carlo's head.

⑧ *Every-*

Trixie looked very funny sitting on Carlo's head. Every-

one

body laughed.

T3.16   *Anne's Miscues*   *Creating Support for Effective Literacy Education* by C. Weaver,
L. Gillmeister-Krause, & G. Vento-Zogby, © 1996. Portsmouth, NH: Heinemann. May be copied for
transparency use only.
From *Reading process and practice* (2nd ed.) by Constance Weaver. Portsmouth, NH: Heinemann, 1994.

First Graders' Miscues on Words in Isolation

has
his   . . . said his father.

hot
not   His father said, "You are not old enough for that."

want
went   The next day Hap and his mother and father went
           to the fair.

which
with   "Hap can come with me."

wig
wag   All morning Peter tried to make the turtle wag its tail.

now
know   "I know you would," said his mother. . . .

don't
didn't   But she didn't bring it back to Peter.

our
your   "Come on, Lassie," said Peter. "Wag your tail."

tall
tail   He wanted the turtle to wag its tail.

made
named Peter named his fish Lassie.

T3.17   *First Graders' Miscues on Words in Isolation*   *Creating Support for Effective Literacy Education* by C. Weaver, L. Gillmeister-Krause, & G. Vento-Zogby, © 1996. Portsmouth, NH: Heinemann. May be copied for transparency use only.

From *Reading process and practice* (2nd ed.) by Constance Weaver. Portsmouth, NH: Heinemann, 1994.

Good Readers' Miscues

1. . . . a voice calling, *him* somewhere above.

2. . . . it was enough to wake *up* the dead.

3. . . . stop driving until we (can) see Los Angeles.

4. . . . I went (over) to his bed.

5. . . . the door *to* of Harry's room *bedroom* . . .

6. . . . a pair of pyjamas (with) blue, *and* brown and *with* white stripes.

T3.18   *Good Readers' Miscues*   *Creating Support for Effective Literacy Education* by C. Weaver, L. Gillmeister-Krause, & G. Vento-Zogby, © 1996. Portsmouth, NH: Heinemann. May be copied for transparency use only.

From Kenneth Goodman, *Theoretically based studies of patterns of miscues in oral reading performance.* Detroit: Wayne State University, 1973. (ERIC: ED 079 708)

Jay's Miscues

After a hearty supper Hayes joined the smokers about *①around*

the fire. His appearance did not settle all the questions in *②at all*

the minds of his brother rangers. They ~~saw~~ simply a loose, *③*

lank young youth with tow-colored sunburned hair and a berry- *ⓒ ④*

brown, ingenuous face that wore a quizzical, good-natured *⑤ ingenious*

smile.

"Fellows," said the new ranger, "I'm goin' to interduce

you to a lady friend of mine. Ain't ever heard anybody *⑥ ⑦ much about*

call her a beauty, but you'll all admit she's got some fine *⑧ ⑨ ⑩ a*

points about her. Come along, Muriel!"

T3.19a *Jay's Miscues* *Creating Support for Effective Literacy Education* by C. Weaver,
L. Gillmeister-Krause, & G. Vento-Zogby, © 1996. Portsmouth, NH: Heinemann. May be copied for
transparency use only.
From *Reading process and practice* (2nd ed.) by Constance Weaver. Portsmouth, NH: Heinemann, 1994.

He held open the front of his blue flannel shirt. Out of

[12] [13] *toad*

it crawled a horned frog. A bright red ribbon was tied

[14] *the*

jauntily around its spiky neck. It crawled to its owner's

[15] *it*

knee and sat there motionless.

[16] *'s*

"This here Muriel," said Hayes, with an oratorical wave

[17] *o She's* [18]

of his hand, "has got qualities. She never talks back, she

[19]

always stays at home, and she's satisfied with one red

dress for everyday and Sunday, too."

[20] *d*

"Look at that blame insect!" said one of the rangers

[21] *toads*

with a grin. "I've seen plenty of them horny frogs, but I

c

never knew anybody to have one for a side partner. Does

the blame thing know you from anybody else?"

[23] *her*

"Take it over there and see," said Hayes.

T3.19b *Jay's Miscues (continuation)*   *Creating Support for Effective Literacy Education* by C. Weaver, L. Gillmeister-Krause, & G. Vento-Zogby, © 1996. Portsmouth, NH: Heinemann. May be copied for transparency use only.

From *Reading process and practice* (2nd ed.) by Constance Weaver. Portsmouth, NH: Heinemann, 1994.

Questions About Strategies

1. Does the reader use prior knowledge and context to <u>predict</u> effectively?

2. Does the reader <u>monitor comprehension</u> and <u>correct</u>, or try to correct, miscues that don't make sense in context?

3. Does the reader use grapho/phonemic cues effectively, <u>along with</u> prior knowledge and context?

4. In summary, does the reader <u>orchestrate</u> prior knowledge with the language cue systems to process text effectively?

Jay's Miscues: Evidence of Predicting

After a hearty supper Hayes joined the smokers about *(around)* the fire.

They saw simply a loose, *(young)* lank/youth with tow-colored sunburned hair . . .

Out of it crawled a horned frog. *(toad)*

It crawled to its owner's / knee and sat there motionless. *(the)* *(it)*

"This here Muriel," said Hayes, with an oratorical wave of his hand, "has got qualities." *('s)* *(She's)*

T3.21 *Jay's Miscues: Evidence of Predicting*   *Creating Support for Effective Literacy Education* by C. Weaver, L. Gillmeister-Krause, & G. Vento-Zogby, © 1996. Portsmouth, NH: Heinemann. May be copied for transparency use only.

From *Reading process and practice* (2nd ed.) by Constance Weaver. Portsmouth, NH: Heinemann, 1994.

Jay's Restructuring of Text

"Ain't ~~ever~~ *much about* heard anybody ~~call~~ her ~~a~~ beauty, but you'll all admit she's got some fine points about her. Come along, Muriel!"

He held open the front of his blue flannel shirt. Out ~~of~~ ~~it~~ crawled a horned frog.

"This here's Muriel," said Hayes, with an oratorical wave of his hand. *She's* "has got qualities."

T3.22   *Jay's Restructuring of Text*   *Creating Support for Effective Literacy Education* by C. Weaver,
L. Gillmeister-Krause, & G. Vento-Zogby, © 1996. Portsmouth, NH: Heinemann. May be copied for
transparency use only.
From *Reading process and practice* (2nd ed.) by Constance Weaver. Portsmouth, NH: Heinemann, 1994.

Characteristics of Good Readers

1. They concentrate more upon constructing meaning from texts than upon identifying all the words correctly.

2. They use prior knowledge and context to predict (perhaps unconsciously) what's coming next. Most of the time, prediction prevents miscues or enables readers to identify words by just sampling the visual information.

3. They are constantly monitoring comprehension, noticing when meaning has gone awry, and, when necessary, doing whatever they can to restore meaningfulness.

T3.23 *Characteristics of Good Readers*   *Creating Support for Effective Literacy Education* by C. Weaver, L. Gillmeister-Krause, & G. Vento-Zogby, © 1996. Portsmouth, NH: Heinemann. May be copied for transparency use only.

From *Reading process and practice* (2nd ed.) by Constance Weaver. Portsmouth, NH: Heinemann, 1994.

Reading Levels

Level	Words decoded	Questions answered
Independent	97–100%	80–90%
Instructional	90–97%	60–80%
Frustration	Below 90%	50–60%

T3.24 *Reading Levels*   *Creating Support for Effective Literacy Education* by C. Weaver, L. Gillmeister-Krause, & G. Vento-Zogby, © 1996. Portsmouth, NH: Heinemann. May be copied for transparency use only.

From *Reading process and practice* (2nd ed.) by Constance Weaver. Portsmouth, NH: Heinemann, 1994.

TEACHING AND LEARNING TO READ

This section is divided into various subsets of transparencies, all usable in helping other people understand why the development of reading is fostered better by whole language practices than by traditional basal reader and skills teaching.

Facilitating Reading Acquisition: Transparency 4.1

In a workshop setting, you might invite participants who learned to read before going to school to explain how they learned to read and how their parents helped them learn to read. In recent years, some younger people have reported that their parents used with them materials like phonics flash cards and programs, or that they themselves are using such materials with their own children. Most middle-generation adults report, however, that the major thing that enabled them to read was their parents reading to them. You might ask *how* they read the book together, for merely reading the book aloud from cover to cover is not nearly as helpful to emergent readers as predicting from the cover picture and title what the book might be about, stopping periodically to make further predictions from text and illustrations, talking about the pictures and making connections between pictures and words and their own lives, and perhaps noticing other aspects of the print as adult and child read and reread favorite books.

Those who learned to read at home commonly report that they first started reading by retelling a favorite story from the pictures and from memory, and/or that they memorized a favorite story and then learned to match the written words with the spoken words they already knew. Though middle-generation readers were typically not taught phonics, such readers commonly have as good a grasp of letter/sound patterns as younger adults who were explicitly taught phonics. They simply induced the relationships and patterns from the words, with or without adults specifically calling their attention to the patterns.

Transparency 4.1 may reinforce some of the points that workshop participants have made, but it will surely introduce some points that they haven't thought about. The second point, about using simple and patterned texts with natural language, can introduce a comparison between the unnatural story "Let's Cook!" in transparency 4.2 and "Walk to the Pond" in transparency 4.3 with more natural and more enjoyable texts, such as the song "Are You Sleeping?" in transparencies 4.4 and 4.5 and in several transparencies near the end of Section 5, "Phonics and the Teaching of Phonics." Points 2, 3, and 5 reflect Brian Cambourne's conditions for learning (see transparency 1.4, in Section 1).

Stilted Versus Natural Texts: Transparencies 4.2 Through 4.5

Transparency 4.2 resembles the generic "story" found in the pre-primers of many basal reading series, at least in the late 1980s. Notice that without pictures, we really cannot tell who is speaking; this, in fact, was typical of many such stories. Notice, too, the impoverished vocabulary and the stilted nature of some of the sentences, such as the last two. The earliest levels of basal reading programs were commonly designed to reflect the principles of a "sight word" approach, a phonic/linguistic approach, or both. With a sight word approach, the vocabulary is initially limited, as much as possible, to so-called basic sight words; each "new" word is commonly repeated several times when first introduced. With a phonic/linguistic approach, the vocabulary is initially limited, as much as possible, to phonically regular words, such as those containing a short vowel sound. The text "Let's Cook!" reflects both these principles. In a workshop, you might lead participants to recognize that such a controlled text is so unnatural as to actually be harder to read than a text with more meaningful vocabulary and more natural sentences. An emergent reader is almost forced to rely only on grapho/phonemic knowledge, which makes reading more difficult than when the reader can use prior knowledge, context, and illustrations as well as grapho/phonemic cues.

Transparency 4.3, "Walk to the Pond," is loosely based on a pre-primer level "story" from an informal reading inventory. This text has the same limitations as the basal reader "story"—at least to some degree. You might cover the bottom part of the transparency and show only the text at first, then cover only the top and ask the comprehension questions. If workshop participants have not been forewarned that they will have to answer questions about the passage, they may find that they cannot answer the first question because they didn't bother with that particular detail. This can help adults realize that it is not necessarily reasonable to expect children to remember every detail that a textbook or teacher might ask about, nor does not remembering such details necessarily mean that the reader has not comprehended the selection.

Transparencies 4.4 and 4.5 were developed in an attempt to help others understand how emergent readers can go from understanding the whole of a text to learning the parts: the words, letter/sound patterns, and so forth. With **transparency 4.4**, you can first cover the French version of "Are You Sleeping?" and together read or sing the familiar English version. Then try reading the French version, or singing it if you are comfortable with leading the group in the French pronunciation. As you examine the text more closely, you will surely realize that the first two lines are essentially the reverse of those in the English version. Furthermore, you will probably realize that "dormez-vous" means "Are you sleeping?" From knowing the meaning, you have figured out the sentence and perhaps the actual words. (*Dormez* means "sleep" and *vous* means "you"; the word order is that of a question.) With the sentence "Sonnez les matines," you may be able to figure out the words from knowing that it means "Morning bells are ringing" and from recognizing the relationship between "sound" and "sonnez" as well as the relationship between "matins" (morning prayers) and "matines."

Of course there are obvious differences between reading this passage if you don't already know French but do know how to read in English, compared with emergent readers who do know the language but don't yet know it in written form. Nevertheless, we think this process of figuring out the French version is somewhat akin to learning to read in one's native language: by reading and rereading meaningful texts and by gradually figuring out individual words (and letter/sound relations too, when the text is being read aloud).

In case many workshop participants are likely to know French, you might use the German version instead on **transparency 4.5**, or the two in sequence. In case you need help, "Schläfst du noch?" translates word-for-word as "Sleep you still?" And "Hörst du nicht die Glocken?" translates as "Hear you not the bells?" Once readers have grasped the meanings of the words, they should be able to read a simple but unfamiliar text, such as the one at the bottom of transparency 4.5. "New" words can be predicted from context and prior knowledge, such as knowledge of syntax and of related words in English. The text reads as follows, translated word-for-word: "My brother sleeps still / and the bells ring still / he hears them not / ding, dang, dong."

Shared Book Experience: Transparencies 4.6 through 4.9

More and more primary grade teachers in the United States and Canada are using the Shared Book Experience procedures developed by Don Holdaway and teachers in New Zealand, or some variation thereof (Holdaway, 1979, 1982; Smith & Elley, 1995; Clark & Miller, 1992). The Shared Book Experience—or shared reading experience, as it may be called—is based upon what many parents do quite naturally in helping their children learn to read. The SBE involves use of a text large enough for all the children in the group to see and read: a commercially produced Big Book, a piece of chart paper, a transparency projected large on a screen or wall, and so forth.

Transparency 4.6 lists key features of the SBE, which involve the teacher and children reading, rereading, and discussing favorite texts and, in the process, focusing on concepts of print like left-to-right directionality, strategies like predicting, and elements like words and letter/sound patterns. Before sharing transparency 4.6 with workshop participants, you might lead them through a shared reading experience with a text in Section 5, "Phonics and the Teaching of Phonics" (any transparency from 5.22 through the rest of Section 5 could be used). You might read the text; reread it while you point to the words and participants read along; discuss how you were able to predict some words, if relevant; and discuss particularly noticeable aspects of letter/sound relations, such as repeated consonants at the beginnings of words (alliteration) or rhyme patterns at the ends of words. You may also want to emphasize that the shared reading experience is used with authentic, interesting

texts that have natural grammatical patterns and use interesting words, not just "basic" words. That is, reading skills are taught within an authentic context.

Transparency 4.7 lists ten things that can be taught and learned during the shared reading experience, though of course there are others, such as the fact that shared texts can provide models and patterns for children's own writing. The ten points are further elaborated in **transparencies 4.8a and 4.8b**; however, the print on these transparencies will be too small to use on the overhead for most workshop settings, so you may want to photocopy these pages for participants instead. (Otherwise, these pages can simply be used for your own reference in discussing the preceding transparency. Before moving to transparency 4.9, you might want to invite participants to suggest advantages of the shared reading experience over, say, round robin reading, in which reading typically is not taught at all. (If you want readers to recall what round robin reading can be like, you might use the passage on chlorecyclizine, transparency 3.10, and have different people read one sentence each.)

Transparency 4.9 may include some of participants' points about the advantages of a shared reading experience, but will likely add other points, too. Here are some points you might want to make in elaborating on points 2 and 3:

Children can read more difficult text than they could read independently, because

- the rhyme, rhythm, and repetition of many texts used for shared reading will make prediction easier
- the teacher and more advanced readers provide support
- children more or less learn the text "by heart" before focusing on individual words or on letters and sounds

Less proficient readers join in as they can. They are not singled out for their lack of proficiency, so they read more confidently. In particular,

- they get support from others
- they feel that their miscues go unnoticed, so they more readily take risks in reading
- they get caught up in the group's enthusiasm

Of course point 4, that every child experiences success, is critical. So is point 5, that children aren't just getting ready to read: they are actually reading. Kasten and Clarke's (1989) research demonstrated that kindergarten children learn far more with the Shared Book Experience than with a reading readiness program emphasizing phonics (and they typically do better on the tests of phonics knowledge, too).

A Literacy Program and Literacy Events: Transparencies 4.10 and 4.11

Transparency 4.10 lists major features of what we believe to be an effective program for developing literacy. Transparency 4.11 suggests ways of making it possible for less proficient readers to participate in literacy events and thus become more proficient at reading and discussing what they read.

Following is some information you might want to share in discussing the points on **transparency 4.10**, components of a total literacy program.

• *Independent Reading*
Students need time to practice the craft of reading. In whole literacy classrooms, children can choose much of what they read, though sometimes these choices are limited by the constraints of the curriculum, community values, and the teacher's professional judgment. Books, magazines, and other print resources are readily available in the classroom. Emergent readers are treated as readers and are expected to read and enjoy books during time set aside for independent reading (even if they mostly predict the story from pictures). Typically all adults in the classroom read independently too, to demonstrate the importance and joy of reading. If needed, a less proficient reader may

be paired with a more proficient one who can help with some problem words and strategies, discuss the emerging meaning, and/or take turns reading a page aloud. (For more ideas, see transparency 4.11 on ways to help children participate in literacy events.)

• *Reading Aloud to Children*
Reading aloud is commonly done on a daily basis. In addition to building a spirit of community in the classroom, the teacher serves as a role model and mentor, instilling the habits and values of a literate life. Being careful not to basalize the literature, the teacher may share personal responses to the literature while eliciting reactions from the children. On occasion, children may confer in pairs, reacting to the parts that they are "dying to talk about." It is important to allow the children to walk in the shoes of the characters and feel close to them.

• *Shared and Guided Reading*
This is primarily done with younger children. The activity begins by rereading one or more favorite selections (Big Books or charts or transparencies containing songs, poems, stories, or information). During these rereadings, a teacher points to the words while reading. This provides an opportunity for the children to be taught predetermined concepts or strategies, such as using everything you know along with the initial letter(s) of a word to predict what the word might be. In addition, the teacher captures the teachable moment, based on children's interests and needs. For older but relatively nonproficient readers, these same techniques may be used with multiple copies of an age-appropriate text, or even a book that is projected onto a screen or wall.

• *Literature Discussion Groups*
Small groups are formed, based on student choice (usually the children choose which of several books they will read). Such discussion groups provide the opportunity for teachers and students to share reactions to the literature, make connections to other books and their own lives, discuss the elements of litera-

ture, and consider strategies for dealing with problem words and other elements of the text. Such discussion enriches understanding, as the group collaboratively constructs and reconstructs meaning. On the topic of literature discussion groups, see transparencies 6.17 through 6.21 and the related suggestions and background information.

• *Choral Reading, Readers' Theater, Drama, Storytelling*

These activities afford children the opportunity to authentically engage with literature and the literacy processes. During choral reading, different parts of a literacy selection are assigned to different groups, who then read their part in unison, or chorus. In readers' theater, the script is written like a play, but the children read their parts with expression (and possibly gestures) instead of memorizing their lines and acting them out, as they would in a drama. Students may engage in storytelling, once they have rehearsed a story for performance.

• *Language Experience*

This is primarily done with younger children. The teacher (or other adult) acts as a scribe for the child or group. Working with individual students, the teacher typically writes under the child's illustration a word or sentence(s) that the child has dictated. With a group, the children usually compose together a poem, story, song, letter, etc., while the teacher writes what is dictated. The chart may be used during a shared reading experience. Teachers have become increasingly selective in engaging in this activity, since mere dictation can all too easily convince children that they are not yet ready to write for themselves. They more often engage the children in independent writing and in guided writing, which has a wider range of benefits.

On the other hand, such language experience activities can be a real breakthrough for older children who are experiencing difficulty with reading and writing. When given help in producing their own texts, they find reading easier because they can draw upon memory and their natural speech patterns to predict

and correct. As they gain confidence, struggling readers become increasingly more proficient.

• *Guided Writing*

Guided writing is one of the best ways for teachers to help emergent readers and writers develop concepts of print, phonics and spelling knowledge, and competence as readers and writers. Teachers help the children decide what they want to write on a sentence-by-sentence basis, then guide the children in making key letter/sound associations as the teacher and/or a child writes the letters to spell each word. With more independent readers and writers, the teacher and students can brainstorm, select ideas, compose, reread, reconsider, revise. They may possibly edit and publish, perhaps by adding the piece to a class collection of writings, displaying it in a prominent place, or including it in a class or school newspaper.

• *Independent Writing*

As with reading, children must have many opportunities to write independently. Early attempts at writing may consist of drawings, scribble writing, or randomly stringing together letters of the alphabet. It is important that these early attempts be valued by teachers. When children begin to hear separate sounds in words, the teacher may help the child write letters that represent the sounds. At first children will commonly represent a whole word with just one letter (typically the first consonant), but the teacher can guide them in representing more of the sounds they hear. As children are exposed to books and other print, to demonstrations and directive instruction, they become more proficient writers, demonstrating more consistent use of conventions of print, spelling, and varied genres. Choice plays a big part in what students write.

• *Journals and Learning Logs*

An important element in many classrooms, journals may take several forms: dialogue journals (wherein student and teacher, or two students, write back and forth to each other about any topic); literature logs or reading journals (literature discussions via journals that focus specifically on literary works); and learning logs (journals in which students respond to a certain subject, such as science or math).

• *Directive Instruction in Skills and Strategies*

The term "directive" is chosen to emphasize the point that explicit teaching commonly occurs in response to students' observed needs and interests, not in a vacuum. Furthermore, it involves demonstrations, guidance, and support, or scaffolding; it is not a one-shot dispensation of information (see, for instance, transparencies 1.9 and 1.10, on minilessons). Readers need guidance in developing various skills and strategies (see particularly the sections on phonics and on reading strategies). Writers, too, need guidance of various sorts, such as guidance in making the breakthrough to phonemic writing (writing in which letters represent sounds), developing a repertoire of spelling words and strategies, revising and editing their work, expanding the genres in which they can write competently, and so forth; see Section 7, "Writing and Learning to Write."

Following is some information you might want to share in discussing **transparency 4.11**, on ways of helping children participate in literacy events. Such activities are helpful for all children, but may prove to be especially beneficial for those experiencing difficulty with reading and writing.

• *Paired Reading*

This may take a variety of forms. Students may choose a friend to read with, even if they are reading different books and mainly reading silently together. They may read and discuss different but related books, or the same book. More proficient readers may be paired with less proficient readers to provide support in developing more effective reading strategies.

• *Echo Reading*

An adult may read aloud while the child who needs support reads along, lagging just slightly behind and thus echoing the adult as needed. Or, students may read nearly in unison, perhaps with a less proficient reader echoing a more proficient reading partner.

• *Listening to Tape Recording of Text While Reading*

This activity may be made available to students at a "listening center" in the classroom. Children may sign out tapes with books to listen to at home. This provides children with yet another opportunity to hear fluent reading. As they follow along in the text, they can also make associations between spoken and written words and between letter and sound patterns.

• *Individually-Tailored Tape Recordings*

Marie Carbo has found that struggling readers can often be helped immensely by listening to a tape recording of a book and following along in the text. The unique feature of her "recorded books" program is that the text is read in chunks of grammar and meaning at a pace that is just a little faster than the child might handle independently. This makes it easier for the child to keep up with the tape and helps the child read in chunks of words, not word by word. As the child becomes more proficient, the same text can be recorded at a somewhat faster pace, with the words chunked into larger syntactic and semantic units (Carbo, 1989). Of course, such tapes should not replace listening to tapes with normal pace and intonation, or listening to books read aloud in the classroom. Such tapes are merely a temporary aid for the struggling reader.

• *Tape Recordings of Child Reading*

Some readers benefit immensely from listening to tape recordings of their own reading. Even without instructional guidance, they may notice when they have said something that doesn't make sense but not corrected it. Listening to themselves read can help readers focus on meaning and fluency, as well as on strategies like self-correction. The teacher can work with the child individually, too, focusing on strategies the child uses well and helping the child develop and strengthen other strategies—strategies such as reading for meaning, predicting, monitoring comprehension, and correcting or trying to correct miscues that don't fit the context. Such tutorial intervention has come to be known as Retrospective Miscue Analysis (e.g., Goodman and Marek, 1996; Marek, 1989; for concrete tutorial strategies, see also Weaver, 1994, where the discussion draws substantially from Marek's work).

The next three activities were developed by Jerry Harste, Kathy Short, and Carolyn Burke. You may want to refer to *Creating Classrooms for Authors and Inquirers* (1995) for a more thorough description.

• *"Sketch to Stretch"*

After reading a selection, children are divided into small groups and invited to sketch what the reading meant to them. They are given ample time to read and sketch. Once the drawings are completed, each group member reveals his or her illustration and allows the members of the group to discuss what the artist is attempting to say. The artist concludes the discussion. Sharing continues until each member has shared his or her sketch.

Lorraine reports that when she has done sketch to stretch in her multiage school, they focused on the beginning, middle, and end of the story (e.g., Cochrane, Cochrane, Scalena, & Buchanan, 1984). The beginning includes setting, time, characters, and a bit of the story; the middle includes the conflict or problem and the rising action, the exciting part; and the end is the denouement, solving the problem. Lorraine typically has children do sketch to stretch in a group of three, with each child drawing a picture on chart paper to reflect one of these parts of the story. They then tape all three pictures together horizontally and use them as a basis for discussion. Lorraine reports that sketch to stretch is one of the most popular and valuable independent activities children choose as a follow-up to independent reading.

• *"Written Conversation"*

Children work in teams. The first participant begins by writing a question on a sheet of paper and passes it to the partner, who reads it, writes a response, and returns it to the first participant. This activity continues until the team decides to quit. The activity can be used in response to a read-aloud or content area lesson, or before writing a first draft. It can also be used in dialogue journals, with the student and teacher writing back and forth. Such written conversations can be especially valuable in classrooms where more than one language is spoken as the native language. Children can write comments about a drawing and clarify their written words (in whatever language) through picture and gesture. Gradually, this helps children learn some of each other's language, and particularly helps children learn English as another language.

• *"Say Something"*

Students work in pairs. They are given text to read and are instructed to stop reading at predetermined paragraphs and react to what was read (to "say something"). This procedure continues until the text is completed. Students may share experiences, predict, and/or continue to make connections to the piece. The teacher's role may be to involve the students in a group discussion focusing on how this strategy—stopping periodically to reflect—may be useful in their own reading. For this activity, teachers may provide a variety of genres: picture books, short stories, poems, fiction, nonfiction, and so forth.

• *Directive Instruction in Skills and Strategies*

For comments on this topic, you can refer to the discussion of transparency 4.10, immediately before this one.

Cross Reference to Transparencies 6.2, 6.3, and 1.7

In concluding a workshop on teaching and learning to read, you might find it useful to use transparencies 6.2 and 6.3, which include quotations that can help convince people that teaching skills in isolation is not the best way to help children develop the skills and strategies they need for reading. Prior to or following these, you might use transparency 1.7, which compares transmission and transactional models of learning and teaching.

Cross Reference to Transparencies 1.9 and 1.10 on Minilessons

Particularly if you use transparencies 6.2 and 6.3 at this point, you may find it useful to return to transparency 1.9 and/or 1.10, which compare behavioral and constructivist ways of teaching minilessons. Minilessons are, of course, one important form of directive instruction in whole language classrooms.

Teaching Reading/Developing Reading: Transparency 4.12

Transparency 4.12 offers a brief summary of some of the contrasts between the teaching of reading via basal reading and skills programs and the development of reading ability via the Shared Book Experience and other components of a literacy program and literacy support activities, as delineated in transparencies 4.10 and 4.11. In connection with the first point, you may want to emphasize that children in emergent literacy classrooms are surrounded by print: environmental print (signs, labels, names on children's mailboxes, etc.), books galore, and other texts such as magazines, catalogues, lists, notices, posters, brochures, and so forth. In connection with point four, you may wish to mention some of the ways that children's reading is assessed. Miscue analysis is one example, but, for instance, you might want to point out ⁺ children's phonics knowledge can be assessed by having them write a list of unfamiliar dictated words. The later section on assessment offers many more ideas, as does the brochure on assessment in Part Two of this book.

Sources and Resources

CAMBOURNE, B. (1988). *The whole story: Natural learning and the acquisition of literacy in the classroom.* New York: Scholastic. See p. 33 for the complete model, which is discussed in Chapter 4.

CARBO, M. (1989). *How to record books for maximum gains.* Roslyn Heights, NY: National Reading Styles Institute.

CLARK, J., & MILLER, J. (1992). The shared reading experience. *Michigan Reading Journal, 25,* 16–21.

COCHRANE, O., COCHRANE, D., SCALENA, S., & BUCHANAN, E. (1984). *Reading, writing and caring.* Winnipeg: Whole Language Consultants. Distributed in the U.S. by Richard C. Owen.

GOODMAN, Y. M., & MAREK, A. M. (Eds.). (1996). *Retrospective miscue analysis: Revalving readers and reading.* Katonah, NY: Richard C. Owen.

HARSTE, J., SHORT, K., WITH BURKE, C. (1995). *Creating classrooms for authors and inquirers* (2nd ed.). Portsmouth, NH: Heinemann.

HOLDAWAY, D. (1979). *The foundations of literacy.* Sydney: Ashton Scholastic. Distributed in the U.S. by Heinemann.

HOLDAWAY, D. (1982). Shared Book Experience: Teaching reading using favorite books. *Theory into Practice, 21,* 293–300.

HOLDAWAY, D. (1986). The structure of natural learning as a basis for literacy instruction. In M. R. Sampson (Ed.), *The pursuit of literacy: Early reading and writing* (pp. 56–72). Dubuque, IA: Kendall / Hunt.

KASTEN, W. C., & CLARKE, B. K. (1989). *Reading/ writing readiness for preschool and kindergarten children: A whole language approach.* Sanibel: Florida Educational Research and Development Council. ERIC: ED 312 041.

MAREK, A. M. (1989). Using evaluation as an instructional strategy for adult readers. In K. S. Goodman, Y. M. Goodman, & W. J. Hood

(Eds.), *The whole language evaluation book* (pp. 157–164). Portsmouth, NH: Heinemann.

SMITH, J. W. A., & ELLEY, W. B. (1995). *Learning to read in New Zealand*. Katonah, NY: Richard C. Owen.

WEAVER, C. (1994). *Reading process and practice: From socio-psycholinguistics to whole language* (2nd ed.). Portsmouth, NH: Heinemann.

Books on Literacy Development

The following books are appropriate for parents as well as teachers. The asterisked books are especially easy and delightful reading:

*Barron, M. (1990). *I learn to read and write the way I learn to talk: A very first book about whole language*. Katonah, NY: Richard C. Owen. Available in both an English version and a Spanish version.

CLAY, M. M. (1987). *Writing begins at home*. Portsmouth, NH: Heinemann.

DOAKE, D. (1991). *Reading begins at birth*. Richmond Hill, Ontario: Scholastic.

*LAMINACK, L. L. (1991). *Learning with Zachary*. Richmond Hill, Ontario: Scholastic.

NEWMAN, J. M. (1984). *The craft of children's writing*. Richmond Hill, Ontario: Scholastic. Distributed in the U.S. by Heinemann.

VILLIERS, U. (1990). *Luk Mume luk Dade I kan rit*. New York: Scholastic. Consists of young children's writing samples, with explanations of their writing development.

How Adults Facilitate Reading Acquisition

1. By reading to children again and again and by demonstrating what it means to be a reader.

2. By reading and rereading with children various simple and patterned texts that have natural language.

3. By responding positively to children's early attempts to read.

4. By providing an emotionally safe environment for risk-taking.

5. By supporting children in reading.

6. By expecting children to succeed at reading, rather than to fail.

"Let's Cook!"

Can I cook?

Yes, you can cook.

I can cook!

Can I cook?

Yes, you can cook.

I can cook too!

Can I cook?

No, you cannot cook.

I am not happy.

I can only look.

T4.2 *Passage to Illustrate Basalese: "Let's Cook!"*   *Creating Support for Effective Literacy Education* by C. Weaver, L. Gillmeister-Krause, & G. Vento-Zogby, © 1996. Portsmouth, NH: Heinemann. May be copied for transparency use only.

"Walk to the Pond"

It was summer. Tim went for a walk. He took his pet pig, Pete. They walked and walked and walked. They saw a pond. There were frogs. Some were green. Some were gray. They were fun to see. Tim and Pete saw ducks, too. Pete did not run after them. He was a good pig.

1. What time of the year or season was it?

2. What did Tim do?

3. Why do you think Tim took his pig for a walk?

4. Why do you think Pete didn't run after the ducks?

5. What does "good" mean?

T4.3   *Passage Resembling Informal Reading Inventory: "Walk to the Pond"*   *Creating Support for Effective Literacy Education* by C. Weaver, L. Gillmeister-Krause, & G. Vento-Zogby, © 1996. Portsmouth, NH: Heinemann. May be copied for transparency use only.

"Are You Sleeping?" (#1)

Song in English

Are you sleeping, are you sleeping,

Brother John, Brother John?

Morning bells are ringing, morning bells are ringing,

Ding, ding, dong! Ding, ding, dong!

Song in French

Frère Jacques, Frère Jacques,

Dormez-vous, dormez-vous?

Sonnez les matines, sonnez les matines,

Din, din, don! Din, din, don!

"Are You Sleeping?" (#2)

Song in German

Bruder Jakob, Bruder Jakob

Schläfst du noch, schläfst du noch?

Hörst du nicht die Glocken, hörst du nicht die
  Glocken?

Ding, dang, dong! Ding, dang, dong!

Simple text

Mein Bruder schläft noch

und die Glocken klingen noch

er hört sie nicht

ding, dang, dong.

T4.5   *"Are You Sleeping?" (#2) (in German, with Another Simple Text in German)*
Creating Support for Effective Literacy Education by C. Weaver, L. Gillmeister-Krause, & G. Vento-Zogby, © 1996.
Portsmouth, NH: Heinemann. May be copied for transparency use only.

Shared Book Experience:
What it typically includes

- the teacher and children rereading familiar texts together

- the teacher running a finger under the words

- focusing on reading strategies and various aspects of the text (words, letter/sound patterns, etc.), through discussion

- the teacher introducing a new text, eliciting predictions, and reading the text aloud

- children independently or in pairs rereading the texts shared (perhaps with an audio recording that accompanies the text)

T4.6 *Shared Book Experience: What It Typically Includes*   *Creating Support for Effective Literacy Education* by C. Weaver, L. Gillmeister-Krause, & G. Vento-Zogby, © 1996. Portsmouth, NH: Heinemann. May be copied for transparency use only.

Shared Book Experience:
What can be taught and learned

1. Book handling and conventions of print

2. Nature of book language

3. Sight vocabulary

4. Letter/sound relationships

5. Word attack skills

6. Strategies for processing written texts, and metacognitive awareness of such strategies

7. Conventions of punctuation, intonation patterns

8. Grammar and text structure in reading

9. Understanding meanings; critical thinking

10. Various genres, including fiction, nonfiction, and poetry

T4.7 *Shared Book Experience: What Can Be Taught and Learned*   *Creating Support for Effective Literacy Education* by C. Weaver, L. Gillmeister-Krause, & G. Vento-Zogby, © 1996. Portsmouth, NH: Heinemann. May be copied for transparency use only.

Shared Book Experience: What can be learned

1. **Book handling and conventions of print**
   - holding a book right side up; where to begin reading; how to turn the pages
   - understanding conventions of print, such as the fact that we read pages from top to bottom and left to right in English
   - understanding the concepts of word and letter

2. **Nature of book language**
   - understanding conventions that don't occur in speech ("he said," "he exclaimed")
   - understanding the different vocabulary found more often in print than speech
   - understanding dialect patterns that may differ from the children's own

3. **Sight vocabulary**
   - developing stock of interesting words that can be recognized on sight
   - developing stock of functional words that can be recognized on sight
   - developing ability to recognize more and more words in predictable contexts

4. **Letter/sound relationships**
   - recognizing letters and letter clusters
   - developing letter/sound knowledge—particularly an ability to read common onsets and rimes
   - developing ability to *use* letter/sound knowledge along with prior knowledge and context to make reasonable predictions

5. **Word attack skills**
   - developing ability to use prior knowledge and context to predict words
   - developing ability to use letter/sound knowledge along with prior knowledge and context to predict words
   - developing ability to confirm predictions by examining the text word in chunks of letters
   - developing ability to get the meanings of words by looking at meaningful parts

6. **Strategies for processing written texts, and metacognitive awareness of such strategies**
   - predicting a logical sequence of events or actions ("What do you think might happen in this story?" "What do you think might happen next?")
   - predicting what would fit next grammatically and semantically ("What would make sense here?")

6. **Strategies, continued**
- monitoring comprehension and appropriate word identification ("Does that sound right?" "Does that make sense?")
- using the visual aspects of words and letter/sound knowledge to check initial identification of words ("Does that word look/sound like . . . ?")
- reprocessing text to clarify meaning and particular words

7. **Conventions of punctuation, intonation patterns**
- developing awareness of terminal punctuation marks (period, question mark, exclamation point) and how they are used
- developing awareness of how terminal punctuation marks relate to intonation patterns
- developing awareness of what is signaled by other punctuation marks, especially quotation marks

8. **Grammar and text structure in reading**
- developing awareness of grammatical markers to signal reference and relationships (e.g. pronouns, prepositions, coordinating and subordinating conjunctions)
- developing awareness of markers that signal grammatical/semantic relationships like plurality and pastness
- understanding the structure of predictable texts
- understanding basic story structure (beginning, middle, end)
- beginning to understand the structures of particular genres ("Once upon a time," etc.)

9. **Understanding meanings; critical thinking**
- reviewing, activating and using schemas to process text; adding to one's repertoire of schemas
- drawing inferences
- analyzing, synthesizing, evaluating; thinking critically
- distinguishing between fact and fantasy or opinion
- exploring the meanings of metaphorical and figurative language
- responding personally and emotionally to texts; relating texts to personal life

10. **Various genres, including fiction, nonfiction, and poetry**
- songs
- poetry
- pattern books
- other predictable books
- folktales
- fables
- myths
- stories
- biography
- informational texts

T4.8b   *Shared Book Experience: What Can Be Learned (continuation)*   *Creating Support for Effective Literacy Education* by C. Weaver, L. Gillmeister-Krause, & G. Vento-Zogby, © 1996. Portsmouth, NH: Heinemann. May be copied for transparency use only.

Shared Book Experience: Advantages

1. Children enjoy reading together.

2. Children can read more difficult text than they could read independently.

3. Less proficient readers join in as they can. They are not singled out for their lack of proficiency, so they read more confidently.

4. Therefore, every child experiences success.

5. Children aren't just getting ready to read. They are actually reading.

T4.9 *Shared Book Experience: Advantages*   *Creating Support for Effective Literacy Education* by C. Weaver, L. Gillmeister-Krause, & G. Vento-Zogby, © 1996. Portsmouth, NH: Heinemann. May be copied for transparency use only.

Components of a Literacy Program

- independent reading

- reading aloud to children

- shared and guided reading

- literature discussion groups

- choral reading, readers' theater, drama, storytelling

- language experience

- guided writing

- independent writing

- journals and learning logs

- directive instruction in skills & strategies

Ways to Help Children Participate in Literacy Events

- paired reading

- echo reading

- listening to tape recording of text
    while reading

- individually tailored tape recordings

- tape recordings of child reading

- "sketch to stretch"

- "written conversation"

- "say something"

- directive instruction in skills & strategies

Teaching Reading

Developing Reading

1. Teacher uses a graded program, with an anthology, workbooks and worksheets, and skills tests.

1. Teacher uses Big Books and charts that all can see. Children also have small books from which to read independently. Trade books are used too.

2. The program determines what will be taught, and when.

2. The teacher determines what will be taught when, based on professional knowledge and observation of and interaction with the children.

3. Children are grouped according to alleged ability.

3. Children needing more help may be grouped for specific instruction and/or paired with a more competent reader, but there is no permanent grouping.

4. Children's reading is assessed via the basal tests.

4. Children's reading is assessed variously, with attention to strategies used.

T4.12   *Comparison Between Teaching Reading and Developing Reading*   *Creating Support for Effective Literacy Education* by C. Weaver, L. Gillmeister-Krause, & G. Vento-Zogby, © 1996. Portsmouth, NH: Heinemann. May be copied for transparency use only.

PHONICS AND THE TEACHING OF PHONICS

Repeatedly in the newspapers we see letters to the editor extolling the virtues of intensive, systematic phonics and blaming illiteracy on whole language. However, research does not support this claim. The research that has compared actual whole language classrooms with skills-intensive and phonics-intensive classrooms typically shows that children develop phonics knowledge as well or better in whole language classrooms and, furthermore, that children in whole language primary grade classrooms typically develop the characteristics of effective readers and writers to a greater degree than children in skills-intensive and phonics-intensive classrooms (see, for instance, Weaver, 1994, ch. 7; Smith & Elley, 1995; Stahl, McKenna, & Pagnucco, 1993). However, it should be emphasized that phonics and other skills are not simply ignored in these whole language classrooms. In fact, most of the whole language primary grade classrooms in the comparative research studies have included the Shared Book Experience, in which phonics and other reading strategies and skills are taught in context. See the fact sheet "On Research on Whole Language Education" in Part Two of this book.

One of the latest "wrinkles" in the phonics debate is the argument that we must teach phonemic awareness—that is, awareness of the "separate" sounds in words. Various researchers have pointed out that there is a strong correlation between phonemic awareness and reading achievement on standardized tests (e.g., Adams & Bruck, 1995; Beck & Juel, 1995; Foorman, 1995). This research on the acquisition of phonemic awareness has led to the argument that many children need

explicit help in developing phonemic awareness—not merely to sound out words, but to recognize words on sight, automatically (see, for example, the teaching suggestions by Yopp, 1992). This argument has reached the public ear and various state boards of education and legislatures—as, for example, in California and Texas.

Adding fuel to the argument for teaching phonics systematically is a recent study by Foorman and others (forthcoming) that at least seems to suggest that teaching phonics in isolation may get children off to a better start in developing phonemic awareness and phonics skills and in using these skills in word identification than a program that embeds phonics into a whole literacy context. However, it is impossible to tell from these "preliminary findings" just how much time was spent focusing on letter/sound relationships in the "embedded phonics" treatment (which sounds a lot like the Shared Book Experience) and the "whole language" treatment. As Connie has written in the fact sheet "On Research on the Teaching of Phonics" (Part Two),

> The study excluded only one independent (multiple-choice) measure of comprehension, on which there were no significant differences among the treatment groups. No other kinds of factors were measured. So the study speaks only to the early acquisition of phonemic awareness and phonics skills, not to the overall issue of becoming a competent and independent reader who uses such skills in the service of constructing meaning. Even then, it is not clear whether phonics was actually taught in context in the whole language class-

rooms, so the instruction may not have been comparable to the whole language classrooms in the aforementioned studies.

The "aforementioned studies" are several studies comparing the effects of whole language classrooms with the effects of traditional, skills-intensive classrooms (again, see the fact sheet "On Research on Whole Language Education").

Because intensive systematic phonics is so widely touted, workshop leaders often find themselves needing to dispel the notion that phonics is *the* route to learning to read, that phonics should be taught first, and/or that phonics will cure illiteracy (though indeed some adults as well as children beyond the primary years may need more help in grasping letter/sound patterns and/or in processing words in chunks of letters, such as syllables).

Since the teaching of phonemic awareness and phonics *first* have become such political issues, it would be wise to familiarize yourself with the issues and with counterarguments before leading a workshop on phonics and teaching phonics in whole language classrooms. In Part Two, the fact sheets that would be most helpful are the three that deal with phonics (especially the long one on research on the teaching of phonics), and the one that deals with research on whole language education. It would also be wise when discussing the learning and teaching of phonics to note especially the particular activities most likely to foster phonemic awareness.

Many of the transparencies in Section 4, "Teaching and Learning to Read," can be used to help people understand that we do not read by phonics alone. The transparencies in Section 5 are designed to extend that insight by focusing on phonics in particular. Many of them are derived from Chapter 5 in Connie's *Reading Process and Practice* (Weaver, 1994c).

Poem About Letter/Sound Relations: Transparency 5.1

We wanted to include the oft-cited poem "Hints on Pronunciation for Foreigners" as the first transparency (as quoted in Chomsky,

1970, or Adams, 1990), but the original publisher couldn't locate the author for permission. Therefore, Connie decided to draft an original poem, "Phonics Fun," which was revised with help from Peter Krause. It should be obvious that the intent in writing the poem was to demonstrate that phonics is not as simple as the public often seems to believe. (Witness Rudolph Flesch's famous 1955 statement, "Teach the child what each letter stands for and he can read.") You might want particularly to comment on the "rule" that is illustrated in the first two stanzas by *bead*, *mislead*, and one pronunciation of *lead*, but contradicted by *heart*, *head*, *dead*, and the other pronunciation of *lead*; this rule holds only about 45% of the time. Another commonly taught "rule" is "When there are two vowels, one of which is final e, the first vowel is long and the *e* is silent." In the third stanza, *plate*, *scene*, *bite*, *cove*, *home*, *tome*, *stove*, and *rove* follow the rule, while *come*, *move*, *love*, *shove*, and one pronunciation of *dove* do not. This rule holds only about 63% of the time. For the rules, see T5.8 and the accompanying discussion.

Spellings and Sounds: Transparencies 5.2 and 5.3

English is an alphabetic language, wherein spellings are based on sound. However, English spellings are not solely based on sound, as **transparency 5.2** is designed to demonstrate. Consider, for instance, the homophones in the first list. These sound-alike words have different spellings, reflecting the fact that their meanings are different.

Or consider the spellings for regular noun plural endings. The words in the first column take an /s/ sound; the words in the second column take a /z/ sound; and the words in the third column take a schwa-like vowel plus a /z/. Instead of representing these differences in sound, though, the spellings reflect the constancy in meaning: the concept of plurality. (In the third column, the singular words that don't end in *-e* do take an *-es* in the plural; still, the /z/ sound is represented with an *-s*.)

At the bottom, the sets of words keep a particular element of the spelling constant across the words that are related in meaning, though the pronunciation is different. For example, *medicine, medic,* and *medical* all retain the letter *c*, though in *medicine* it is pronounced with an /s/ sound and in *medic* and *medical* it is pronounced as /k/. The second *t* remains the same in *situate* and *situation*, even though its pronunciation differs. There are two *b*s in both *bomb* and *bombard*, though the second *b* is pronounced only in *bombard*. In these and other related sets of words, the spelling reflects the constancy in meaning rather than the difference in sound.

Transparency 5.3 is designed to further emphasize the fact that there is great inconsistency between spellings and pronunciations, even from one dialect region to another within the United States (e.g., Shuy, 1967; Wolfram, 1991). For example:

• Words ending in *-og* are not pronounced the same everywhere. In some dialects, the vowels are all the same; in others, there are at least two differing sets.
• *Merry, marry,* and *Mary* are all pronounced the same in some dialects; others make two or even three distinctions.
• *Far, father,* and *awe* have the same "a" sound in some dialects, but not in others.
• *Pin* and *pen* are different in most dialect areas, but not all.
• *Wash* and *Washington* take an added /r/ for many South Midlanders, who say the words as "warsh" and "Warshington." Bostonians, on the other hand, may add an /r/ to words like *idea* ("the idear is") and Cuba ("Cubar is"). In some areas of the South and the Northeast, speakers typically omit /r/ after a vowel and before a consonant, as in "cahd" for *card*, and "bahn" for *barn* (this pattern also occurs in Black English Vernacular).
• *Root* and *route* are pronounced the same in some dialect areas, but not all.

While these pronunciation differences are in one sense trivial, they are not at all trivial for children from one dialect area being taught phonics from a program or by a teacher reflecting a different dialect area. This is another argument against teaching children to read by phonics, as well as evidence that the same spellings are not always pronounced in the same way.

Thus examining the various patterns illustrated in these two transparencies clearly demonstrates the ridiculousness of Rudolph Flesch's claim in *Why Johnny Can't Read*: "Teach the child what each letter stands for and he can read" (Flesch, 1955, pp. 10, 31). In fact, as Connie's colleague Beverly Regelman has pointed out, one couldn't even read the cover of Flesch's book by phonics alone.

Phonics and Words: Transparencies 5.4 and 5.5

As previously implied, adults often have the mistaken notion that sounding out words is easy once we've learned phonics, and that phonics magically enables us to "get" the word. This, of course, is not necessarily true, unless we already know the word. Sometimes we can pronounce unfamiliar words correctly, yet have little or no idea what they mean. Sometimes we have some sense of the meaning, but do not pronounce the words correctly. And sometimes we have difficulty with both pronunciation and meaning. The two transparencies in this set are designed to elicit these responses from workshop participants.

Transparency 5.4 has three sets of words. Many participants may pronounce most of the words correctly in the sets headed by *caracara* and *picopicogram*, yet have little idea what most of the words mean. On the other hand, words in the third set are slightly more common, we think, and have meanings that some individuals may have gleaned from the context of their reading (as in *machinations, paroxysm,* and *parsimony*). The other word in that set, *isochronal*, contains meaningful elements that some people may recognize: *iso-* ('the same') and *chron-* ('time'); thus they may conclude, correctly, that the word refers to equal intervals of time. On the other hand, some or all of these words may be pronounced incorrectly, even if they are understood. (Mispronunciation may result, in part, from putting the accent on the wrong syllable.)

Of course there is no guarantee that the first two sets will be relatively pronounceable but little understood, while the third set will be the opposite. For this reason, workshop leaders who see value in thus leading participants to the conclusion that phonics is not everything may prefer to try the columns of words in **transparency 5.5**, which are arranged simply in alphabetical order. Participants could be invited to read the columns aloud, while the workshop leader listens for and later comments on some of the mispronounced words. Participants could also be invited to comment on some of the words whose meaning they don't know, even after being told the dictionary pronunciation. We have found that activities like this help people realize that phonics is, indeed, only one language cue system, not a preventative or cure for illiteracy, as some people have claimed.

The dictionaries used for the following words and definitions were the *American Heritage College Dictionary* (1993) and *Webster's Third New International Dictionary* (1961/1981).

The Words and Their Pronunciations and Definitions

Note: The accent marks are boldfaced in the dictionary, to indicate primary stress.

- arenaceous   ăr′ ə-nā′ shəs

resembling, derived from, or containing sand; growing in sandy areas

- bosquet   bŏs′ kĭt

a small grove; a thicket

- caracara   kăr′ ə-kär′ ə

any of several large carrion-eating or predatory hawks of the subfamily Caracarinae, *native to South and Central America and the southern United States*

- chiffonier   shĭf′ ə-nîr′

a tall, narrow chest of drawers or bureau, often with a mirror

- coriaceous   kôr′ē-ā′ shəs

of or like leather, especially in texture

- deliquesce   dĕl′ĭ-kwĕs′

to melt away; to disappear, as if by melting; also has definitions relating to chemistry and botany

- demesne   dĭ-mān′   or   dĭ-mēn′

from old French de maine: *manorial land retained for the private use of a feudal lord; the grounds belonging to a mansion or country house; an estate; a district; a territory; a realm; a domain*

- evotomys   ə -văd′ ə-məs

synonym of clethrionomys, *which has Greek roots meaning "the entrance of the windpipe" and "to close"*

a genus of rodents consisting of the red-backed mice

- excoriate   ĭk-skôr′ ē-āt′   or   -skōr-

to tear or wear off the skin of; to censure strongly; denounce

- expunge   ĭk- spŭnj′

to erase or strike out; to eliminate completely; annihilate

- fiduciary fĭ-do͞o′shē-ĕr′ē or
  –shə-rē or –dyo͞o– or fī—

adjective: holding, held, or founded in trust or confidence; of, having to do with, or involving a confidence or trust: of the nature of a trust ("a fiduciary capacity," "a fiduciary relation"); resting upon public confidence for value or currency ("fiduciary fiat money")

noun: one (as a corporate trust company or the trust department of a bank) that holds a fiduciary relation or acts in a fiduciary capacity to another (as to one whose funds are entrusted to it for investment)

- fissiparous fĭ-sĭp′ər-əs

reproducing by biological fission; tending to break up into parts or break away from a main body

- flabellate flə-bĕl′ĭt or
  flăb′ə-lāt

fan-shaped

- fulminate fo͝ol′ mə nāt′ or
  fŭl–

to issue a thunderous verbal attack or denunciation; to explode or detonate

- isochronal ī-sŏk′rə-nəl

equal in duration; marked by or occurring at equal intervals of time

- machination măk′-ə-nā′shən
  or măsh—

the act of plotting; a crafty scheme or cunning design for accomplishing a sinister end

- mezereon mə-zîr′ē-ən

a poisonous Eurasian ornamental shrub

- ozostomia ō′za-stō′mē-ə

foulness of breath ("bad breath")

- palimpsest păl′əm (p)-sĕst′

noun: writing material (such as parchment or paper) so prepared that the writing can be erased and the material reused

- paroxysm păr′ək-sĭz′əm

a sudden, uncontrollable outburst of emotion: for example, paroxysms of laughter, paroxysms of grief

- parsimony pär′sə-mō′nē

unusual or excessive frugality; stinginess; adoption of the simplest assumption, as in the formulation of a theory

- picopicogram pēkō′pēkō′gram′

from pico (one trillionth, or 10 to the minus 12th power) + gram

a unit of mass equal to 10 to the minus 24th power (abbreviated ppg)

- pretermit prē′tər-mĭt′

preter derives from Latin praeter, beyond; mit is from Latin mittere, to let go

to disregard intentionally or allow to pass unnoticed or unmentioned; to fail to do or include; omit; to interrupt or terminate

Example: "Angry with his children, he deliberately pretermitted them from his will."

- preternatural   prē– tər– nǎch´ər– əl
  or   nǎch´rəl

preter derives from Latin praeter, *beyond*

out of or beyond the normal course of nature; differing from the natural; surpassing the normal or usual; extraordinary; transcending the natural or material order; supernatural

- roisterous   roi´ stər– rəs   or
  rois– t(ə) rəs

noisy, boisterous merrymaking, as in "It was a roisterous party."

- serendipity   sěr´ ən– dǐp´ǐ– tē

the faculty of making fortunate discoveries by accident (from the characters in the Persian fairy tale The Three Princes of Serendip, *who made such discoveries)*

- stereobate   stěr´ē– ō– bāt´   or
  stîr´

from Greek stereo–, *solid, and* batēs, *walker: the foundation of a stone building*

- tintinnabulation

  tǐn´tǐ– nǎb´ yə– lā´shən

the ringing or sounding of bells

- tinzenite   tǐn´ zə– nīt

a mineral consisting of a silicate of manganese, aluminum, and calcium and occurring in yellow

monoclinic crystals at Tinzen, Grisons, Switzerland

- tortuosity   tôr´ chōō– ǒs´ǐ– tē

the quality or condition of being tortuous; twistedness or crookedness; a trait of deviousness or crookedness in a person

- transpalatine   trǎnz´ pal´ə– tǐn´

from Latin trans + palātum, *roof of the mouth: of, relating to, or being the transverse bone of the skull of a reptile*

- transubstantiate

  trǎn´ səb– stǎn´ shē– āt´

to change one substance into another; transmute

Vowel Rules: Transparencies 5.6 Through 5.9

Simple rules for pronouncing vowels are often taught in school, typically in the first grade. What most people don't realize, however, is that the commonly taught rules don't apply with a high degree of frequency while, on the other hand, at least some vowel pronunciations are more stable in "rime" patterns like -*ate*, -*ent*, -*ive*, -*ish*, -*ook*. Furthermore, reading such "chunks" of letters is much easier than trying to sound out words letter by letter. (See the next set of transparencies for further explanation and discussion of "rimes" and "onsets.")

Several studies of the reliability of phonics rules or generalizations have been done, but perhaps the best known is that by Theodore Clymer (1963). Take, for instance, the rule "When two vowels go walking, the first one does the talking," a rule that even many adults remember. You might first elicit from workshop participants examples of words that do and don't fit the rule before telling them that the rule applied only 45 percent of the time in the word sample examined by Clymer. (Some examples of and exceptions to the rule are listed at the bottom of **transparency 5.6**.)

How about the "silent *e*" rule, that "When a word ends in a vowel + consonant + *e*, the *e* is usually silent and the other vowel is long"? How frequently does that rule apply? Somewhat more frequently, as workshop participants may conclude—but still only 63 percent of the time, according to Clymer's study (**transparency 5.7**).

Transparencies 5.8 and 5.9 are different in that they supply the percentage of applicability found by Clymer. The first of these transparencies demonstrates that some of the most common phonics "rules" apply less than 65 percent of the time. The second transparency shows some of the rules that are the most consistent—but they hardly need to be learned as rules.

Isolated Phonics Lessons: Transparency 5.10

Transparency 5.10 illustrates some of the kinds of lessons found in popular or readily available phonics programs. In the first example, the child is expected to name the object in the picture, listen to its beginning, middle, and final sounds, and circle the correct letters (*tr* + *a* + *p*, in this case). But what if the child doesn't name the picture correctly? Also, many children who *can* read will nevertheless have difficulty hearing the "separate" sounds in words. Being able to do exercises like this has little to do with being able to read, or even with being able to use letter/sound knowledge to sound out words. Yet activities like this are common in phonics programs. The second example is similar in its demands, but requires recognizing some visually similar words as well as identifying what is happening in the picture and associating the two.

Incidentally, we concluded that when reduced in size, the artist's sketches of the mouse-

trap and the girl skipping and spinning were anything but clear. However, we decided to retain the drawings because their ambiguity illustrates a key problem with such exercises. Children—and many adults—often can't tell what the picture is supposed to be depicting, or what part of the picture they are supposed to attend to; sometimes, a related difficulty is that they would name the object differently ("coat" rather than "jacket," for instance—or "mouse-trap" rather than just "trap").

The kind of activity we've labeled as "Reading words" emphasizes the sounding out of words. This is the technique emphasized in the famed *Reading Mastery: DISTAR* program (1988), and in the book derived from it for home use (Engelmann, Haddox, & Bruner, 1983).

The list of words that begin with *sq-* illustrates the approach in Samuel Blumenfeld's *Alpha-Phonics* (1983), also designed especially for home use. The book consists primarily of lists of words that have some letter/sound relationship in common. While a good reader will indeed have developed phonics skills that facilitate the reading of such lists, you may want again to point out to workshop participants that letter/sound knowledge reflects only one language cue system learned and used in reading, and that overemphasizing phonics can result in readers merely trying to say or sound out words instead of trying to construct meaning from texts. Phonics knowledge may best be considered a *result* of learning to read, rather than a prerequisite to reading.

Onsets and Rimes: Transparencies 5.11 Through 5.15

In *Beginning to Read: Thinking and Learning About Print* (1990), Marilyn Adams summarized a substantial body of research suggesting that syllables are easier for emergent readers to hear and isolate than are individual sounds, and that the major parts of syllables, the onsets and rimes, are likewise easier to process. Furthermore, various studies have shown that when proficient readers sound out words, they do so in "chunks" of letters—often syllables or onsets and rimes. Thus it seems far more productive to focus children's attention on such units than on individual sounds, though individual letter sounds must be grasped too, especially for writing and spelling by ear, in the early stages of learning to write and spell.

The *rime* of a syllable consists of the vowel sound plus any consonants that may follow it (**I**, **eye**, m**ight**, **isle**, for instance). The *onset* is what precedes the rime—a consonant (as in **b**ig, **t**op, **w**in), a consonant digraph (two letters but one sound, as in **th**ick, **ch**ip, **wr**inkle), or a consonant blend (a cluster, as in **fr**ight or **sl**ay). **Transparency 5.11** illustrates digraphs and blends that commonly occur as the onsets of syllables. **Transparency 5.12** likewise illustrates common rime patterns, in which the vowel pronunciation is relatively constant. Nearly five hundred "primary grade words" can be derived from this set of only thirty-seven rimes (Wylie and Durrell, 1970).

It would be tempting, of course, to teach all the common onset and rime patterns, or to have children read lists of words illustrating them; that way, we could be sure of "covering" most of the phonics that children need. However, what we know about language and literacy acquisition demonstrates that children do not have to be directly taught everything they need to know. Thus attention to a sampling of onsets and rimes should suffice, for almost all students.

Transparency 5.13 illustrates one kind of activity that teachers may use with emergent readers. Starting with a frequently occurring onset like *fl-*, they may brainstorm for words that begin with this onset—and in the process, illustrate a number of rime patterns. **Transparency 5.14** suggests another way of doing this: by starting with a list of the thirty-seven common rime patterns and seeing which ones make a word when *fl-* is added as the onset. **Transparency 5.15** takes just one rime, *-ake*, and shows various onsets that can go with it to make a word. Such collaborative word play is usually more productive than just reading lists

of words, partly because it emphasizes the separateness of the onsets and rimes as well as their combination into one-syllable words. Such word play is perhaps most successful when it derives from examining repeated onset patterns (alliteration) and rime patterns (rhyme) in something the children have been reading together during a shared reading experience. See, for example, the songs and poems from transparency 5.22 through the rest of Section 5.

Determining Lesson: Transparencies 5.16a and 5.16b

In Connie's original 1988 edition of *Reading Process and Practice*, Dorothy Watson and Paul Crowley wrote a chapter in which they discussed the Determining Lesson presented on **transparencies 5.16a and b** (see Watson, 1996). In a workshop setting, you might begin by showing the list of *ea* words, reading the directions with participants, and discussing whether the fourth grader attempting to do this exercise really does have a problem with *ea* words. Participants often point out that the directions are not easy to follow and that many of the words are not ones that fourth graders are likely to know. In short, people are often not convinced from this exercise that this child had a problem with *ea* words. However, Jan's teacher apparently thought so, based on Jan's errors and her not completing the exercise.

Because of her difficulties with the worksheet, Jan cried herself to sleep that night. Fortunately, her parents consulted a teacher with expert knowledge in the reading process. To determine whether Jan really had difficulty reading words with the digraph *ea*, this teacher developed a passage with several *ea* words—a passage based on the fact that Jan's father and uncle often went pheasant hunting. In reading about a familiar situation, Jan could draw upon her prior knowledge and context as well as her word and phonics knowledge.

Transparency 5.16b shows Jan's miscues on this passage. While she did miscue on some *ea* words, she corrected almost all of them—

though not the miscue on *deafening*, which she did at least try to correct. Jan's explanation for her attempted correction, the nonword "deefing," was to cite the rule "When two vowels go walking, the first one does the talking"! Notice that while Jan did omit the word *steady* in the rather unusual and unpredictable phrase *steady leash*, she read the word correctly in the somewhat more predictable context of *Babe and Bingo's steady stream of barking*. When she could use meaning as an aid to identifying words (in reading the passage) instead of listening for sounds within words that she had to pronounce out of context (in order to do the worksheet), Jan had little trouble with words that contained the digraph *ea*. Perhaps it is not surprising, then, that Jan was generally successful in school and considered herself a good reader—a view that was shared by her teacher and her parents.

As Watson and Crowley point out, before assuming from isolated skills exercises that a reader has difficulty with a particular skill or phonics element, teachers should assess that skill or the ability to read that element within coherent and meaningful text. Perhaps many parents will be less anxious about their children's difficulties with phonics worksheets if they see this demonstration that children do not have to be able to "do" phonics in isolation in order to use phonics knowledge in reading authentic texts. Indeed, perhaps many more parents will begin questioning the need for such worksheets.

Why Not to Teach Phonics Intensively and Systematically: Transparency 5.17

Many of the transparencies in this section on phonics should logically lead to the conclusion that it is not necessary or desirable to teach phonics and phonemic awareness intensively and systematically. Further information on relevant research is provided in the fact sheet titled "On Research on the Teaching of Phonics" and the fact sheet "On Research on Whole Language Education."

Recently the intensive and systematic teaching of phonics and phonemic awareness has been demanded by various special interest groups, such as the National Right to Read Foundation, the Eagle Forum, and, of course, companies that sell phonics programs like *Hooked on Phonics*. However, various lines of research demonstrate that children do not need intensive phonics instruction to develop the functional command of letter/sound patterns that they need as readers. Explicit attention to letter/sound patterns can be important, but such instruction does not need to be intensive and systematic (Beck & Juel, 1995; Adams & Bruck, 1995).

Young children are amazing learners. In the first few years of their lives, they learn to feed themselves, to walk, and to speak their native language—all with little, if any, direct instruction. These accomplishments are all the more impressive when we consider in detail the nature of these acts. In learning to speak English, for example, young children learn, at an unconscious level, the rule for making regular verbs past tense: add a / t / sound if the verb ends in an unvoiced consonant (*laughed, talked*), a / d / sound if the verb ends in a voiced consonant or a vowel (*giggled, sewed*), or a schwa-like vowel plus / d / if the verb already ends in / t / or / d / (*waited, waded*); see transparency 2.2. We know children have learned this as a rule when they abandon previously "correct" past tenses like *went* and *bought* for the regular but "incorrect" *goed* and *buyed*. Similarly, young children internalize and utilize the basic syntactic patterns of the language, such as subject + verb + object. They also learn many other patterns that we adults rarely are conscious of, such as the order of auxiliary verbs (if we have two or three auxiliaries, they occur in this order: modal auxiliary like *can* or *will*, then a form of *to have*, then a form of *to be*—as in "She might have been driving").

Such evidence demonstrates beyond a doubt the powerful learning abilities of young children. The fact that they normally learn highly complex processes and systems by merely interacting with the external world is perhaps the most important reason why children do not need to be taught phonics intensively and systematically. This and other reasons will be listed and briefly described below, with references to supporting research; most of this is taken from Connie's ERIC document, *Phonics revisited*, which is based on her *Reading Process and Practice* (Weaver, 1994b, 1994c). **Transparency 5.17** lists most but not quite all of the following reasons not to teach phonics intensively and systematically.

1. Kids don't need such thorough, direct, and systematic teaching. Their learning as babies, toddlers, and preschoolers gives ample evidence that we do not need to directly teach everything that children need to know, and that indeed the most complex processes—such as speaking their native language and learning to read and write—are among those processes which can be much better learned through experience, with the support of adults but with little direct teaching. As Don Holdaway explains it, such natural learning involves four major phases: observation of demonstrations, guided participation, unsupervised practice in the entire process, and performance—that is, the sharing of one's accomplishments (Holdaway, 1986; see transparency 1.5). Further extending Holdaway's model into the development of literacy, Brian Cambourne (1988) implies that one of the most important roles adults play in fostering children's development is encouraging children to take risks as learners, to "have a go" at reading, and not to worry initially about identifying or sounding out every word (see transparency 1.4). Phonics knowledge develops within the context of real reading and writing and oral language.

2. English is an alphabetic language, but by no means a phonetic or phonemic one in which one sound equals only one symbol, and vice versa. For one thing, meaning rather than sound determines many of our spellings (see transparency 5.2). Consider some common homonyms: *son, sun; break, brake; no, know; meat, meet, mete; right, write, rite.* Further evidence of the meaning basis of some of our spellings comes from pairs or sets of words that spell meaning-related parts the same way, despite the differences in sound: *medicine, medical; music, musician; site, situation; sign, signal; bomb, bombardier.* Clearly not all letters have one and only one sound. Consonants are the most reliable, but take *t,* for instance: it sounds like / t / in some contexts, but it combines with other letters to make other sounds, as well (as in *thin, those, catch, lotion*). As if these examples were not enough to discourage a heavy phonics approach to reading, there are also dialects to complicate the picture: for example, *-og* words like *frog, dog, smog, log,* and *hog* are not pronounced the same throughout the country (transparency 5.3). Heavy emphasis on phonics makes learning to read unnecessarily difficult for those children whose oral language patterns differ from the patterns assumed in the instructional materials.

3. It is much more effective and more efficient to focus on chunks of letters than on isolated letters. This is true in part because it is much easier for young children to hear and grasp syllables and syllablelike units in written language than to hear separate letter sounds. Also, proficient readers seem to process letters in syllablelike or smaller chunks, especially onsets and rimes. Therefore it seems best to emphasize not the sounds of single letters and digraphs per se, but syllables and the most salient parts into which they can be divided: the onsets and rimes of syllables (for summaries of relevant research, see Goswami & Bryant, 1990; Adams, 1990). The onset consists of any consonants that might precede the vowel (**t**op, **fr**ight, **sl**ay, **ch**ain). The rime consists of a vowel sound (the only obligatory part of a syllable), plus any consonant sounds that might optionally follow the vowel (**I**, **eye**, m**ight**, **isle**, for instance). It is relatively easy for even emergent readers to process unknown print words in onset and rime chunks, if they already know a fair number of print words (Moustafa, 1996). Thus in calling children's attention to letter/sound relationships, we should probably emphasize on-

sets and rimes, to facilitate the learning of common letter/sound patterns and the sounding out of words. However, research on emergent literacy (e.g., Hall, 1987) demonstrates that even these patterns do not necessarily need to be taught systematically or intensively. Most children learn them from repeated immersion in shared reading experiences (Holdaway, 1982) and rereading of favorite texts.

4. Proficient reading involves using everything you know to get words and construct meaning from a text. Fluent readers can identify many words on sight, even in word lists (e.g., Stanovich, 1991), yet identifying words by letter/sound patterns alone does not seem to be the way proficient readers normally read connected text (Goodman, 1973, 1982; for a line of reasoning that reconciles seemingly conflicting evidence, see Weaver, 1994c, Chapter 5). In a study with first graders, for instance, Freppon (1991) found that children taught reading through a traditional skills-based curriculum tried to sound out words more than twice as often as the children in literature-based classrooms where skills were not taught in isolation. However, the children in the literature-based classrooms were much more successful in sounding out words (53 percent of the time, compared with 32 percent), because they were simultaneously using prior knowledge and context in an effort to construct meaning from the text, not merely trying to sound out the word as if it stood in isolation. Learning phonics skills in isolation is not nearly as valuable as learning to read words in context—and thereby learning letter/sound patterns, too. We need to help children use letter/sound knowledge along with meaning as they read authentic texts.

5. Too much emphasis on phonics encourages children to use "sound it out" as their first and possibly only independent strategy for dealing with problem words (Applebee, Langer, & Mullis, 1988). Similarly, overemphasizing phonics may be especially damaging for children who have had few experiences with books prior to school. Of course they need to develop a functional grasp of letter/sound patterns and relationships, but first and concomitantly, they need numerous experiences of being read to, and of themselves reading along with the text while stories, poems, and rhymes are read to them.

6. Many emergent readers are not good at learning analytically, abstractly, or auditorily. For them, the study of phonics in isolation is difficult, if not impossible. This conclusion is suggested partly by Piagetian studies of child development (e.g., Wadsworth, 1989), but also by research into learning styles and reading styles (e.g., Carbo, 1987, both references). Thus teaching and testing phonics patterns and rules may result in many children quickly being labeled as dyslexic or reading disabled, or simply as slow readers, when the main problem is the mismatch between the children's learning style and the instructional program.

7. You don't have to be able to demonstrate phonics skills in isolation in order to have and use letter/sound knowledge while reading, along with context and everything you know. This can be shown with the Determining Lesson in transparencies 5.16a and b.

8. The research purporting to demonstrate the superiority of intensive systematic phonics over incidental phonics (e.g., Chall, 1983) is not very impressive. The best of these studies were reexamined by testing expert Richard Turner, who concluded from these nine randomized field studies "that systematic phonics falls into that vast category of weak instructional treatments with which education is perennially plagued." In comparison with basal-reader/whole-word instruction, systematic phonics produced a slight and early advantage on standardized tests, but "this difference does not last long and has no clear meaning for the acquisition of literacy" (Turner, 1989, p. 283). Most of these studies were undertaken before 1967, long before the advent of classrooms where natural, whole language learning has been emphasized. Even researchers who once advocated intensive, systematic phonics have

backed off from this recommendation, simply recommending now that teachers give explicit attention to phonemic awareness (awareness of sounds) and to phonics (e.g., Beck and Juel, 1995; Adams & Bruck, 1995).

9. More recent research comparing whole language classrooms with traditional skills-based classrooms (including those that emphasize phonics) has found that children develop phonics skills as well or better in whole language classrooms, as measured on standardized tests. (The oft-cited 1989 Stahl & Miller study must be discounted because it lumped whole language together with language experience, which is at most only one technique used within a whole language classroom.) Furthermore, Stahl, McKenna, and Pagnucco in their 1993 article indicate from their more thorough and up-to-date investigation of the research that phonics may be taught as effectively in whole language classrooms as in any other. (On the other hand, a recent study by Foorman [forthcoming] is now being touted as evidence that intensive phonics is superior to whole language. See the fact sheet "On research on the teaching of phonics" for more details.)

In whole language classrooms, phonics and phonemic awareness are taught and learned in the context of authentic reading and writing. Most important, however, are the other differences that demonstrate the real power of natural, whole language learning and teaching (e.g., Dahl & Freppon, 1992; Stice & Bertrand, 1990; Kasten & Clarke, 1989; Freppon, 1993, 1991; Clarke, 1988; Ribowsky, 1985). The six studies summarized in Weaver, 1994c (see also Weaver, 1990; Stephens, 1991) and the nine studies of learning English as a second language summarized in Elley (1991) seem to warrant the following additional generalizations about children in whole language classrooms, compared with those in skills-based classrooms that (to a greater or lesser degree) teach phonics in isolation. The whole language children seem (1) to develop greater facility in using phonics knowledge effectively; (2) to develop vocabulary, spelling, grammar,

and punctuation skills as well as or better than children in more traditional classrooms; (3) to be more inclined and able to read for meaning, rather than just to identify words; (4) to develop more strategies for dealing with problems in reading, such as problems in identifying words; (5) to develop greater facility in writing; (6) to develop a stronger sense of themselves as readers and writers; and (7) to develop greater independence as readers and writers. Based upon research with children from preschool through grade two, these generalizations must still be considered tentative. However, the results from these studies strongly suggest the superiority of a natural, whole language emphasis that develops phonics knowledge in the context of authentic reading and writing.

Once convinced that children don't need intensive, systematic phonics in order to learn the phonics they need for reading, people still sometimes think that children should be taught phonics systematically so that they will learn to spell. One way to help workshop participants reconsider this assumption is to give them a spelling test like the one in Connie's *Reading Process and Practice* (1994c, pp. 170–71). This "test" consists of some homonyms (*sun, brake, rowed, mete*, which of course the tester would not illustrate in the context of a sentence); some nonsense words (such as *keak, pite, wraim*); and some longer real words that most people are not likely to know (*coriaceous, deraign, escharotic, gaudeamus*, and *piceous*; examples could also be taken from the word list on transparency 5.5). Most people find that they have not spelled correctly more than a fourth to a third of such a list.

Of course, some people object that this is a contrived test, which it is. However, in a study that applied phonics rules in reverse, Cronnell found that these rules generated correct spellings less than half the time (Cronnell, 1970, as cited in Adams, 1990). Furthermore, using the three hundred spelling/sound rules developed by Hanna et al. (1966), fewer than 50 percent of the seventeen-thousand words in their corpus would be spelled correctly. And, as

Adams notes (1990), "in a spelling bee between fourth graders and a computer that had been programmed with these rules, the fourth graders handily won out" (p. 390). Perhaps such information will help workshop participants realize that phonics knowledge helps only in the beginning stages of writing, when children are spelling words as they hear them in order to get their ideas down on paper.

How Children Learn Phonics: Transparency 5.18

The material in this section draws from Connie's ERIC digest, *Phonics in Whole Language Classrooms*, which is based on her *Reading Process and Practice* (Weaver, 1994a, 1994c). In a workshop setting, you might find it useful to draw upon some of the following comments.

It has sometimes been asserted that children do not learn phonics in whole language classrooms, since phonics is not taught intensively and systematically. However, various lines of research demonstrate that children do not need intensive phonics instruction in order to develop the functional command of letter/sound patterns that they need as readers (Weaver, 1994b, 1994c; Goodman, 1993). Not the least of this evidence is the research demonstrating that children develop and use phonics knowledge better in whole language classrooms than in traditional skills-based classrooms, including those that emphasize phonics (as summarized in Weaver, 1994c). Here are some of the ways children develop functional phonics knowledge in the context of authentic reading and writing. Most of these points are listed on **transparency 5.18**, "How Children Learn Phonics." You may want to point out the activities that seem especially likely to develop phonemic awareness—that is, an awareness of the "separate" sounds in words. Children develop phonics knowledge:

1. By being encouraged to write independently. Of course, primary grade children should be writing in whatever way they can,

whether it be scribble writing, random letters and symbols, or letters that at least begin to be decipherable as words. But when they can use letters to represent sounds, they begin to promote their own phonics development through writing (Temple, Nathan, Temple, & Burris, 1993; McGee & Richgels, 1990; Clay, 1987).

2. By observing the teacher write down the children's ideas, or the teacher's own. For example, the teacher may model his or her own writing process, lead the children in guided writing, and/or write something from the children's dictation. In each instance, the children may not only observe but may also participate by suggesting appropriate letters for representing given sounds in a word. And, of course, the teacher may facilitate learning by calling attention to particular letter/sound patterns, especially of onsets and rimes.

3. By noticing print while the teacher reads a Big Book or large chart aloud. Children need to have familiar and favorite stories (poems, rhymes, etc.) read to them again and again, during a shared reading experience wherein they can see the text and see the teacher point to words as they are spoken (Holdaway, 1979, 1982). This process facilitates the learning of words and of letter/sound patterns, as well as an understanding of print and how it is read in English.

4. By discussing interesting elements of sound in a reading selection. Teachers can facilitate such discussion within the shared reading experience, using Big Books, charts, or transparencies that all the children can see. Alphabet books also invite the discussion of letter/sound relationships.

5. By engaging in self-chosen activities with words having similar sound elements, commonly as an outgrowth of the shared reading experience. For example, children might make charts of words exhibiting letter/sound patterns of particular interest to them. After two or more charts have been compiled, children could make related graphs comparing appro-

priate data (Whitin, Mills, & O'Keefe, 1990). Children can also be guided in making their own alphabet books.

6. By learning to use letter/sound cues along with prior knowledge and context. Proficient readers seem unconsciously to use initial letters plus prior knowledge and context to predict what a word might be, before focusing on more of the word or the following context to confirm or correct. The teacher may demonstrate this strategy in the context of a shared reading experience and may likewise engage children in predicting words from prior knowledge, context, and the initial letter(s).

7. By receiving individual help in using phonics cues along with prior knowledge and context, in order to get meaning. This strategy seems to come naturally for many children, but others may need instructional assistance in first using the strategy consciously. Children who seem not to be developing this strategy may need individual tutorial assistance in using prior knowledge, context, and the initial letter(s) of a word to predict what would fit, then looking at the rest of the word to confirm or correct.

8. By rereading familiar materials and inferring phonics relationships. Emergent readers need to read and reread favorite stories, songs, and poems, lists of classmates' names, and so forth, and to read them independently or with a peer. This independent practice contributes greatly to solidifying children's growing understanding of print, including their internalization of letter/sound patterns. The rereading is facilitated if children have individual copies of the text, and if they can listen to a tape recording of the text as they read. It's especially helpful if the tape recording is appropriately paced (Carbo, 1989).

Contrasting Models of Learning Phonics: Transparencies 5.19 and 5.20

The intensive, systematic teaching of phonics that is so widely promoted reflects a transmis-

sion model of learning, while a whole language approach—fostering phonics knowledge within the context of authentic reading and writing—reflects a transactional model of learning. Therefore, **transparency 5.19** repeats the contrast in transparency 1.7, but this time with the heading "Intensive phonics" instead of "Transmission" and "Whole language" instead of "Transactional." Using some of the intervening transparencies with workshop participants should make it easier for them to understand what it means for children to "attempt the whole and gradually refine the parts," and how this applies to phonics in particular.

Transparency 5.20 reflects some of the differences in the research assumptions and assessment measures between phonics advocates and whole language advocates (though both groups of researchers typically recognize the importance of developing phonics knowledge in the context of authentic language experiences). Because the research of phonics advocates typically uses standardized tests as the only measure of reading proficiency (or rather, of reading "achievement"), their research is not as comprehensive as that of whole language advocates. The latter have demonstrated through comparative research in primary grade classrooms that children in whole language classrooms learn phonics as well as or better than children in skills-oriented classrooms and that, in addition, children in whole language classrooms typically make better use of their phonics knowledge, develop more strategies for dealing with problem words, read for meaning better, write better at an early age, and become more independent as readers and writers. For more information, see the fact sheets "On Research on Whole Language Education" and "On Research on the Teaching of Phonics," in Part Two of this book.

Ways of Helping Children Learn Phonics: Transparency 5.21

Transparency 5.21 is in effect the flip side of transparency 5.18, "How Children Learn

Phonics." In a workshop setting you might use first 5.18 and then this one, or use this one on "teaching" phonics instead of 5.18. Again, the following elaboration on these points is drawn from Connie's ERIC digest, *Phonics in Whole Language Classrooms* (Weaver,1994a). Below are some of the ways teachers can help children develop phonics knowledge. Again, you might want to point out which activities seem especially likely to develop phonemic awareness.

1. First, have faith in children as learners. They can and usually will develop a grasp of letter/sound patterns and relationships with explicit guidance and support but little direct instruction, just as they learned to talk without direct instruction in the rules of the English language. Also, don't assume that because children cannot do worksheets on particular phonics elements that they cannot read words with those same patterns (e.g., the Determining Lesson in transparencies 5.16a and b).

2. Discuss onset and rime patterns within songs, poems, and stories that are read to and with children, typically in the context of shared reading experiences. Among the stories, poems, rhymes, and songs chosen to share with children should be some that emphasize alliteration (the repetition of one or more onsets) and rhyme (rimes). One of the best ways to generate children's interest in the sound elements of a selection may be to ask simply, "What do you notice about this poem?" or, more specifically, "What do you notice about the sounds in this poem?" (Mills, O'Keefe, & Stephens, 1992). Though children may notice different sound elements from what the teacher anticipated, this procedure gives children ownership over their own learning. Of course much of the poetry that rhymes is humorous poetry—one thinks, for example, of Shel Silverstein's poetry, or Jack Prelutsky's, though humorous poetry should comprise only a modest proportion of the poetry to which children are introduced. One book particularly rich in poems with alliteration, rhyme, and onomatopoeia (words that sound like the sound they designate) is *Noisy Poems*, collected by Jill Bennett (1987). Collections of poetry like *The Random House Book of Poetry for Children*, selected by Jack Prelutsky (1983), are often good sources for poems in which sound elements are prominent. Other such collections include *Sing a Song of Popcorn*, selected by Beatrice Schenk de Regniers (1988), and *Poems Children Will Sit Still For*, also selected by Beatrice Schenk de Regniers (1969). A cumulative book with wonderfully alliterative and onomatopoeic verbs is *Deep Down Underground*, by Olivier Dunrea (1989).

3. Guide collaborative activities focusing on onsets and rimes, typically as an outgrowth of the shared reading experience. This will reinforce children's natural learning of letter/sound relationships and patterns. Mathematically related ideas can involve the making of charts that list words with particular sound patterns, and graphs based upon the charts (for example, teachers and children might chart all the *sl-* and *sp-* and *st-* words in several poems, then make a class graph showing the relative frequency of the words in each list; see, for instance, Whitin, Mills, & O'Keefe, 1990, and some of the poems in Bennett's *Noisy Poems*). Children may especially enjoy collaborating in such activities— and in creating their own alphabet books, too. In *Looking Closely: Exploring the Role of Phonics in One Whole Language Classroom* (Mills, O'Keefe, & Stephens, 1992), we see various phonics-enhancing activities that can stem from and enhance enjoyment of literature, as well as activities involving children's names. See also *Learning Phonics and Spelling in a Whole Language Classroom* (Powell & Hornsby, 1993), which offers many procedures and examples similar to the ones presented here.

4. Demonstrate the use of context and initial letter cues to predict a word. There are several ways teachers can do this, such as: (1) by modeling how they themselves use meaning (and grammar) along with initial letters to predict what a word might be; (2) by repeatedly encouraging children to think "What would make

sense here?" before trying to sound out a word; (3) by engaging together in oral cloze activities based on their shared readings ("What would fit in this sentence, I put c_____ in the soup?"); and (4) by discussing, in literature discussion groups, how various children dealt with problem words. It is critical to help children develop and use letter/sound knowledge in the context of constructing meaning from texts.

5. Reread favorite stories, poems, songs, and tongue twisters from large texts that the children can follow; point to words while reading together. Large texts can include commercial Big Books, books or other writings the children have developed, or other writings on posterboard, paper, or even transparency: the point is that the texts must be large enough for all the children to read together. Pointing to the words while reading together helps children develop awareness of individual words and thereby promotes letter/sound awareness too.

6. Provide small texts and tape recordings, so the children can listen and follow the text. It is important for children to have their own copies of familiar and favorite texts so that they can practice reading. Providing for children to listen to tape recordings of the texts will again facilitate word and phonics knowledge.

7. Do guided writing with the children, and support their efforts to write independently. Both are absolutely critical. During guided writing, the teacher helps children shape their ideas and choose what words and sentences they want to have written for them as a group, then solicits the children's help with the spelling and writing. When children and teacher work together to hear and write the sounds in words, the children's grasp of letter/sound relationships is confirmed and enhanced. When children are just beginning to hear the separate sounds in words, they need guidance in writing the letters for the sounds they hear. At first, a child just beginning to write phonemically will usually represent only one sound per word, typically the first sound.

The teacher or a more proficient writer can help children make the breakthrough to this phase and then help them write more and more of the sounds in words. (See the discussion of transparency 1.8, "Development of Language and Literacy." See also Section 7, "Writing and Learning to Write."

8. Provide additional help and materials for the children who need it: for example, books with alliteration and rhyme, such as Dr. Seuss books. Children who are exceptionally slow in grasping letter/sound relationships may benefit from tutorial assistance, such as that offered in the Reading Recovery Program (e.g., Clay, 1993). Also, teachers should be alert for children's idiosyncratic ways of developing phonics knowledge and support those. Jevon's learning of letter/sound relationships through his classmates' names is but one example (White, 1990).

Cross Reference to Transparencies 1.9 and 1.10 on Teaching Minilessons

At this point you might find it useful to summarize how minilessons in transactional classrooms differ from those in a transmission classroom, using transparency 1.9 and/or 1.10. Notice that the teacher actually does more teaching in the transactional, whole language classroom.

Before using these two transparencies, you might use transparency 1.7, which contrasts a transmission model of learning, derived from behavioral psychology, with a transactional model of learning, based on cognitive psychology. These two models underlie the differing models of skills instruction contrasted in transparencies 1.9 and 1.10.

Songs and Poems for Learning Phonics: Transparencies 5.22 Through 5.28b

Transparencies 5.22 through 5.28b consist of traditional songs and poems that can be used in classroom settings or in workshops to demonstrate some of the ways that phonics is taught in the context of reading and enjoying authentic texts. Typically the songs and poems emphasize alliteration (same beginning sounds), rhyme (same ending sounds), and sometimes onomatopoeia as well (words that sound like what they designate). Children usually enjoy noticing, discussing, and savoring such sound elements. Thus the songs and poems lend themselves to some of the extension activities previously described.

One particularly enjoyable poem we could not get permission to put on a transparency page is Rhoda Bacmeister's "Galoshes," which is printed here instead:

"Galoshes"

Susie's galoshes
Make splishes and sploshes
And slooshes and sloshes
As Susie steps slowly
Along in the slush.

They stamp and they tramp
On the ice and concrete,
They get stuck in the muck and the mud;
But Susie likes much best to hear

The slippery slush
As it slooshes and sloshes,
And splishes and sploshes,
All around her galoshes!

Of course children enjoy pantomiming the actions in the poem, but it also offers opportunities to discuss recurring sound elements. Sometimes what children especially notice is sounds like -ish, -osh, -ush, -oosh, and they may enjoy making lists of words with similar sounds. In workshops, Connie has demonstrated how you can begin lists of sp- and spl- words from the words in this poem, then start adding to the list by drawing from Jack Prelutsky's poem "Spaghetti" (anthologized in Bennett's *Noisy Poems*). These lists can be further extended and charted by the children. (They can even add words in invented spellings on a piece of chart paper designated for that purpose—words that can later be added to the class chart in conventional spelling during class discussion.)

Another poem we regret being unable to include on a transparency page is "Fishes' Evening Song," by Dahlov Ipcar (in Bennett's *Noisy Poems*). There are several key words that begin with *f-*, or with *fl-*; with *pl-*; with *s-*, or with *s* plus another consonant. Thus, there are many opportunities to make charts of words with the same onset, to make word cards with the same onset that can be sorted into piles according to the onset, and so forth. There are also some rimes that notably reoccur: *-ap, -ip, -op, and -ish*, for example. In addition, some of the words are examples of onomatopoeia: that is, they *sound* something like what they designate. Examples are *splash, splish, swush, swash, swish*, and at least some of the words ending in *-ap, -ip*, and *-op*.

Transparency 5.22 is the poem "Cheeky Chipmunk," by Miriam Bat-Ami. This and "Wet Worm" on **transparency 5.23** are part of her projected book *The Underground Alphabet Book*. Both poems contain alliteration and can be used in a workshop setting to explain how initial consonant sounds can be taught through observation and discussion during a shared reading experience and, if desired, through related follow-up activities of the kinds described previously. **Transparency 5.24**, a poem Connie's son John verbalized at age seven, can be used similarly. (Connie captured the poem on paper and they submitted it to a local Poetry on Buses contest. As a winning entry, the poem was displayed on local metro buses for a month.)

Transparency 5.25 is a variant of the traditional song "This Old Man." It was developed using the six basic colors as the first line of each new stanza. In sharing and discussing this variant with other people, you might note that a nonsense word (*burple*) and a fictitious place name (*LaFlorange*) were created as rhyming words. The intent here was to create a poem in which the rhyming words are spelled the same.

In using the song with children, however, you will probably find that they enjoy offering other rhyme words, in which the rhyming part may not be spelled the same. This is a good opportunity to start making a chart of the different ways certain rhymes can be spelled. Notice that some of these rhymes have two syllables and therefore two "rimes": *-ellow*, for instance, plus *-urple* and *orange* (in some dialects).

Children will also enjoy making up new verses of their own, as in **transparency 5.26**, which includes a version created by Deborah Payne's fourth graders at Sauquoit Valley Elementary in Sauquoit, New York. Another possibility: together, teacher and students might begin brainstorming body parts to end the second rhyming line and then brainstorm for rhyme words to end the first, creating, for instance, lines like "This old man had a band / He played knick knack on my hand." New variants will, of course, offer new opportunities for charts on the different spellings of the rhymes. Furthermore, graphs can be derived from the charts, thus combining language arts with mathematics.

One important way to foster phonics knowledge and teach the strategy of predicting is to cover all but the onset of the word in a line that rhymes with a preceding line. For example, "This old man, he played red, / He played knick knack on my b—." Discussion of their predictions helps children become metacognitively aware of using prior knowledge, context, and initial letters to predict words, after which they can look at the rest of the letters to confirm or correct.

One poem that can be used the same way is "The Pines," in **transparency 5.27**. This poem was chosen to illustrate the fact that not all poems that rhyme are singsongy or humorous; rhyme can be used in poems with serious intent, and such poems should also be shared with children.

Transparencies 5.28a and 5.28b include the traditional poem "Susie Moriar," which is also especially good for predicting rhyme words. (If you have trouble predicting any of these rhymes, each one is included in the first line of the next couplet.) DLM Teaching Resources has published a Big Book wherein the rhyming word is cued by a picture at the bottom of the page, before being printed in the first line of the next page (*Susie Moriar*, 1987).

Sources and Resources

Items marked with an asterisk emphasize concrete ideas for developing letter/sound knowledge in the context of literacy.

ADAMS, J. J., & BRUCK, M. (1995). Resolving the "Great Debate." *American Educator, 19* (2), 7, 10–20.

ADAMS, M. J. (1990). *Beginning to read: Thinking and learning about print.* Cambridge: Harvard University Press.

APPLEBEE, A. N., LANGER, J. A., & MULLIS, I. V. S. (1988). *Learning to be literate in America: Reading, writing, and reasoning.* The nation's report card. Princeton, NJ: National Assessment of Educational Progress, Educational Testing Service. ERIC: ED 281 162.

BECK, I. L., & JUEL, C. (1995). The role of decoding in learning to read. *American Educator, 19* (2), 8–9, 21–25, 39–42.

BERDIANSKY, B., CRONNELL, B., & KOEHLER, J. (1969). *Spelling-sound relations and primary form-class descriptions for speech-comprehension vocabularies of 6–9 year-olds.* Technical Report no. 15. Inglewood, CA: Southwest Regional Laboratory for Educational Research and Development. ERIC: ED 030 109.

BLUMENFELD, S. L. (1983). *Alpha-phonics: A primer for beginning readers.* Boise, ID: The Paradigm Company.

CAMBOURNE, B. (1988). *The whole story: Natural learning and the acquisition of literacy in the classroom.* Auckland, NZ: Scholastic. ERIC: ED 359 497.

CARBO, M. (1987). Deprogramming reading failure: Giving unequal learners an equal chance. *Phi Delta Kappan, 69,* 197–202.

CARBO, M. (1987). Reading style research: "What works" isn't always phonics. *Phi Delta Kappan, 68,* 431–35.

CARBO, M. (1989). *How to record books for maximum reading gains.* National Reading Styles Institute, P.O. Box 39, Roslyn Heights, NY 11577.

CHALL, J. (1983). *Learning to read: The great debate* (2nd ed.). New York: McGraw-Hill.

CHOMSKY, C. (1970). Reading, writing, and phonology. *Harvard Educational Review, 40,* 287–309.

CLARKE, L. K. (1988). Invented versus traditional spelling in first graders' writings: Effects on learning to spell and read. *Research in the Teaching of English, 22,* 281–309.

CLAY, M. (1987). *Writing begins at home.* Portsmouth, NH: Heinemann.

CLAY, M. (1993). *Reading Recovery: A guidebook for teachers in training.* Portsmouth, NH: Heinemann.

CLYMER, T. L. (1963). The utility of phonic generalizations in the primary grades. *The Reading Teacher, 16,* 252–258.

CRONNELL, B. A. (1970). *Spelling-to-sound correspondences for reading vs. sound-to-spelling correspondences.* Technical Note TN2-70-15. Los Alamitos, CA: Southwest Regional Laboratory.

DAHL, K. L., & FREPPON, P. A. (1992). *Learning to read and write in inner-city schools: A comparison of children's sense-making in skills-based and whole language classrooms* (Final Report to the Office of Educational Research and Improvement, U.S. Office of Education Grant Award No. R117E00134). Cincinnati, OH: University of Cincinnati.

ELLEY, W. B. (1991). Acquiring literacy in a second language: The effect of book-based programs. *Language Learning, 41* (3), 375–411.

ENGELMANN, S., HADDOX, P., & BRUNER, E. (1983). *Teach your child to read in 100 easy lessons.* New York: Simon & Schuster.

FLESCH. R. (1955). *Why Johnny can't read.* New York: Harper & Row.

FOORMAN, B. R., FRANCIS, D. J., BEELER, T., WINIKATES, D., & FLETCHER, J. M. (Forthcoming). Early intervention for children with reading problems: Study designs and preliminary findings. *Learning Disabilities: A Multi-Disciplinary Journal.*

FREPPON, P. A. (1991). Children's concepts of the nature and purpose of reading in different instructional settings. *Journal of Reading Behavior, 23,* 139–163.

FREPPON, P. A. (1993). *Making sense of reading and writing in urban classrooms: Understanding at-risk children's knowledge construction in different curricula* (Final Report to the Office of Educational Research and Improvement). Washington: U.S. Office of Education, OERI. ERIC: ED 361 433.

*FREPPON, P. A., & DAHL, K. L. (1991). Learning about phonics in a whole language classroom. *Language Arts, 68,* 190–197.

GOODMAN, K. S. (1973). *Theoretically based studies of patterns of miscues in oral reading performance.* Detroit: Wayne State University. Educational Resources Information Clearinghouse: ERIC: ED 079 708.

GOODMAN, K. S. (1982). *Language and literacy: The selected writings of Kenneth S. Goodman.* (Ed. Frederick V. Gollasch). 2 vols. Boston: Routledge and Kegan Paul. ERIC: ED 261 358.

GOODMAN, K. S. (1993). *Phonics phacts.* Richmond, Ontario: Scholastic, and Portsmouth, NH: Heinemann.

GOSWAMI, U., & BRYANT, P. (1990). *Phonological skills and learning to read.* Hove, East Sussex: Lawrence Erlbaum.

HALL, N. (1987). *The emergence of literacy.* Portsmouth, NH: Heinemann.

HANNA, P. R., et al. (1966). *Phoneme-grapheme correspondences as cues to spelling improvement*. USOE Publication No. 32008. Washington, DC: Government Printing Office.

HOLDAWAY, D. (1979). *The foundations of literacy*. Sydney: Ashton-Scholastic. Available in the U.S. from Heinemann.

HOLDAWAY, D. (1982). Shared Book Experience: Teaching reading using favorite books. *Theory into Practice, 21*, 293–300.

HOLDAWAY, D. (1986). The structure of natural learning as a basis for literacy instruction. In M. R. Sampson, *The pursuit of literacy: Early reading and writing* (pp. 56–72). Dubuque, IA: Kendall / Hunt.

Hooked on Phonics. Orange, CA: Gateway Educational Products.

KASTEN, W. C., & CLARKE, B. K. (1989). *Reading/writing readiness for preschool and kindergarten children: A whole language approach*. Sanibel: Florida Educational Research and Development Council. ERIC: ED 312 041.

McGEE, L. M., & RICHGELS, D. J. (1990). *Literacy's beginnings: Supporting young readers and writers*. Needham Heights, MA: Allyn & Bacon.

*MILLS, H., O'KEEFE, T., & STEPHENS, D. (1992). *Looking closely: Exploring the role of phonics in one whole language classroom*. Urbana, IL: National Council of Teachers of English.

MOUSTAFA, M. (1996). *Reconceptualizing phonics instruction in a balanced approach to reading*. Unpublished manuscript. San Jose, CA: San Jose State University.

*POWELL, D., & HORNSBY, D. (1993). *Learning phonics and spelling in a whole language classroom*. New York: Scholastic.

Reading Mastery: DISTAR. (1988). Chicago: SRA.

RIBOWSKY, H. (1985). *The effects of a code emphasis approach and a whole language approach upon emergent literacy of kindergarten children*. Alexandria, VA: ERIC: ED 269 720.

RICHGELS, D., POREMBA, R., & McGEE, L. (1996). Kindergartners talk about print: Phonemic awareness in meaningful contexts. *The Reading Teacher, 49*, 632–641.

ROUTMAN, R., & BUTLER, A. (1995). Phonics fuss: Facts, fiction, phonemes, and fun. *School Talk, 1* (2). National Council of Teachers of English.

SHUY, R. W. (1967). *Discovering American dialects*. Urbana, IL: National Council of Teachers of English.

SMITH, J. W. A., & ELLEY, W. B. (1995). *Learning to read in New Zealand*. Katonah, NY: Richard C. Owen.

STAHL, S. A., McKENNA, M. C., & PAGNUCCO, J. R. (1993). The effects of whole-language instruction: An update and a reappraisal. *Educational Psychologist, 29*, 175–185.

STAHL, S. A., & MILLER, P. D. (1989). Whole language and language experience approaches for beginning reading: A quantitative research synthesis. *Review of Educational Research, 59*, 87–116.

STANOVICH, K. E. (1991). Word recognition: Changing perspectives. In R. Barr, M. L. Kamil, P. B. Mosenthal, & P. D. Pearson (Eds.), *Handbook of reading research*, Vol. 2 (pp. 418–452). New York: Longman.

STEPHENS, D. (1991). *Research on whole language: Support for a new curriculum*. Katonah, NY: Richard C. Owen.

STICE, C. F., & BERTRAND, N. P. (1990). *Whole language and the emergent literacy of at-risk children: A two-year comparative study*. Nashville: Center of Excellence: Basic Skills, Tennessee State University. ERIC: ED 324 636.

TEMPLE, C., NATHAN, R., TEMPLE, F., & BURRIS, N. (1993). *The beginnings of writing* (3rd ed.). Boston: Allyn & Bacon.

TURNER, R. L. 1989. The "Great" debate—Can both Carbo and Chall be right? *Phi Delta Kappan, 71*, 276–283.

WADSWORTH, B. J. (1989). *Piaget's theory of cognitive and affective development.* New York: Longman.

WAGSTAFF, J. (n.d.). *Phonics that work: New strategies for the reading/writing classroom.* New York: Scholastic.

WATSON, D. (1996). *Making a difference: Selected writings by Dorothy Watson.* (Ed. S. Wilde). Portsmouth, NH: Heinemann.

WATSON, D., & CROWLEY, P. (1988). How can we implement a whole-language approach? In C. Weaver, *Reading process and practice: From socio-psycholinguistics to whole language* (pp. 232–279). Portsmouth, NH: Heinemann.

*WEAVER, C. (1990). *Understanding whole language: From principles to practice.* Portsmouth, NH: Heinemann.

*WEAVER, C. (1994a). *Phonics in whole language classrooms.* ERIC digest. ERIC: ED 372 375.

WEAVER, C. (1994b). *Phonics revisited.* ERIC: ED 370 090.

*WEAVER, C. (1994c). *Reading process and practice: From socio-psycholinguistics to whole language* (2nd ed.). Portsmouth, NH: Heinemann.

*WHITE, C. (1990). *Jevon doesn't sit at the back anymore.* Richmond Hill, Ontario: Scholastic.

WHITIN, D. J., MILLS, H., & O'KEEFE, T. (1990). *Living and learning mathematics: Stories and strategies for supporting mathematical literacy.* Portsmouth, NH: Heinemann.

WILDE, S. (1992). *You kan red this! Spelling and punctuation for whole language classrooms, K–6.* Portsmouth, NH: Heinemann.

WOLFRAM, W. (1991). *Dialects and American English. A publication of the Center for Applied Linguistics.* Englewood Cliffs, NJ: Prentice Hall.

WYLIE, R. E., & DURRELL, D. D. (1970). Teaching vowels through phonograms. *Elementary English, 47,* 787–791.

YOPP, H. (1992). Developing phonemic awareness in young children. *The Reading Teacher, 45,* 696–703.

Children's Literature Cited

BENNETT, J. (Collector). (1987). *Noisy poems.* Illus. Nick Sharratt. New York: Oxford University Press.

DE REGNIERS, B. S. (Collector). (1969). *Poems children will sit still for: A selection for the primary grades.* New York: Citation.

DE REGNIERS, B. S. (Collector). (1988). *Sing a song of popcorn: Every child's book of poems.* New York: Scholastic.

DUNREA, O. (1989). *Deep down underground.* New York: Macmillan.

PRELUTSKY, J. (Collector). (1983). *The Random House book of poetry for children.* New York: Random House.

Susie Moriar: An Old Rhyme. (1987). Illus. by M. Foreman. Allen, TX: DLM Teaching Resources.

"Phonics Fun"

Let's see now: Where, oh where, to start?
Some say the head and some the heart.

Heart, as a maverick, rhymes with *hart*.
Head rhymes with *bed*, but not with *bead*—
And *lead* with either *dead* OR *deed*.
How spelling doth mislead: indeed!

We see the rule of silent *e*
In *plate* and *scene* and *bite* and *cove*,
But *come* rhymes not with *home* and *tome*,
Nor *move* with *love* and *shove*, or *stove*.
While *dove*, a word more versatile,
Can rhyme with either *love* OR *rove*.

A's not the same in *bat* and *bank*,
no matter what the books may say.
And *fat*'s not *fat* at all in *father*,
Nor *moth* in *mother*, *broth* in *brother*.
Indeed, what rhymes with *father*? *Bother*!

A *cough* is not a *cough* in *hiccough*
Nor *-ough* the same in *tough* and *though*.
Though rhymes, in fact, with *slow* and *grow*,
And also rhymes with *no* and *know*.
Know rhymes with *hoe*, but not with *chow*;
But *bow* can rhyme with *no* OR *now*.

And then there's *route*, which rhymes with *snoot*—
But also rhymes with *snout* and *shout*!

A hundred rules or so will do
To account for *sue*, and *shoe*, and *shoo*
For *flew* and *flue* and others *too*.
Dear me, 'tis enough to make me blue.
                    —Connie Weaver

T5.1   *"Phonics Fun"*   *Creating Support for Effective Literacy Education* by C. Weaver, L. Gillmeister-Krause, & G. Vento-Zogby, © 1996. Portsmouth, NH: Heinemann. May be copied for transparency use only.

Spelling/Sound Relationships

Homophones

son, sun	rap, wrap
break, brake	by, buy, bye
no, know	rowed, rode, road
new, knew	meat, meet, mete
peace, piece	write, right, rite

Noun plural endings

/s/ ending	/z/ ending	/ɨ z/ ending
caps	cabs	horses
cats	cads	fizzes
likes	pigs	churches
laughs	loves	judges
thoughts	dreams	wishes

Words related in meaning

medicine	/s/	medic; medical	/k/
music	/k/	musician	/sh/
logic	/k/	logician	/sh/
situate	/t/	situation	/sh/
bomb	/0/	bombard	/b/
resign	/0/	resignation	/g/

T5.2   *Spelling/Sound Relationships*   *Creating Support for Effective Literacy Education* by C. Weaver, L. Gillmeister-Krause, & G. Vento-Zogby, © 1996. Portsmouth, NH: Heinemann. May be copied for transparency use only.

From *Reading process and practice* (2nd ed.) by Constance Weaver. Portsmouth, NH: Heinemann, 1994.

Dialect Differences

words ending in -og:
    frog, fog, dog, hog, log, bog, cog, smog, clog, tog

merry, marry, Mary

far, father and awe

pin, pen

wash, Washington

idea, Cuba

root, route

Getting Words (#1)

caracara

fiduciary

flabellate

fulminate

mezereon

isochronal

machinations

paroxysm

parsimony

picopicogram

pretermit

stereobate

tinzenite

transpalatine

Getting Words (#2)

arenaceous

bosquet

caracara

chiffonier

coriaceous

deliquesce

demesne

evotomys

excoriate

expunge

fiduciary

fissiparous

flabellate

fulminate

isochronal

machination

mezereon

ozostomia

palimpsest

paroxysm

parsimony

picopicogram

pretermit

preternatural

roisterous

serendipity

stereobate

tintinnabulation

tinzenite

tortuosity

transpalatine

transubstantiate

Vowel Rules (#1)

"When two vowels go walking, the first one does the talking."

Yes   No

Examples:

nail, bead, ceiling, pie, boat, suit

Exceptions:

said, head, neighbor, chief, cupboard, build

Vowel Rules (#2)

"When a word ends in vowel + consonant + e̲,
the e̲ is usually silent and the other vowel is long."

Yes   No

Examples:

cake, late, scene, chime, bone, June

Exceptions:

have, bare, come, move

Vowel Rules (#3)

Rule	% utility
When there are two vowels together, the first one is long and the second is silent.	45%
When there are two vowels, one of which is final *e*, the first is long and the *e* is silent.	63%
When a vowel is in the middle of a one-syllable word, the vowel is short.	62%
When a word has only one vowel letter, the vowel sound is likely to be short.	57%

T5.8   *Vowel Rules (#3)*   *Creating Support for Effective Literacy Education* by C. Weaver, L. Gillmeister-Krause, & G. Vento-Zogby, © 1996. Portsmouth, NH: Heinemann. May be copied for transparency use only.

From Theodore Clymer, The utility of phonic generalizations in the primary grades. *The Reading Teacher, 16* (January 1963): 252–258.

Vowel Rules (#4)

Rule	% utility
The combination *ee* is likely pronounced with a long *e* sound.	98%
The combination *oa* is likely pronounced with a long *o*.	97%
When *y* is the last letter in a word, it usually has a vowel sound.	84%
An *r* gives the preceding vowel a sound that is neither long nor short.	78%
In *ay*, the *y* is silent and *a* has a long sound.	78%

T5.9   *Vowel Rules (#4)*   *Creating Support for Effective Literacy Education* by C. Weaver,
L. Gillmeister-Krause, & G. Vento-Zogby, © 1996. Portsmouth, NH: Heinemann. May be copied for
transparency use only.
From Theodore Clymer, The utility of phonic generalizations in the primary grades. *The Reading Teacher, 16*
(January 1963): 252–258.

Phonics Lessons

	fr	tr	i	a	p	b

The girl skips and spins. ☐

The girl skates and spits. ☐

Reading words

"Sounds it out."   his = hiiisss

squash	squander	square
squeak	squeamish	squall
squish	squiggle	squeeze
squirrel	squeal	squirm

 Creating Support for Effective Literacy Education by C. Weaver, L. Gillmeister-Krause, & G. Vento-Zogby, © 1996. Portsmouth, NH: Heinemann. May be copied for transparency use only.

Some Common Onsets

Single consonant letters

Two letters, one sound	Consonant blends		
th-	br-	bl-	sc-
ch-	cr-	cl-	sk-
sh-	dr-		sm-
wh-	fr-	fl-	sn-
ph-	pr-	pl-	sp-
gh-	tr-		
wr-	chr-	qu-	squ-
sc-	scr-		
pn-	shr-	dw	
kn-	spr-	gw-	
gn-	str-	sw-	
ps-	thr-	tw-	

Some Common Rimes

-ack	-ide
-ail	-ight
-ain	-ill
-ake	-in
-ale	-ine
-ame	-ing
-an	-ink
-ank	-ip
-ap	-ir
-ash	-ock
-at	-oke
-ate	-op
-aw	-ore
-ay	-or
-eat	-uck
-ell	-ug
-est	-ump
-ice	-unk
-ick	

T5.12   *Some Common Rimes*   *Creating Support for Effective Literacy Education* by C. Weaver, L. Gillmeister-Krause, & G. Vento-Zogby, © 1996. Portsmouth, NH: Heinemann. May be copied for transparency use only.

Nearly 500 "primary grade words" can be derived from this set of only 37 rimes. From R. E. Wylie and D. D. Durrell, Teaching vowels through phonograms, *Elementary English, 47*, 787–791. Copyright 1970 by the National Council of Teachers of English. Reprinted with permission.

Onsets and Rimes (#1)

What rimes go with *fl-*?

fl-ack	fl-aw
fl-ail	fl-ay
fl-ake	fl-ick
fl-ame	fl-ight
fl-an	fl-ing
fl-ank	fl-ip
fl-ap	fl-ock
fl-ash	fl-op
fl-at	fl-unk

T5.13   *Onsets and Rimes (#1)*   *Creating Support for Effective Literacy Education* by C. Weaver, L. Gillmeister-Krause, & G. Vento-Zogby, © 1996. Portsmouth, NH: Heinemann. May be copied for transparency use only.

Onsets and Rimes (#2)

What rimes go with *fl-*?

fl-ack	-ide
fl-ail	fl-ight
-ain	-ill
fl-ake	-in
-ale	-ine
fl-ame	fl-ing
fl-an	-ink
fl-ank	fl-ip
fl-ap	-ir
fl-ash	fl-ock
fl-at	-oke
-ate	fl-op
fl-aw	-ore
fl-ay	-or
-eat	-uck
-ell	-ug
-est	-ump
-ice	fl-unk
fl-ick	

Onsets and Rimes (#3)

What onsets go with *-ake*?

b-ake	br-ake
c-ake	
	dr-ake
f-ake	fl-ake
J-ake	
l-ake	
m-ake	
qu-ake	
r-ake	
s-ake	sh-ake sn-ake st-ake
t-ake	
w-ake	

Determining Lesson (Part 1): Vowel digraph ea

The vowel digraph ea has three sounds: long e, short e, and long a. If a word is unfamiliar, try each of the three sounds. You should then recognize the word. Show the sound of ea on the line after each word. Show the sound of a short e with an unmarked e.

—14 (–41)   KEY: EACH ē   HEAD e   GREAT ā

1. TREATMENT ē
2. STEADIER a ✓
3. STEALTHY ✓
4. TEAK ā ✓
5. GREATEST ā
6. WREATH ē
7. DEALT e
8. CONGEAL ē
9. SHEATH ✓
10. CREASED ā ✓
11. MEASLES ē
12. BEACON ā ✓
13. BREAKNECK ā –
14. HEATHEN e ✓
15. HEAVENLY e
16. EASEL ē
17. SWEAT ē ✓
18. UNHEALTHY e
19. SEASONING ē
20. CHESAPEAKE ✓
21. STREAMLINED ē
22. TREACHERY ā ✓
23. DEFEATED ē
24. PHEASANTS ē ✓

25. CREAKING ē
26. JEALOUSY ✓
27. APPEAL e ✓
28. DECREASE ē
29. BEEFSTEAK e
30. PEASANT e
31. PEACEABLE ✓
32. REVEAL
33. WEAPON
34. CLEANSING
35. BEAGLE
36. SNEAKERS
37. FEATHERY
38. FEAT
39. FLEA
40. MEANWHILE
41. CEASE
42. HEAVILY
43. PEALED
44. WEASEL
45. DREAD
46. EATABLE
47. INCREASING
48. DEALER

finish your work! (–41)

49. TREACHEROUS
50. HEADQUARTERS
51. CLEANLINESS
52. MEANT
53. UNDERNEATH
54. BREAKTHROUGH
55. REPEAL
56. STREAKED
57. WEATHERED
58. MEANTIME
59. EAGERNESS
60. EAVES
61. THREATENED
62. LEASED
63. LEASH
64. BREAKWATER
65. DEAFEN
66. EASTERN
67. RETREATING
68. BLEACHERS
69. DEATHLESS
70. HEADACHE
71. LEAKY
72. SNEAKY

T5.16a *Determining Lesson (Part 1)* *Creating Support for Effective Literacy Education* by C. Weaver, L. Gillmeister-Krause, & G. Vento-Zogby, © 1996. Portsmouth, NH: Heinemann. May be copied for transparency use only.

From Dorothy J. Watson, *Making a difference: Selected writings of Dorothy Watson* (Ed. Sandra Wilde). Portsmouth, NH: Heinemann, 1996. Reprinted with permission.

Determining Lesson (Part 2)

(R)

When hunting season comes Uncle Bill is almost as eager

to head for the woods as Babe and Bingo are. Babe and Bingo

are beautiful beagles, but Uncle Bill calls them eager beavers

when it comes to pheasant hunting.

(C) re—

When Uncle Bill releases those dogs from their (steady) *P*

(C) break—

leash, you should see them streak across the meadow at break-

neck speed. They can really work up a sweat!

Aunt Joan dreads hunting season. Babe and Bingo's

2 deefing
1 deaf
a

steady stream of barking is deafening and gives her headaches

(C) b—

She can't bear to think of one feather on a a bird being harmed.

Uncle Bill gives the pheasants to a neighbor. Babe and Bingo

howl.

T5.16b   *Determining Lesson (Part 2)*   *Creating Support for Effective Literacy Education* by
C. Weaver, L. Gillmeister-Krause, & G. Vento-Zogby, © 1996. Portsmouth, NH: Heinemann. May be copied for
transparency use only.
From Dorothy J. Watson, *Making a difference: Selected writings of Dorothy Watson* (Ed. Sandra Wilde).
Portsmouth, NH: Heinemann, 1996. Reprinted with permission.

Why Not to Teach Phonics Intensively and Systematically

1. Kids don't need such thorough, direct, and systematic teaching.

2. English is an alphabetic language, but by no means a phonetic one.

3. It is more effective and more efficient to focus on chunks of letters than on isolated letters or on rules.

4. Proficient reading involves using everything you know to get words and construct meaning from text.

5. Too much emphasis on phonics encourages children to "sound it out" as their first and possibly only independent strategy for dealing with problem words.

6. Many emergent readers are not good at learning analytically, abstractly, or auditorily. For them, the study of phonics is difficult, if not impossible.

7. You don't have to be able to demonstrate phonics skills in isolation in order to have and *use* letter/sound knowledge while reading, along with context and everything you know.

8. The research purporting to demonstrate the superiority of intensive systematic phonics over incidental phonics is not very impressive.

T5.17 *Why Not to Teach Phonics Intensively and Systematically* Creating Support for *Effective Literacy Education* by C. Weaver, L. Gillmeister-Krause, & G. Vento-Zogby, © 1996. Portsmouth, NH: Heinemann. May be copied for transparency use only.
From *Reading process and practice* (2nd ed.) by Constance Weaver. Portsmouth, NH: Heinemann, 1994.

How Children Learn Phonics

1. By being encouraged to write independently.

2. By observing the teacher write down the children's ideas, or the teacher's own.

3. By noticing print while the teacher reads a Big Book or large chart aloud.

4. By discussing interesting elements of sound in a reading selection (e.g., alliteration, rhyme, onomatopoeia).

5. By engaging in self-chosen activities with words having similar sound elements.

6. By hearing and participating in discussions of the use of phonics cues in the context of meaningful reading.

7. By receiving individual help in using phonics cues along with prior knowledge and context, in order to get meaning.

8. By rereading familiar materials and inferring phonics relationships.

T5.18 *How Children Learn Phonics*   *Creating Support for Effective Literacy Education* by C. Weaver, L. Gillmeister-Krause, & G. Vento-Zogby, © 1996. Portsmouth, NH: Heinemann. May be copied for transparency use only.

From *Reading process and practice* (2nd ed.) by Constance Weaver. Portsmouth, NH: Heinemann, 1994.

Intensive Phonics	Whole Language
behavioral, reductionistic	constructivist, holistic
habit formation, simple association	hypothesis formation, developing cognitive structures (schemas)
practice one thing at a time, progress step by step	attempt the "whole"; gradually refine the parts
teach; practice/memorize; test	demonstrate, assist; apply; observe, record
part + part + part = whole	whole part part part

T5.19   *Intensive Phonics versus Whole Language Models*   *Creating Support for Effective Literacy Education* by C. Weaver, L. Gillmeister-Krause, & G. Vento-Zogby, © 1996. Portsmouth, NH: Heinemann. May be copied for transparency use only.

Intensive Phonics Advocates	Whole Language Advocates
1. Believe that the most important characteristic of good readers is that they identify most words in a text correctly and automatically.	1. Believe that the most important characteristic of good readers is that they read to construct meaning from texts, using context and prior knowledge as well as grapho/phonemic cues.
2. Set up research studies as if readers' performance on standardized tests of isolated skills is an accurate and adequate measure of reading.	2. Consider standardized tests to be relatively uninformative. In research, various kinds of data are considered more useful—especially a miscue analysis with retelling.
3. Set up their research studies as if they believe that readers must be able to demonstrate a skill in isolation in order to control that skill during actual reading of coherent and appropriate text.	3. Know from their research into the process of reading whole texts that readers do NOT have to be able to demonstrate a skill in isolation in order to use it in actual reading, and set up further research studies accordingly.
4. Research emphasizes short-term performance on tests; does not assess progress toward most long-term goals for readers, nor consider whether teaching to the tests helps or hinders in the long run.	4. Research emphasizes long-term effects: reading authentic texts proficiently and with understanding, and becoming an independent lifelong reader who enjoys reading and DOES read.
5. Generally operate from a stage theory of learning to read.	5. Operate from an emergent literacy perspective.

Ways of Helping Children Learn Phonics

1. Have faith in children as learners.

2. Discuss onset and rime patterns within songs, poems, stories that are read to and with the children.

3. Guide collaborative activities focusing on onsets and rimes.

4. Share and make alphabet books with children.

5. Demonstrate the use of context and initial letter cues to predict a word.

6. Reread favorite stories, poems, and songs from large texts that the children can follow; point to words while reading together.

7. Provide small texts and tape recordings, so the children can listen and follow the text.

8. Do guided writing with the children, and support their efforts to write independently.

9. Provide additional help and materials for the children who need it: for example, books with alliteration and rhyme, such as Dr. Seuss books.

10. Support children's own ways of learning phonics.

T5.21   *Ways of Helping Children Learn Phonics*   *Creating Support for Effective Literacy Education* by C. Weaver, L. Gillmeister-Krause, & G. Vento-Zogby, © 1996. Portsmouth, NH: Heinemann. May be copied for transparency use only.
From *Reading process and practice* (2nd ed.) by Constance Weaver. Portsmouth, NH: Heinemann, 1994.

"Cheeky Chipmunk"

Inside a chipmunk's cheeks:
    Deep pockets
    purse pouches
    tight lockets
    screwed sockets
                    are
    minced mice,
    moist mushrooms,
    snacks
    of berries
    and nuts
    and succulent
    snake.

Under a chipmunk's mattress:
ceiling high headboard
bedboard
winter weather hoard-board
                    are
    mashed mice
    mouldy mushrooms,
    succulent snacks
    of berries
    and nuts
    and snake.

—Miriam Bat-Ami

T5.22   "Cheeky Chipmunk"   *Creating Support for Effective Literacy Education* by C. Weaver, L. Gillmeister-Krause, & G. Vento-Zogby, © 1996. Portsmouth, NH: Heinemann. May be copied for transparency use only.
Miriam Bat-Ami, *The underground alphabet book*. Manuscript. Kalamazoo, MI, 1996.

"Wet Worm"

After a rainstorm,

when the world is wet-alive,

from under the brush,

HUSH!

up from his rain-washed hole

the wet worm wiggles

free

through the wood.

—Miriam Bat-Ami

T5.23 *"Wet Worm"* *Creating Support for Effective Literacy Education* by C. Weaver, L. Gillmeister-Krause, & G. Vento-Zogby, © 1996. Portsmouth, NH: Heinemann. May be copied for transparency use only.
Miriam Bat-Ami, *The underground alphabet book*. Manuscript. Kalamazoo, MI, 1996.

"Daisy Dreams"

Sleep, sleep

    Deep down

In the daisy dreams.

    —John Weaver, at age seven

Rhyming Song: "Knick Knack Paddy Wack" (#1)

This old man, he played red,
He played knick knack on my bed,
With a knick knack paddy wack
Give the dog a bone,
This old man came rolling home.

Additional verses:

This old man, he played blue,
He played knick knack with our glue.

This old man, he played yellow,
He played knick knack with a fellow.

This old man, he played purple,
He played knick knack with a burple.

This old man, he played green,
He played knick knack with the queen.

This old man, he played orange,
He played knick knack in LaFlorange.

Rhyming Song: "Knick Knack Paddy Wack" (#2)

This old man, was so nice,
He played knick knack with the mice.
With a knick knack paddy wack
Give the dog a bone,
This old man came rolling home.

Additional verses:

This old man, went to sleep,
He played knick knack counting sheep.

This old man, liked to run,
He played knick knack just for fun.

This old man, swam all day,
He played knick knack by the bay.

This old man, danced all night,
He played knick knack by the light.

This old man, jumped way up,
He played knick knack with his pup.

This old man, wasn't greedy,
He played knick knack with the needy.

T5.26   *Rhyming Song: "Knick Knack Paddy Wack" (#2)*   *Creating Support for Effective Literacy*
Education by C. Weaver, L. Gillmeister-Krause, & G. Vento-Zogby, © 1996. Portsmouth, NH: Heinemann. May
be copied for transparency use only.
Written by Deborah Payne's fourth graders for their kindergarten buddies. Sauquoit Valley Elementary,
Sauquoit, New York.

"The Pines"

Hear the rumble,
Oh, hear the crash.
The great trees tumble
The strong boughs smash.

Men with saws
Are cutting the pines—
That marched like soldiers
In straight green lines.

Seventy years
Have made them tall.
It takes ten minutes
To make them fall.

And, breaking free
With never a care,
The pine cones leap
Through the clear, bright air.

    —Margaret Mahy

T5.27   "The Pines"   *Creating Support for Effective Literacy Education* by C. Weaver,
L. Gillmeister-Krause, & G. Vento-Zogby, © 1996. Portsmouth, NH: Heinemann. May be copied for
transparency use only.
From *The first Margaret Mahy story book*. London: J. M. Dent & Sons Ltd., Publishers.

"Susie Moriar"

This is the story of Susie Moriar.

It started one night
As she sat by the f____.

The fire was so hot,
Susie climbed in a p____.

The pot was so black,
Susie dropped in a cr____.

The crack was so narrow,
Susie climbed in a wh____.

The wheelbarrow was so low,
Susie fell in the sn____.

The snow was so white,
Susie stayed there all n____.

The night was so long,
Susie sang a s____.

The song was so sweet,
Susie ran down the str____.

The street was so big,
Susie jumped on a p____.

The pig jumped so high,
He touched the sk____.

He touched the sk____.

He touched the sk____.
And he couldn't jump any higher.

And oh! what a ride had . . .
Susie M____.

STRATEGIES AND THE TEACHING OF STRATEGIES

The transparencies in this section can be used in a workshop focusing on *what* and *how* effective teachers teach in helping children learn to read or to further expand and refine their repertoire of reading strategies. Of course other things are taught too, such as letter/sound relationships and the skill of relating letters to sounds.

Reading Skills and Strategies: Transparency 6.1

Parents and many teachers commonly talk about reading "skills," such as recognizing words on sight, sounding out words, inferring cause-effect relationships, and other so-called comprehension skills. What we think of as skills commonly involve (or *seem* to involve) just one language cueing system, such as the grapho/phonemic or the semantic. In doing a workshop on strategies, then, you might want to differentiate skills from what, in the last couple of decades, have been called strategies.

When readers orchestrate skills to accomplish some larger aim, they can be said to use *strategies*—-whether these strategies are conscious or merely unconscious cognitive processes. For example, readers coordinate prior knowledge, context (both syntactic and semantic), word knowledge, and letter/sound knowledge to predict, monitor comprehension, correct or try to correct when necessary. Thus prediction, monitoring comprehension, and correction may all be considered strategies for processing language—both oral and written. Unlike skills, such strategies are more a matter of knowing—at least intuitively—what to do and when and how to do it, in processing language. Of course, these strategies may have substrategies, too: for instance, monitoring comprehension typically involves comparing new information and ideas with old, integrating the two, and/or rejecting one or the other. When readers are conscious of the strategies they use, they are said to have *metacognitive* awareness of their strategies.

Teaching Reading Skills: Transparencies 6.2 and 6.3

In addition to or instead of using transparency 6.1, you might use transparency 6.2 and/or 6.3. **Transparency 6.2** includes some quotes from Barak Rosenshine's article summarizing the results of his attempt to determine how many separately identifiable comprehension skills there might be. **Transparency 6.3** includes a quote about the skills taught in basal reading series. Based on K. Goodman, Shannon, Freeman, and Murphy's *Report Card on Basal Readers* (1988), this quote from a position statement on basal readers alleges that "The sequence of skills in a basal reading series exists not because this is how children learn to read, but simply because of the logistics of developing a series of lessons that can be taught sequentially, day after day, week after week, year after year" (Commission on Reading, 1988; this position statement is reproduced in its entirety in Part 2). One or both of these transparencies could be good leads into the observation that it is more profitable to help children develop reading strategies than to teach skills in isolation, and that *needed* skills—an important qualification—can be taught within the context of authentic reading and writing.

Another option would be to use at this point transparency 6.10 on proficient reading strategies. You might first brainstorm with workshop participants some possible reading strategies once you've introduced the concept of strategy, *and then* share this list of strategies that are orchestrated by proficient readers.

Strategies for Problem Words: Transparencies 6.4a Through 6.9b

Because it may seem relatively obvious to most people that they need and use strategies for dealing with problem words, we have decided to put this cluster of transparencies next. However, you might prefer to use first transparency 6.10, on proficient reading strategies, and perhaps transparency 6.11, on predicting, illustrated by transparencies with the poem "Susie Moriar" (transparencies 5.28a and b).

Before using **transparency 6.4**, you may want to brainstorm with workshop participants the various strategies they know they use for dealing with problem words. Of course, some people may insist that they look up every word they don't know in a dictionary—but if they do, they may also admit that they don't read very much! Most groups of adults will readily admit not only to trying to sound out the word or see if they can derive meaning from word parts, but to rereading, reading on to see if that helps, and just plain skipping the word if its absence doesn't seem to affect meaning (**transparency 6.4** lists such strategies that typically arise during discussion). Of course, skipping a word is particularly common in reading fiction. When reading something like a textbook or technical manual, we are less likely to skip words, particularly if they are boldface or otherwise

flagged as being important terms. In any case, asking someone and using a dictionary are usually the last resorts of most adults.

From this brainstorming, it is usually easy to convince most adults that it makes sense to share this whole repertoire of strategies with children and not leave them thinking, as so many do, that the only strategies they can or should use are "sound it out" and "ask someone." (Of course we do not want emergent readers to skip a high percentage of the words, as some may do. The point needs to be made that this is only one strategy and that it is often better to try other strategies first.)

Transparencies 6.5 through 6.7 include prompts that parents, teachers, and others can use in helping a child develop effective reading strategies, as the child reads aloud and the adult listens. For emergent readers (**transparency 6.5**) one might first invite the child who stops and hesitates at a word to check the picture, think what would make sense, and *then* look at the first letter(s) to think again what word would make sense. In other words, the adult can help the child orchestrate picture cues, prior knowledge and context, and letter/sound cues in the strategy of predicting. This will then make it easier for the child to get the whole word right by looking at the rest of the word and, if necessary, sounding it out in chunks of letters. The suggestions are similar for helping independent readers who have stopped at a word, except that the third idea is to call the reader's attention to one or more meaningful parts of the word. Of course this works only with some words, but it is an important skill for independent readers to learn as they increasingly deal with words having elements derived from Latin and Greek. This skill, too, is part of the overall strategy of orchestrating everything you know to predict and identify the word.

Strategies to suggest to all readers as appropriate are given on **transparency 6.6**. "Try it again" is of course the strategy of rereading, and the adult can point to a good place to begin rereading: the phrase containing the word, or perhaps the beginning of the sentence. In the process of helping a reader develop his or her repertoire of strategies, an adult might ask "Why did you stop?" when the reader halts at a word, then invite the reader to "Show me the tricky part." Asking and following up with these questions can enable the adult to better understand what strategies the reader is trying to use, and therefore what strategies might still need to be taught. The other strategies are, we think, self-evident.

Transparency 6.7 includes questions that can be asked when the reader has already made a miscue. If the word (or more complex miscue) does not make sense in context, the adult can ask "Does that make sense?" If the miscue doesn't fit the grammar of the sentence, the adult can ask "Does that sound right?" (Y. Goodman, Watson, & Burke, 1987). Asking these questions demonstrates to the child an important strategy for monitoring comprehension. Of course the ultimate goal is to get children to ask themselves such questions. Thus the adult may wean children from the adult-generated question by asking, after a miscue that doesn't fit the context, "What should you ask yourself?" This will help the child not only use the strategies but become metacognitively aware of the value of doing so.

Transparency 6.8 includes strategies for dealing with problem words that can be copied onto bookmarks for children to use as prompts; each list is meant to reflect the suggestions on transparencies 6.5 and 6.6. The column on the left is for emergent readers, and may serve as a reminder to parents who are listening as their child reads. As the child gains skill and confidence, the parent or other adult may encourage the child to look at other letters in the word, in order to confirm or correct a prediction. The column on the right is for independent readers. **Transparencies 6.9a and b** repeat the same material, but in smaller type that may be more suitable for copying into bookmarks (6.9a is for boys, 6.9b for girls). In a workshop setting, it may be useful to copy and distribute one of the parent brochures titled "How to help your child become a reader" (in Part Two).

Strategies for Processing Text: Transparencies 6.10 and 6.11

After reminding participants of some reading strategies already mentioned (such as predicting and monitoring comprehension), you might invite them to brainstorm for other important reading strategies before sharing **transparency 6.10**, which includes these and other strategies orchestrated by good readers.

One of the most important strategies, and one of the first learned, is using everything you know to predict what is coming next. This includes not only predicting the events or character changes, but predicting words. Of course most people are unaware of predicting words, but their miscues suggest that in fact good readers use prior knowledge, preceding context (grammar and meaning), and sometimes a sampling of letter cues (typically the initial letters, or onset) to predict what the word may be (**transparency 6.11**). In other words, for proficient readers the brain is ahead of the eyes. Because of this, good readers make miscues that preserve meaning and grammar, including some miscues that reflect their expectations but don't go with the following context. In such cases, good readers typically correct or try to correct the miscue—at least silently. Here are some examples of good readers' miscues that you might share with participants:

After a hearty supper Hayes joined the

around
smokers about the fire. *[around* for *about]*

. . . stop driving until we can̲ see Los Angeles

[can was omitted]*

the
Carlo put Trixie on a box. *[the* for *a]*

We ourselves find that our miscues often reflect predicting from prior knowledge and context, while only sampling the visual cues of the word itself. When what we "read" doesn't make sense, we of course are prompted to re-process the word. Children need to know that good readers make these kinds of miscues but also try to correct them.

Cross Reference to Transparencies 5.28a and 5.28b

To clarify how teachers and parents can help children use everything they know to predict a word before processing it in its entirety, you might refer to transparencies 5.28a and b, with the poem "Susie Moriar."

Minilessons for Various Strategies: Transparencies 6.12 Through 6.16

Obviously the transparency for brainstorming the rhyming words in "Susie Moriar" generates a minilesson, an observation that you might want to share with workshop participants. The transparencies in the present set provide materials to illustrate other kinds of minilessons. (For an explanation of how minilessons may be handled in transaction-oriented classrooms, see again transparencies 1.9 and 1.10; transparency 1.7 provides background for these, if needed.)

Transparency 6.12 comes from an article Connie read a few years ago. When she encountered the unfamiliar word *fissiparous* in the fifth line, she tried using the meaning of word parts to get the word. *Fissiparous* reminded her of *fissure*, so she tested the meaning 'crevice' or 'crack' to see if it would fit. Since the preceding sentence mentioned dividing higher education into increasingly isolated departments and disciplines, a meaning akin to 'crack' seemed relevant. Subsequently, Connie has discovered that examining this word and passage can be effective in helping adults consider the strategies they use for dealing with problem words.

If you use this transparency in a workshop setting, you might first cover all but the sepa-rately printed word *fissiparous* and ask partici-pants how they would deal with it. Someone usually suggests sounding it out, but the group quickly concludes that this procedure—whether the pronunciation is right or not—won't help in understanding the word. Our most promising strategy is to look at word parts, particularly *fiss-*, as Connie did. Typically someone will suggest the word *fission*, as in nuclear division (dividing of the atom), and of course this meaning is rele-vant. Sometimes *fissure* is also suggested. Next, you can uncover the paragraph and have partic-ipants read the sentence preceding the one with *fissiparous*, to see if the suggested meanings make sense in context. This activity can lead into a discussion of the strategies that we use, as proficient readers, to deal with problem words (see transparency 6.4). You might find that workshop participants want to try to deal with *negentropic*, too. Have fun!

Transparencies 6.13 through 6.15 are all from the novel *Johnny Tremain*, by Esther Forbes (1943). In a workshop setting, you might use **transparency 6.13** to see whether participants can predict the word that goes in each of the blanks (it's the word *apprentice*). This activity can be used to introduce the point that many whole language teachers avoid preteaching key vocabulary words whenever possible. Instead, they encourage students to use context to infer the meanings of words, a strategy that is important for independent and proficient readers. In the novel, young Johnny Tremain is an apprentice silversmith (eventu-ally an apprentice to the famed silversmith Paul Revere), so the term is critical to under-standing Johnny's situation. In the first few pages of the novel, however, Forbes uses the word four times, each time giving more cues as to the word's meaning.

A whole language teacher might introduce the book by telling about the setting (Boston, just before the Revolutionary War). However, the teacher might refrain from defining the word *apprentice* and instead ask the students to write in their literature journals each occurrence of the word in these early pages, and what they can infer about its meaning each time (see transparency **6.14**). Their journal entries will thus become a starting point for discussing not only the meaning of the word, but the strategy of using context to clarify a word's meaning.

Transparency 6.15 can be used first for one kind of activity and then another. First, you might have workshop participants read the passage and see whether they can get some meaning for the words *ethereal* and *apoplectic* from the context. Those who "know" the meaning of either word are asked not to volunteer yet. After soliciting ideas and discussing what words and phrases suggested the meanings offered, you can supply the meanings. (From previous encounters with the word *apoplectic*, Connie thinks of the relevant meaning as "pale, like a ghost," though this isn't exactly the way it's defined in a dictionary. *Apoplectic* means looking extremely angry or enraged (and therefore probably red-faced), as if one has had a cerebral hemorrhage, a stroke. So, Dorcas is trying to look pale, delicate, refined, but looks red-faced instead.)

After such a discussion, you can ask participants whether much meaning would be lost if the reader were to skip these words entirely. Typically the answer is no, for the preceding and following sentences give good clues to Dorcas's pretention to gentility. Connie has also successfully done these activities in reverse order, asking first whether it appears that a reader could simply skip these two words without losing substantial meaning. This discussion can lead into further consideration of how we as proficient readers know when it's okay to skip a word. How, then, can we lead children to the same kinds of conclusions? Obviously an activity like this is part of the solution.

The activity in **transparency 6.16** has been adapted from a handout at a Michigan Department of Education workshop in 1986 (author unknown). This activity can be used to demonstrate one way of helping readers realize that they need to draw upon prior knowledge to construct meaning from texts—that the meaning is not "in" the text, but in the transaction between reader and text. First, you can explain that there is in effect a continuum characterizing our re-

sponses to the questions in the sample text on this page: some responses will at least seem to be drawn directly from the text, others will come entirely from our prior knowledge and assumptions, while most can be viewed as falling somewhere in between on the continuum.

One thing that's interesting about this activity is that even the first question can elicit responses that reflect prior knowledge as much as or more than the text itself. One can simply repeat the words of the text, "at the window," but often people will allude to a "ticket office" because the rest of the passage suggests that, given their prior experience. Generally speaking, the farther down the list of questions, the more respondents will have to draw upon prior knowledge and reasoning. While this passage was developed for use with children, it entertainingly illustrates to adults as well the fact that we do not merely get meaning *from* the text. For anyone who needs it, the activity also serves as a reminder that we have to think about what we're reading to get meaning from it; identifying the words is not enough.

Literature Discussions: Transparencies 6.17 Through 6.21

Many whole language teachers organize literature discussion groups or circles (e.g., Short & Pierce, 1990; Pierce & Gilles, 1993; Harste & Short, with Burke, 1988/1995), or literature study groups in which children hold "grand conversations" about literature (Peterson & Eeds, 1990). The transparencies in this set are designed to illustrate the nature of such literature discussions and their benefits.

When Connie uses "The Moth and the Star" (**transparency 6.17**) with workshop participants, she invites them to read the fable and then discuss it with neighbors, in much the same way they might discuss a good movie over pizza afterward. Then in whole group discussion, one can elicit some of the group's responses. What connections did they make—with other literature? with their own lives or beliefs? What questions did they raise?

You can then invite participants to explore their process of interacting during the initial discussion. Typically they made comments or asked questions about how the other person(s) responded; they did not ask literal recall questions or picky detail questions such as questions 1 and 2 on **transparency 6.18**, which can be shared to demonstrate the trivial and arbitrary nature of typical "comprehension" questions, compared with the genuineness and thoughtfulness of the free-flowing discussion about the fable.

Transparency 6.19 lists the so-called higher-level thinking skills typically prompted by literature discussions of this sort. **Transparency 6.20** further lists some of the intellectual activities that occur. Finally, **transparency 6.21** lists a few of the benefits from literature discussions of this nature, including the benefits of hearing others discuss their reading strategies. (Eeds & Wells, 1989, was a valuable source in compiling these lists.)

If desired, transparency 6.17, containing "The Moth and the Star," can be further used to explain how teachers might focus on reading strategies in the context of authentic reading. For example, before inviting students to read this fable, the teacher might ask students to write down any words they have trouble with, and what they do to deal with the problem. Such words might include *singed*, for instance. Many readers unfamiliar with the word may use context to conclude that it is more or less synonymous with *burned* even if they pronounce it like "sing" with a /d/ sound added.

Sources and Resources

Commission on Reading. (1988–89). *Basal readers and the state of American reading instruction: A call for action*. Position statement. Urbana, IL: National Council of Teachers of English.

EEDS, M., & WELLS, D. (1989). Grand conversations: An exploration of meaning construction in literature study groups. *Research in the Teaching of English, 23*, 4–29.

GILLES, C., et al. (Eds.). (1988). *Whole language strategies for secondary students*. Katonah, NY: Richard C. Owen.

GOODMAN, K. S., SHANNON, P., FREEMAN, Y., & MURPHY, S. (1988). *The Report Card on Basal Readers*. Katonah, NY: Richard C. Owen.

GOODMAN, Y. M., & BURKE, C. (1980). *Reading strategies: Focus on comprehension*. Katonah, NY: Richard C. Owen.

GOODMAN, Y. M., WATSON, D. J., & BURKE, C. L. (1987). *Reading miscue inventory: Alternative procedures*. Katonah, NY: Richard C. Owen.

HARSTE, J., SHORT, K., WITH BURKE, C. (1995). *Creating classrooms for authors and inquirers* (2nd ed.). Portsmouth, NH: Heinemann.

PETERSON, R., & EEDS, M. (1990). *Grand conversations: Literature groups in action*. Richmond Hill, Ontario: Scholastic.

PIERCE, K. M., & GILLES, C. (Eds.). (1993). *Cycles of meaning: Exploring the potential of talk in learning communities*. Portsmouth, NH: Heinemann.

ROSENSHINE, B. (1980). Skill heirarchies in reading comprehension. In R. J. Spiro, B. C. Bruce, & W. F. Brewer (Eds.), *Theoretical issues in reading*. Hillsdale, NJ: Lawrence Erlbaum.

SHORT, K. G., & PIERCE, K. M. (Eds.). (1990). *Talking about books: Creating literate communities*. Portsmouth, NH: Heinemann.

WATSON, D. J. (Ed.). (1987). *Ideas and insights: Language arts in the elementary school*. Urbana, IL: National Council of Teachers of English.

WEAVER, C. (1994). *Reading process and practice: From socio-psycholinguistics to whole language* (2nd ed.). Portsmouth, NH: Heinemann.

Literature Used

FORBES, E. (1943). *Johnny Tremain*. New York: Dell.

THURBER, J. (1940). *Fables for our time*. New York: HarperCollins.

Reading Skills and Strategies

What are some reading skills?

What are some reading strategies?

Comprehension Skills

It is difficult to confidently put forth any set of discrete comprehension skills. . . .

We are not even clear that the skill of deriving explicit meaning from texts is separate from skills of deriving implicit meaning.

At this point, there is simply no clear evidence to support the naming of discrete skills in reading comprehension.

T6.2   *Comprehension Skills: Rosenshine on Discrete Reading Skills*   *Creating Support for Effective Literacy Education* by C. Weaver, L. Gillmeister-Krause, & G. Vento-Zogby, © 1996. Portsmouth, NH: Heinemann. May be copied for transparency use only.

From Barak Rosenshine, Skill hierarchies in reading comprehension. In R. J. Spiro, B. C. Bruce, & W. F. Brewer (Eds.), *Theoretical issues in reading*. Hillsdale, NJ: Lawrence Erlbaum, 1980.

Skills in Basal Reading Programs

The sequence of skills in a basal reading series exists not because this is how children learn to read but simply because of the logistics of developing a series of lessons that can be taught sequentially, day after day, week after week, year after year.

T6.3 *Skills in Basal Reading Programs*   *Creating Support for Effective Literacy Education* by C. Weaver, L. Gillmeister-Krause, & G. Vento-Zogby, © 1996. Portsmouth, NH: Heinemann. May be copied for transparency use only.

From *Basal readers and the state of American reading instruction: A call for action*. Position statement of the Commission on Reading of the National Council of Teachers of English. Urbana, IL, 1988. Used with permission of the National Council of Teachers of English.

Strategies for Dealing with Problem Words

THINK WHAT WOULD MAKE SENSE HERE, AND . . .

1. Sound it out, and/or

2. Look at meaningful word parts, and/or

3. Regress and reread, and/or

4. Continue—see if following context clarifies

    If YES, continue reading.

    If NO, decide if the word is important.

      If NO, continue reading.

      If YES,

5. Regress and reread, and/or

6. Ask someone, and/or

7. Look it up.

T6.4 *Strategies for Dealing with Problem Words*   *Creating Support for Effective Literacy Education* by C. Weaver, L. Gillmeister-Krause, & G. Vento-Zogby, © 1996. Portsmouth, NH: Heinemann. May be copied for transparency use only.

From *Understanding whole language* by Constance Weaver. Portsmouth, NH: Heinemann, 1990.

Prompts When a Child Stops and Hesitates at a Word (#1)

For emergent readers

- "Check the picture."
  "Think what would make sense." Then—
  "Look at the first letter(s). What word would fit here?"

(With children who have learned to look at the first letter(s), you may want to direct them to the other letters.)

For independent readers

- "Think what would make sense." Then—
  "Try to sound out the word in chunks" *and/or*
  "See if you can figure out what this part of the word means."

Prompts When a Child Stops and Hesitates at a Word (#2)

For all readers

- "Try it again."

(That is, start the sentence or the phrase over again, to get a running start on the word. For developing readers, show the child with your finger where to begin rereading.)

- "Why did you stop?" "Show me the tricky part."

(You can reread the sentence or phrase and point to the first letter(s) of the problem word. If the child still cannot get the word, ask "Could it be. . . ?" and provide the word. Then ask the child to reread that part, or you reread it to the child, to establish the meaning before going on.)

- "Skip the word and go on to the end of the sentence."
  "Now go back and reread."
  "Think, what would make sense here?"

- "Does the sentence make sense without the word?"
  If yes, then . . .
     "You can put in something else that fits or just go on."
  If no, then . . .
     "You can ask someone or look it up in a dictionary."

T6.6   *Prompts When a Child Stops and Hesitates at a Word (#2)*   *Creating Support for Effective Literacy Education* by C. Weaver, L. Gillmeister-Krause, & G. Vento-Zogby, © 1996. Portsmouth, NH: Heinemann. May be copied for transparency use only.

Prompts When a Child Has Made a Miscue that Doesn't Fit the Context

- "Does that make sense?" (When the miscue doesn't make sense in context.)

- "Does that sound right?" (When the miscue doesn't fit the grammar of the sentence.)

T6.7   *Prompts When a Child Has Made a Miscue that Doesn't Fit the Context*
Creating Support for Effective Literacy Education by C. Weaver, L. Gillmeister-Krause, & G. Vento-Zogby, © 1996.
Portsmouth, NH: Heinemann. May be copied for transparency use only.

What to do?

Check the picture.

Think what would
  make sense.

Look at the first
  letters. What
  word would
  fit here?

Back up and try
  again.

Skip the word and
  go on to the end
  of the sentence.
Then come back
  and try again.

Put in something
  that makes sense.

If necessary. . .
  just go on, or
  ask someone.

What to do?

Think what would
  make sense.

Then, try to sound out
  the word in chunks
  and/or
See if you can figure
  out what the parts
  of the word mean.

Back up and try the
  word again.

Skip the word and
  go on to the end
  of the sentence.
Then come back
  and try again.

Put in something
  that makes sense.

If necessary . . .
  just go on, or
  ask someone, or
  use a dictionary.

T6.8 *Bookmarks (#1)*   *Creating Support for Effective Literacy Education* by C. Weaver, L. Gillmeister-Krause, & G. Vento-Zogby, © 1996. Portsmouth, NH: Heinemann. May be copied for transparency use only.

What to do?

Check the picture.

Think what would
    make sense.

Look at the first
    letters. What
    word would
    fit here?

Back up and try
    again.

Skip the word and
    go on to the end
    of the sentence.
Then come back
    and try again.

Put in something
    that makes sense.

If necessary. . .
    just go on, or
    ask someone.

What to do?

Think what would
    make sense.

Then, try to sound out
    the word in chunks
    and/or
See if you can figure
    out what the parts
    of the word mean.

Back up and try the
    word again.

Skip the word and
    go on to the end
    of the sentence.
Then come back
    and try again.

Put in something
    that makes sense.

If necessary . . .
    just go on, or
    ask someone, or
    use a dictionary.

T6.9a *Bookmarks (#2)* *Creating Support for Effective Literacy Education* by C. Weaver, L. Gillmeister-Krause, & G. Vento-Zogby, © 1996. Portsmouth, NH: Heinemann. May be copied for transparency use only.

What to do?

Check the picture.

Think what would
    make sense.

Look at the first
    letters. What
    word would
    fit here?

Back up and try
    again.

Skip the word and
    go on to the end
    of the sentence.
Then come back
    and try again.

Put in something
    that makes sense.

If necessary. . .
    just go on, or
    ask someone.

What to do?

Think what would
    make sense.

Then, try to sound out
    the word in chunks
    and/or
See if you can figure
    out what the parts
    of the word mean.

Back up and try the
    word again.

Skip the word and
    go on to the end
    of the sentence.
Then come back
    and try again.

Put in something
    that makes sense.

If necessary . . .
    just go on, or
    ask someone, or
    use a dictionary.

T6.9b *Bookmarks (#3)*   *Creating Support for Effective Literacy Education* by C. Weaver, L. Gillmeister-Krause, & G. Vento-Zogby, © 1996. Portsmouth, NH: Heinemann. May be copied for transparency use only.

Proficient Reading Requires the Orchestration of Various Strategies

Strategies for reading with a <u>purpose</u> . . .

Strategies for drawing upon <u>prior knowledge</u> . . .

Strategies for <u>predicting</u> . . .

Strategies for <u>selectively sampling</u> the visual display . . .

Strategies for <u>confirming</u> . . .

Strategies for <u>dealing with problem words</u> . . .

Strategies for <u>monitoring comprehension</u> . . .

Strategies for <u>correcting</u> when something doesn't sound right or make sense . . .

Strategies for <u>reviewing and retaining</u> desired information or concepts . . .

Strategies for <u>adjusting</u> rate and approach . . .

T6.10 *Proficient Reading Requires the Orchestration of Various Strategies* *Creating Support for Effective Literacy Education* by C. Weaver, L. Gillmeister-Krause, & G. Vento-Zogby, © 1996. Portsmouth, NH: Heinemann. May be copied for transparency use only.

From *Reading process and practice* (2nd ed.) by Constance Weaver. Portsmouth, NH: Heinemann, 1994.

Strategies for *Predicting* Include

Drawing upon <u>prior knowledge</u> . . .

Drawing upon <u>preceding context</u> (both grammar and meaning) . . .

Using letter cues, especially <u>initial letters</u> . . .

Word Parts and Words in Context ("Fissiparous")

fissiparous

STS [Science, Technology, and Society] and Education

One does not need to document the awareness of the great difficulties which arose in the early decades of this century as the seamless robe of "high education" was divided even further into narrower and increasingly insular departments and disciplines. This fissiparous tendency can be linked perhaps to the reductionism inherent in "science." The writer has made the case elsewhere that another fundamental cause lay simply in the explosion in the amount of "knowledge" easily available via books and journals, etc., in any one field, compared to the fixed negentropic capability of the human brain.

Learning Words from Context (#1)
(*Johnny Tremain*)

pp. 7–8   And so, in a crooked little house at the head of Hancock's Wharf on crowded Fish Street, Mrs. Lapham stood at the foot of a ladder leading to the attic where her father-in-law's _____ slept. These boys were luckier than most _____. Their master was too feeble to climb ladders; the middle-aged mistress too stout.

p. 9   Dusty Miller was eleven. It was easy for Johnny to say "Look sharp, Dusty," and little Dusty looked sharp. But Dove (his first name had long ago been forgotten) hated the way the younger _____ lorded it over him, telling him when to go to bed, when to get up, criticizing his work in the silversmith's shop as though he were already a master smith.

p. 11   As an _____, he [Johnny] was little more than a slave until he had served his master seven years. He had no wages. The very clothes upon his back belonged to his master, but he did not, as he himself said, "take much."

Learning Words from Context (#2)
(*Johnny Tremain*)

pp. 7–8   And so, in a crooked little house at the head of Hancock's Wharf on crowded Fish Street, Mrs. Lapham stood at the foot of a ladder leading to the attic where her father-in-law's <u>apprentices</u> slept. These boys were luckier than most <u>apprentices</u>. Their master was too feeble to climb ladders; the middle-aged mistress too stout.

p. 9   Dusty Miller was eleven. It was easy for Johnny to say "Look sharp, Dusty," and little Dusty looked sharp. But Dove (his first name had long ago been forgotten) hated the way the younger <u>apprentice</u> lorded it over him, telling him when to go to bed, when to get up, criticizing his work in the silversmith's shop as though he were already a master smith.

p. 11   As an <u>apprentice</u>, he [Johnny] was little more than a slave until he had served his master seven years. He had no wages. The very clothes upon his back belonged to his master, but he did not, as he himself said, "take much."

Deciding What to Do about Unknown Words
(*Johnny Tremain*)

p. 12   In the kitchen he [Johnny] could see his formidable mistress bent doubl over the hearth. Madge, in time, would look like her mother, but at eighteen she was handsome in a coarse-grained, red-faced, thick-waisted way. Dorcas was sixteen, built like Madge, but not so loud-voiced, nor as roughly good-natured. Poor Dorcas thirsted for elegance. She would rub flour on her face, trying to look pale, like the fashionable ladies she saw on the street. She wore her clothes so tight (hoping to look <u>ethereal</u>), she looked <u>apoplectic</u>. How they all had laughed when her stays burst in the middle of a meeting with a loud pop!

T6.15   *Deciding What to Do About Unknown Words (Johnny Tremain)*   *Creating Support for Effective Literacy Education* by C. Weaver, L. Gillmeister-Krause, & G. Vento-Zogby, © 1996. Portsmouth, NH: Heinemann. May be copied for transparency use only.
From *Johnny Tremain* by Esther Forbes. Reprinted by permission of Frances Collin, Literary Agent. Copyright © 1943 by Esther Forbes Hoskins. Copyright © renewed 1971 by Linwood M. Erskine, Jr., Executor of the Estate.

Where Comprehension Comes From

Directions

Discuss "where we get" our responses to these and related questions: from the text itself? from our own prior knowledge and experience? from both, in varying proportions?

Text _____Reader

Text to read and discuss

He plunked down $8.00 at the window. She tried to give him $4.00, but he refused to take it. So when they got inside, she bought him a large bag of popcorn.

1. Where did he plunk down the $8.00?
2. What kind of window was it?
3. How much was the entrance fee for each person?
4. Why wouldn't he take the $4.00?
5. Why did she try to pay her own entrance fee?
6. Does he like popcorn?
7. How old are these people?

"The Moth and the Star" by James Thurber

A young and impressionable moth once set his heart on a certain star.

He told his mother about this and she counselled him to set his heart on a bridge lamp instead. "Stars aren't the thing to hang around," she said; "lamps are the thing to hang around."

"You get somewhere that way," said the moth's father. "You don't get anywhere chasing stars." But the moth would not heed the words of either parent. Every evening at dusk when the star came out he would start flying toward it and every morning at dawn he would crawl back home worn out with his vain endeavor. One day his father said to him, "You haven't burned a wing in months, boy, and it looks to me as if you were never going to. All your brothers have been badly burned hanging around street lamps, and all your sisters have been terribly singed flying around house lamps. Come on, now, get out of here and get yourself scorched! A big strapping moth like you without a mark on him!"

The moth left his father's house, but he would not fly around street lamps and he would not fly around house lamps. He went right on trying to reach the star, which was four and one-third light years, or twenty-five trillion miles, away. The moth thought it was just caught in the top branches of an elm. He never did reach the star, but he went right on trying, night after night, and when he was a very, very old moth he began to think that he really had reached the star and he went around saying so. This gave him a deep and lasting pleasure, and he lived to a great old age. His parents and his brothers and his sisters had all been burned to death when they were quite young.

Questions on "The Moth and the Star"

Choose the one best answer for each question.

1. The moth's mother wanted him to set his heart on

    a. a table lamp
    b. a lighthouse

    c. a bridge lamp
    d. a yard light

2. The moth's father wanted him

    a. to get a job
    b. to get scorched

    c. to get married
    d. to get scarred

3. The moth lived to a great old age because

    a. he finally reached the star
    b. he kept trying to do what he'd set his heart on

    c. he disobeyed his parents
    d. he didn't fly around lamps

4. A good title for this story would be

    a. Never Stop Trying
    b. Don't Set Your Sights Too Low

    c. The Moth That Didn't Get Singed
    d. Doing Your Own Thing

T6.18 *Questions on "The Moth and the Star"* *Creating Support for Effective Literacy Education* by C. Weaver, L. Gillmeister-Krause, & G. Vento-Zogby, © 1996. Portsmouth, NH: Heinemann. May be copied for transparency use only.

Literature Discussions Involve Students In . . .

. . . revisiting the text to clarify meanings

. . . thinking critically about characters and events

. . . sharing strategies for dealing with problem words and other aspects of the text

. . . considering elements of the writer's craft

. . . comparing books with similar themes and characters

. . . evaluating books and aspects of the writer's craft

. . . relating books to their own lives

Literature Discussions and Thinking Skills

The students naturally review events and details from the text (recall), while

  analyzing,
  synthesizing,
  drawing inferences,
  making hypotheses,
  interpreting,

and, of course,
  responding critically and personally.

Benefits of Literature Discussions

1. Literature discussions get children excited about reading books. They read more and enjoy reading more.

2. Misunderstandings are clarified through discussion and by returning to the text as needed.

3. Children will develop a richer understanding of the work of literature and the author's craft through discussion.

4. Children are not evaluated on their recall of small details but rather on their ability to discuss the work thoughtfully and insightfully, while interacting appropriately with peers. This is especially important for the more global learners.

5. There are no worksheets or artificial activities to complete, as evidence of comprehension or of finishing the book.

6. Less proficient readers gain from hearing others discuss their reading strategies. All readers benefit from not being grilled about what they have read.

T6.21 *Benefits of Literature Discussions*   *Creating Support for Effective Literacy Education* by C. Weaver, L. Gillmeister-Krause, & G. Vento-Zogby, © 1996. Portsmouth, NH: Heinemann. May be copied for transparency use only.

WRITING AND LEARNING TO WRITE

Preceding the transparencies in this section is an anticipation guide on writing, which you can use with workshop participants. The transparencies are included to help you demonstrate to parents and others the developmental nature of the writing process, including points such as these:

• Writing ability develops gradually, like learning to talk and to read.
• Children need to engage in the "whole" of writing from the outset, and gradually refine the "parts"—just as they did in learning to talk.
• Permitting "incorrect" forms in the early stages is no more harmful than letting toddlers utter approximations for single words ("da" for *daddy*, "wa" for *water*) or to use two-word sentences.
• We need to help children view writing as a multiphase process—not a process that requires getting it right the first time, but a process of rehearsing, drafting, revising, editing, and often "publishing." Paradoxically, over time, focusing on the process helps children get it more nearly right the first time.
• When children learn to take their writing through various phases of the writing process, their first drafts do become better and better in quality and more and more conventional in language use.
• By encouraging risk-taking and approximations in writing, we promote increasing skill in writing (much more so than by insisting on conventionality from emergent writers and in first-and-only drafts).

Because it is often easier to understand these points when adults recognize how they learned their native language and how they have promoted their children's oral language acquisition, you may find it helpful to begin a workshop on emergent writing with at least some of the transparencies in Section 1, "Learning Theory and the Acquisition of Language and Literacy," and Section 2, "Language Acquisition: Learning to Talk." For a brief introduction to these topics, you might want to use or choose from among the following:

Learning skills: Transparencies 1.1 through 1.3 and/or "Learning the Language," transparency 2.1

Models of learning: Transparencies 1.4 through 1.7

How adults facilitate language acquisition: Transparency 2.5, and/or the cartoon on 2.6

The chart on development of language and literacy (transparency 1.8) should also be helpful and may be copied as a handout for a workshop.

Incidentally, the writing samples in this section and in Section 8, "Assessment," were all from average or below-average students, not from the most proficient writers in their classes. Of course, you may want to use your own writing samples to illustrate various points, but we have included several on the transparency pages for your convenience.

Learning to Write: Transparencies 7.1 and 7.2

These transparencies are similar to transparency 2.1 on learning the language and transparency 3.1 on learning to read. **Transparency 7.1** invites workshop participants to consider whether learning to write is most like designing a bridge, learning to swim, the Suzuki method of learning the violin, or dancing with an invisible partner. Of course various astute responses are possible. We might say that writing itself (if not learning to write) is a lot like designing a bridge, because we plan in advance; writing is also like dancing with an invisible partner, when the audience or the audience's reactions are unknown. Learning to write is also like learning to swim and learning to play the violin by the Suzuki method, both of which typically involve trying the "whole" of the activity and gradually refining the parts or skills.

Transparency 7.2 is similar in inviting participants to consider a different set of analogies: whether learning to write is most like making a cake, building a tower of blocks, learning to ride a bike, or dancing. Again, some responses may apply more to the act of writing itself, rather than to the process of learning to write. This can enrich the discussion.

Discussion Questions on Writing: Transparency 7.3

The questions on **transparency 7.3** are designed to stimulate discussion on how participants learned to write; it parallels transparency 3.2, "Discussion Questions on Reading." Again you can use the "think/pair/share" technique: invite participants to reflect upon these questions and jot down some of their responses, then pair off with someone nearby and share their reflections.

Many adults do not do much writing voluntarily and do not feel good about themselves as writers. Why? Often because in school they rarely wrote anything they were interested in and/or they wrote one and only one draft, which the teacher red-inked with corrections. Such a discussion can help prepare parents to understand the value of encouraging emergent writers to write and spell as best they can, and focusing on correction while helping children revise selected pieces for publication, rather than on marking up everything with corrections.

How Adults Facilitate Writing Acquisition: Transparency 7.4

Transparency 7.4 parallels transparency 2.5 on how adults facilitate language acquisition and transparency 4.1 on how adults facilitate reading acquisition. All of the points on **transparency 7.4** reflect what we know about how parents successfully foster writing in the home, before children have begun school. You may want to share with parents the relevant flier and/or brochure titled "How to Help Your Child Become a Writer" (Part Two of this book) as well others that are relevant, such as the brochure "How Will My Child Learn Phonics, Spelling, and Grammar?"

By using transparency 7.4 to discuss the connections between speaking and writing development, workshop participants can better understand how whole language teachers strive to provide the conditions that help children develop as writers. The following are some points that you may want to address with participants about how adults facilitate writing development:

1. **By calling children's attention to print in the environment and reading it to and with them.**

2. **By modeling what it means to be a writer: letting children see you write.**
Our world is filled with print. Children are exposed to environmental print and realize very early that it contains meaning. (Try passing a McDonald's or a Burger King without a child "reading" the logo.) Many children are natu-

rally exposed to adults writing lists, letters, and notes. Such demonstrations help children understand what writing is all about: those marks on the page stand for or symbolize things we can say. Other environmental print is important, too. How many of us remember, as children, being given paper and pen to "write" with, junk mail to "read," and so forth—things our parents gave us to occupy our time while they continued with their chores? This exposure to print in the context of daily life developed for us a basis in literacy.

3. By encouraging children's experimentations with writing and responding positively to their efforts and risk-taking.

4. By providing an emotionally safe environment for risk-taking.

These two points are closely related. Children need to be able to experiment with written language in much the same way that we allow them to experiment with spoken language, with support for risk-taking and with an initial focus on meaning and communication rather than correctness. Experimentation is essential for learning to speak, read, and write. We did not learn to speak by producing exact, "correct" language at first. When there is pressure on emergent readers and writers to "get it right," the cost of making errors is too great and their natural reaction is to stop taking risks. Children need a safe environment where their attempts at experimenting with form, format, spelling, and punctuation are not only accepted but valued, and their increasing growth toward adult competence is celebrated. It is important not to respond correctively or punitively to the "correctness" of a child's spelling or letter formation, but rather to give support for continued growth in later pieces.

5. By supporting the child's engagement in the writing process.

We can encourage and support children in their writing development by inviting them to write to and with us. Even a child whose writing is represented by scribbles or letters can talk about his or her writing. By providing children with feedback and praise for what they *can* do, we are not only responding to the meaning of their writing but encouraging them to continue writing. As children begin to hear the separate sounds in words, they benefit from encouragement and help in writing letters for the sounds they hear. As they become more sophisticated as writers and spellers, they also become increasingly able to edit their writing for things like including their name, adding periods, and so forth. (See transparencies 7.16 through 7.18 on errors as signs of progress, and see the editing checklist in transparency 7.30.)

It is important, too, for us to continue to provide authentic demonstrations for children. The more that children are allowed to watch us write for a variety of purposes, the more they are exposed to demonstrations of how written language is used. Writing involves sharing ideas, talking about what is written, getting feedback, and (depending upon the purpose) revising and editing. Children need to see us engage in the process.

6. By expecting the child to eventually learn to write like an adult.

It is important that parents and teachers not worry prematurely about adult correctness in writing.

Whole language teachers are often accused of not emphasizing the mechanics of writing and of ignoring the basics. Nothing could be farther from the truth. Whole language teachers do expect that children will eventually learn the conventions of written language, just as they eventually replaced "da da" with "daddy" (or something else) in learning to speak. However, whole language teachers do not merely sit on the sidelines waiting for development to happen. As emergent writers progress in writing, whole language teachers serve as allies and mentors, helping them discover what they want to say and teaching them the conventions needed to make their message clear to their reader. As children become more proficient writers, their teachers help them focus and strengthen the content of their writing and master more and more of the conventions of written language. They also help children polish their pieces and celebrate their writing beyond the classroom community.

Writings from Different Classrooms: Transparencies 7.5 and 7.6

The writing samples in transparencies 7.5 and 7.6 are taken from a study by Diane DeFord (1981). DeFord compared the writings of children from three different classrooms: a phonics classroom, where the reading materials apparently emphasized basic letter/sound correspondences (the "Nan can fan Dan" sort of fare); a skills classroom, where beginning reading instruction focused on the development of sight vocabulary using flash cards and simple stories made up of these words; and a whole language classroom, where the children read and wrote various kinds of real material, such as stories, songs, poems, and informational text. DeFord noted that about a third of the children in the phonics classroom and about three fourths of those in the skills or "look-say" classroom produced the limited kinds of writing illustrated in **transparency 7.5**. She implies that the majority of children in the whole language classroom produced writing more like Jason's in **transparency 7.6**.

To many people in a workshop setting, it will appear obvious that Jason's kind of writing is preferable, if for no other reason than that it reflects a genuine attempt to communicate. However, some workshop participants may prefer Jeffrey's and Amy's samples, in which all or most of the words are spelled correctly, even though few different words are used. In that case, you might try examining Jason's writing to notice the variety of words he has spelled correctly. These include not only "basic" words like *is, we, have, down, them, like, a, the,* and *of* but more challenging words like *fighting, bombers,* and the contraction *it's*. In fact, more than twenty different words are spelled cor-

rectly. Most of the other words show high-quality approximate spellings: for example, *droped* for "dropped," *hostges* for "hostages," and *checers* for "checkers." This comparison reflects what Linda Clarke (1988) discovered by comparing the spelling development (and certain aspects of the reading achievement) of first-grade children who experienced contrasting approaches to spelling: one in which the children were to write only the words they could spell correctly and one in which children were encouraged to use invented (approximated, functional, temporary, constructive) spelling. In their writings, the children in the invented-spelling classrooms did spell more words that were not spelled according to adult conventions—of course, given the differing instructional approaches. However, their writings were significantly longer overall and contained a significantly greater variety of words, just as Jason's writing does in transparency 7.6. Furthermore, the children encouraged to use invented spellings typically scored as well or better on standardized tests of spelling than children allowed only to use correct spellings in first drafts (Clarke, 1988).

The values of invented spelling will be most obvious to adults who understand that learning and language acquisition are gradual processes wherein one typically engages in the "whole" of the act and gradually refines the "parts," or skills. Thus these transparencies logically build upon the insights that should be generated by some of the earlier ones in the sections on learning theory and on language acquisition. Before using transparencies 7.5 and 7.6—or after, if need be—you might use transparencies like 1.1 through 1.5, which deal with learning skills naturally, or transparencies 2.5 and 2.6, which deal with how adults facilitate language acquisition.

Stages in Spelling Development: Transparencies 7.7 Through 7.10

You may find it helpful to relate the stages of spelling development in transparencies 7.7

through 7.10 to the terms used in transparency 1.8, development of language and literacy. This chart may be photocopied for easy reference in a workshop setting.

Transparency 7.7 includes two early samples of Cory's writing, the first written in the spring of his kindergarten year and the second written on October 17 of his first-grade year. According to Cory, the first sample says "I am pushing my tractor." This seems to reflect our "incipient" stage of writing development, during which the child may write words with little if any relationship between letters and sounds. Note, though, that this sample may show at least the beginnings of phonemic writing (perhaps *M* for "am"; *P* and maybe *g* for "pushing"; and maybe *tRR* for "tractor"). The second writing sample clearly illustrates the "developing" phase, wherein children typically represent whole words with their initial letter and (perhaps later) begin to space words.

Transparency 7.8 was written on the first of November, about two weeks after the early phonemic sample "I M P S." This piece reads "I went trick or treating with my friends." Notice that at this point, Cory is moving into the "approximate" stage, characterized at first by the representation of first and last consonant sounds and some of the vowels. Just six weeks later (December 12), Cory's spellings are much more developed, though still probably in the "approximate" stage. The sample on **transparency 7.9** reads "I want to go to the North Pole and back home before Christmas morning." Here, Cory is using more consonants and a vowel in almost every word. He also spells some words correctly. By January 11 (**transparency 7.10**), we might consider his writing to have at least begun the breakthrough to the "independent" stage. He has obviously begun to build a repertoire of sight words that he can spell conventionally.

It seems worthy of mention that every day the child was read to, engaged in sustained silent reading, had opportunities to write, and received many minilessons in hearing and writing sounds. He has had many opportunities to learn about spelling and writing.

Ways of Teaching Spelling: Transparencies 7.11 to 7.16

Because of the prevailing myth that whole language teachers don't teach spelling, **transparency 7.11** includes some of the ways that spelling is taught in such classrooms. You may find it useful to share and discuss these with parents and administrators.

You will notice that "give spelling tests" is not on this list. Many teachers are aware that students progress in spelling naturally and with these other kinds of help, while on the other hand, practicing words for spelling tests does not guarantee that children will spell the words correctly in their writing, even if they get them right on the spelling test (e.g., Gentry, 1987). Therefore, some informed teachers may have abandoned spelling tests. Other teachers do use spelling tests, but the tests may be personalized. For instance, each child may be invited to choose a certain number of words to study per week. The number may be varied according to the child and/or the difficulty of the words. Children can then be paired to help each other practice the words and to test each other on the words at the end of the week. In some schools, such as Grace's, the teachers have agreed to help children master a certain list of words each year, with the number of words relatively limited but frequently occurring.

Transparency 7.12 contains a critique of the spelling in "Frozen Fire," a piece by Houston. First, Lorraine listed the misspelled words, along with the correct spellings. Then she analyzed the patterns within the misspellings. Note, for instance, that both "sentenses" and "exsiting" have an *s* where the letter *c* is used conventionally; this is one pattern that the teacher could focus on in working with Houston. There are four words that have doubled letters in the conventional spelling, but only one letter in Houston's (*too, beginning, better, getting*); these constitute another pattern worthy of particular attention. Since the word *with* is a frequently used word, Lorraine will also point out that it starts with just a *w*, not with *wh* (unlike words such as *who, which, when*).

Transparencies 7.13 and 7.14 are from Tia, a first grader in Lorraine's class. As Lorraine explains in the sample letter on teaching writing (see Part Two), children in her class each have a spelling box that holds words they want to use in their writing. Tia was new to the school, and French was her home language; she was especially concerned about spelling correctly. In **transparency 7.13**, Tia expresses her pleasure in having a spelling box of words. In writing her journal entry two days later (**transparency 7.14**), Tia located the word *Saturday* from among the words typed in the front of her book, used the spelling box to help her write *we had a*, and tried *festival* on her own, spelling it *festeval*. Notice that in replying, Lorraine included the word *festival* spelled correctly. Thus these examples from Tia illustrate three of Lorraine's ways of teaching spelling: by having children develop personalized spelling resources (the spelling box), by encouraging them to use environmental print, and by demonstrating the conventional spelling of a word, in responding naturally to the child's writing.

In the sample letter on teaching children to write (Part Two), Lorraine explains the spelling box as follows:

Obviously, spelling is an integral part of this writing program. Each child is responsible for developing his or her own word list throughout the year. Specifically, I supply each child with a recipe box, alphabetized dividers, and blank 3 x 5 index cards on which they record the words that they want to spell conventionally as they write. The process begins with the child *trying* to write the word on this card. If difficulty is encountered, the rule in the classroom is "Ask three, then ask me." If none of the three classmates knows for certain how to spell the word, then all four children come to me and we discover together how the word is spelled. At this point, this word goes on a card for each of the four children and is filed in their spelling boxes. This word is then added to the lists typed onto each child's computer disk for further use. Each of the four children is then responsible for spelling this word cor-

rectly each time it is used in the child's writing. It's amazing how many words are accumulated by each child in the class. This personal word list is used for spelling tests.

Some teachers have children practice individualized spelling lists, sometimes using paper with three columns. For example, Lorraine's students write the words correctly in the middle column, study them, fold over one side to cover the words, and write them in another column as the words are dictated by a peer, using the set of words that the child originally typed into the computer. A similar procedure can be used for individualized spelling tests.

Strategies for Correcting Spelling: Transparency 7.15

Transparency 7.15 includes several strategies for correcting spelling, several of which are mentioned on transparency 7.11, "Ways of Teaching Spelling." Critical, of course, is developing an awareness of when a word might not be spelled correctly; that's why the first strategy listed is to circle words that might not be spelled correctly. The first two, circling possibly misspelled words and having a go at the spelling, may be the first taught to emergent writers. Many teachers use "have-a-go" sheets with four columns (an idea that comes from Australia). The child writes the word identified as misspelled in the first column, tries a different spelling in the second column and maybe the third column; gets confirmation and or help from the teacher or peers; and writes the word conventionally in the fourth column. A simpler alternative is making at least one attempt to rewrite the misspelled word in a "trying book." Then the child brings the book to the teacher, who reinforces the correctly spelled parts of the word and helps the child complete the correct spelling. We would not recommend using even these strategies, though, until the writer is well established in the "independent" spelling stage.

The three strategies in the middle might be the next ones recommended and taught (not necessarily in this order, though). Using a regular dictionary is more difficult, though using a class-made dictionary may be relatively easy. When children are able to compose on computer, using a spelling-checker is helpful. If available, a hand-held electronic spell checker can also be useful. However, teachers still need to guide children in learning to edit for spelling, because no correctly spelled word will be caught by the spelling checker, even if it's the wrong spelling for the context and the word's meaning (as happens so frequently with homonyms).

Errors as Signs of Progress: Transparencies 7.16 Through 7.18

More than a decade ago, Connie became intrigued by the notion that progress in learning language is inevitably accompanied by "error," such as the temporary overgeneralizing of regular past tense and plural endings, producing forms like *goed, buyed, mans*, and *childrens*. Such errors as signs of progress were noted for writing by Mina Shaughnessy (1977), who emphasized that "It is not unusual for people acquiring a skill to get 'worse' before they get better and for writers to err more as they venture more" (p. 119). Such observations led Connie to undertake some classroom research, and in the article reporting that research she wrote a still applicable conclusion: "The key, I believe, is to think of writing as involving more than one draft. In the first draft(s) we can then afford to encourage writers to take risks, the risks that will result in both growth and error. By allowing for error, we can encourage growth" (Weaver, 1982; see also Chapter 4 in Weaver, 1996).

Since emergent writers would commonly be overwhelmed by being asked or invited to produce a second draft, with young writers like the first graders in transparencies 7.16 through 7.18, we can simply give the individual child the clarifying explanation and examples needed, again and again if necessary, so that eventually the new knowledge and skills will be incorporated in first drafts. Daily exposure to stories and other print will also serve to teach the punctuation that emergent writers need to learn.

The writing samples in transparencies 7.16 through 7.18 show some of the kinds of errors that occur as a natural result of instruction. Grace had taught first grader Rachel that periods go at the ends of sentences, so Rachel dutifully put periods at the end—of the lines, that is (**transparency 7.16**). This is a not uncommon kind of "error" for emergent writers just learning to use periods (Cordeiro, 1988; Cordeiro, Giacobbe, & Cazden, 1983). In **transparency 7.17**, we see that Andrew had been taught to use an apostrophe in possessives—and he used one in the plural *cow's* also. As he began to learn a new skill, he overgeneralized his application of it—just as children overgeneralize regular past tense and plural endings in learning to talk (transparency 2.2). This overgeneralization is a sign of progress. Another first grader had been taught to use commas to separate items in a series, so she did—but they look more like apostrophes (**transparency 7.18**). This child had learned only part of what was involved in using commas in a series. Such partial learning is likewise common among children and adults just beginning to learn a new skill.

The fact that progress generates new kinds of errors is one bit of evidence against the behavioral theory of learning, according to which the teacher would teach something and the children would learn it, or be considered deficient. Such examples help us understand that it is the behavioral learning theory instead that is deficient, that is inadequate to account for how people *really* learn complex skills, strategies, and processes. Learning is gradual, approximate, and fraught with "new" kinds of errors that reflect progress. Teaching that supports learning will reflect the transactional kinds of minilessons and follow-up outlined in transparencies 1.9 and 1.10, which may be useful at this point in a workshop setting. You may also want to let workshop participants know that research supports our conviction that writing skills are best taught in the context of helping children write, revise, and edit, not in isolation (DiStefano & Killion, 1984; also Calkins, 1980).

From Observation to Teaching: Transparencies 7.19 Through 7.21

In order to determine what kind of help writers are ready for, whole language teachers have become knowledgeable "kidwatchers," informed about the reading and writing processes and how they develop, as well as about how children learn. Transparencies 7.19 through 7.21 and the following commentary can help workshop participants understand how teachers examine children's writing to see what kinds of help they are ready for.

In **transparency 7.19**, Danielle, a second grader, wrote (on October 16), "I have a puppy. We are going for a run." It was Danielle who wrote over what she had originally written. But the words are run together, which is not particularly common when the spelling is as sophisticated as Danielle's. This would appear, then, to be the "teachable moment" for showing Danielle how to space between words. At Danielle's request, Lorraine wrote under Danielle's writing what the child herself had written, with spacing between words. Danielle's October 20 journal entry suggests that she has begun to apply what she's been taught about leaving spaces between words (**transparency 7.20**).

In **transparency 7.21**, David, a third grader, uses mostly conventional spellings. However, the spellings "giveing" for *giving* and "cranberrys" for *cranberries* suggest that he might be ready to learn the rule for dropping a silent *e* when adding *-ing,* and the rule for changing *y* to *i* when adding *-es* to form the plural. Typically such rules are best taught through multiple examples. Does David need help hearing and noticing the *r* in words like *turkey* and *gravy*? We might need further evidence to make a decision yes or no.

Examining and Guiding Progress over Time: Transparencies 7.22 Through 7.28

You can use writing samples over a longer period of time to demonstrate to workshop participants how a child is developing more and more in the use of written language. For knowledgeable teachers, it is easy to determine what the child knows and what the child seems to need in the way of directive teaching. Thus, the power of this process is that the teacher constantly builds on children's prior knowledge, reinforcing their own perception of what they know how to do by extending it. Furthermore, having children's writing portfolios accompany them from grade to grade enables parents and teachers to see the growth of the children's writing ability and to determine how best to continue fostering their learning. The portfolio is like a continuous video of the child's writing abilities, as opposed to occasional snapshots.

When examining writing samples obtained over an extended period of time, some questions that can be explored with workshop participants are:

What does the child know already?

What do you think he or she needs to learn next?

What strategies could and should we use to facilitate the child's learning?

These questions can be asked of the writing samples in the next seven transparencies, which show Robbie's writing development from kindergarten to grade two. In **transparency 7.22**, from October of his kindergarten year, Robbie has drawn a picture and written his name. He knows some capital and lowercase letters, knows how to spell his name, and knows that print in English is written horizontally. Like many another kindergartner, he has written his name backwards, from right to left. This suggests he may benefit from having demonstrations of how to write his name from left to right.

You might invite workshop participants to see if they can tell what Robbie has written in **transparency 7.23**, also from October of his kindergarten year. According to Robbie, it says, "Once upon a time there was a dragon and there was a sword fighter and he lived in a big castle with the princess." (Notice that he says "dragon" but has written "monster," MSTR.) What does Robbie already know about writing? Clearly he has learned the alphabetic principle, that there is a connection between sounds and letters. His spelling seems to reflect the developing to approximate stages of our chart in transparency 1.8. He has written the first line from left to right, but instead of starting the second line on the left he has begun it on the right, writing "fighter" backwards, as RTF. Would directionality be the thing to work on next? And how: by demonstrating and explaining?

Transparency 7.24 is a sample of Robbie's writing from almost a year later, September of his first-grade year. Obviously he has learned a great deal about the writing process, both from natural development and directive teaching as relevant.

What understandings does he now demonstrate in his writing? He knows about titles and chapters. He knows upper- and lowercase letters and knows that writing goes from left to right—on each line. He has a sense of audience, engaging the reader with "Bot you havto guess it your self" at the end of Chapter 1. He knows that illustrations are often used to support the text (**transparency 7.25**). What does he need to learn next? Perhaps punctuation (periods) and/or the placement of a chapter heading and title. Perhaps the spelling of *oa* words like *boat*; perhaps the difference in spelling between the homonyms *threw* and *through*.

What strategies should we use to facilitate his learning? For punctuation, use other books, other children's writing, his own sample of writing photocopied with the intent of using it to add periods where they are needed. For chapter titles and headings, other books may be best. For spelling, look at *oa* words in con-

text and maybe write several examples for him; for the homonyms, show examples of these and other homonyms in context (e.g., *to, too, two; see, sea*).

The next writing sample (**transparencies 7.26a through 7.26c**) is from September of Robbie's second-grade year. What understandings does he now demonstrate in his writing? The use of punctuation (periods), though he is not yet consistent in their use. Generally appropriate use of upper- and lowercase letters. The use of humor. Note that his story resembles a narrative, with familiar beginnings and endings, as he writes on a personal topic, a real event.

What does he need to learn next? Perhaps the use of quotation marks, or the use of capitals for words such as *I* and for days of the week. The conventional ordering of letters in the spellings of some words (he wrote "agian" for *again*, "wacth" for *watch*). The spelling of some relatively common words, such as *after, touch,* and *snack*. The spelling of contractions, such as *I'm* and *that's*. What strategies should we use to facilitate his learning? Picture books would be good for noticing the conventional use of quotation marks, which he could then try adding in his own writing when appropriate. The use of capitals for words like *I* and for days of the week could be located in books and/or in environmental print, in other children's writing, or simply demonstrated by the teacher. He could use his own spelling box (see the discussion accompanying transparencies 7.13 and 7.14) to examine the conventional spellings of some words and to add needed ones to his personal word bank, with help from classmates and the teacher as needed.

Stages in the Writing Process: Transparencies 7.27 Through 7.29b

The next five transparencies illustrate a student's ability to edit for content as well as mechanics. Jeff, a sixth grader, was involved in a process-oriented classroom where students wrote daily for approximately an hour each day. A daily sharing session, along with teacher and peer conferencing, allowed students to receive constructive feedback. Students also had access to computers and had word processing skills. Each new draft was saved under a new name, thus providing a history of each piece. Although the use of a computer is not necessary, a sequence of typed drafts proves to be especially beneficial and efficient during parent/teacher conferences. Students can print out each draft of a favorite piece that is taken to completion, as they did in Jeff's classroom. The process can then be shared with parents, who typically develop a better understanding and appreciation of their child's efforts and writing growth.

Jeff's original drafts were typed; they have simply been retyped here in larger size type, for transparency use.

Jeff's first draft lacked a sense of voice. He wrote the piece and shared it with the class. After some supportive feedback, Jeff made several revisions, both in content and mechanics. His final draft reflects several hours of rewriting.

In a workshop setting, you might underline selected parts for comparison and elicit participants' response as to how the draft has been improved. An important point to be made is that while primary-grade students cannot yet engage in such extensive revision, this is a goal toward which students are guided, beginning with minimal editing in the primary grades. Learning to write is not merely left to chance.

Editing Checklist: Transparency 7.30

This editing checklist is modeled after the kind done by Mary Ellen Giacobbe's first graders (Giacobbe, 1984). The checklist in **transparency 7.30**, however, was completed by Ivan, a first grader whom Grace worked with (see transparencies 8.11 through 8.15). Ivan was then in what we have called the *independent* stage of writing (transparency 1.8). The editing skills for which he claims responsibility in this checklist are as follows:

- I can write my name.
- I can put a period at the end.
- I can leave spaces.
- I can use -ed, -ing, -er.
- I can use a question mark, comma, exclamation mark.

In writing this checklist, Ivan realized that the second entry was difficult to read, so he added dashes between words. With further support and practice in spacing, Ivan was able to add the third entry. He now refers to this list when reviewing his work. And as he gains the ability to consistently demonstrate a skill, he adds the skill to the list.

Sources and Resources

BOLTON, F., & SNOWBALL, D. (1993). *Teaching spelling: A practical resource.* Portsmouth, NH: Heinemann.

BUCHANAN, E. (1989). *Spelling for whole language classrooms.* Katonah, NY: Richard C. Owen.

CALKINS, L. M. (1980). When children want to punctuate: Basic skills belong in context. *Language Arts, 57,* 567–573.

CALKINS, L. M. (1994). *The art of teaching writing* (2nd ed.). Portsmouth, NH: Heinemann.

CLARKE, L. (1988). Invented versus traditional spelling in first graders' writings: Effects on learning to spell and read. *Research in the Teaching of English, 22,* 281–309.

CORDEIRO, P. (1988). Children's punctuation: An analysis of errors in period placement. *Research in the Teaching of English, 22,* 62–74.

CORDEIRO, P., GIACOBBE, M. E., & CAZDEN, C. (1983). Apostrophes, quotation marks, and periods: Learning punctuation in the first grade. *Language Arts, 60,* 323–332.

DEFORD, D. E. (1981). Literacy: Reading, writing, and other essentials. *Language Arts, 58,* 652–658.

DiStefano, P., & Killion, J. (1984). Assessing writing skills through a process approach. *English Education, 16* (4), 203–207.

Duke, Kate. (1992). *Aunt Isabel tells a good one.* New York: Dutton.

Gentry, J. R. (1987). *Spel . . . is a four-letter word.* Richmond Hill, Ontario: Scholastic. (Available in the U.S. from Heinemann.)

Giacobbe, M. E. (1984). Helping children become more responsible for their own writing. *LiveWire, 1* (1), 7–9. (National Council of Teachers of English publication.)

Graves, Donald M. (1994). *A fresh look at writing.* Portsmouth, NH: Heinemann.

Laminack, L. L., & Wood, K. (1996). *Spelling in use.* Urbana, IL: National Council of Teachers of English.

Shaughnessy, M. P. (1977). *Errors and expectations: A guide for the teacher of basic writing.* New York: Oxford University Press.

Weaver, C. (1982). Welcoming errors as signs of growth. *Language Arts, 59,* 438–444.

Weaver, C. (1996). *Teaching grammar in context.* Portsmouth, NH: Boynton/Cook.

Wilde, S. (1992). *You kan red this! Spelling and punctuation for whole language classrooms, grades K–6.* Portsmouth, NH: Heinemann.

Books on Literacy Development

The following books are appropriate for parents as well as teachers. The asterisked books are especially easy and delightful reading.

*Barron, M. (1990). *I learn to read and write the way I learn to talk: A very first book about whole language.* Katonah, NY: Richard C. Owen. Available in both an English version and a Spanish version.

Clay, M. M. (1987). *Writing begins at home.* Portsmouth, NH: Heinemann.

Doake, D. (1991). *Reading begins at birth.* Richmond Hill, Ontario: Scholastic.

*Laminack, L. L. (1991). *Learning with Zachary.* Richmond Hill, Ontario: Scholastic.

Newman, J. M. (1984). *The craft of children's writing.* Richmond Hill, Ontario: Scholastic. (Available in the U S from Heinemann.)

Villiers, U. (1990). *Luk Mume luk Dade I kan rit.* New York: Scholastic. Consists of young children's writing samples, with explanations of their writing development.

The following anticipation guide is designed to raise questions. Please begin by indicating your response in the "Before" column. You may use the following key: SA for "strongly agree"; A for "agree"; U for "uncertain"; D for "disagree"; and SD for "strongly disagree."

When you have finished, please circle three or four items you particularly want to have clarified by today's workshop, and/or list some other questions that you have generated.

Before   After

_____   _____   1. It is important to spell all the words correctly when you are writing.

_____   _____   2. Children need to be drilled with skills, rules, and procedures in spelling and writing.

_____   _____   3. Reading aloud to children can have a direct effect on their writing abilities.

_____   _____   4. It's more important to give a child a spelling strategy than to have a child memorize spelling words.

_____   _____   5. Correcting writers' errors helps convince them that they cannot write independently.

_____   _____   6. Children need to be encouraged to experiment with written language.

_____   _____   7. One important way to teach phonics is by encouraging approximated spelling.

_____   _____   8. We should be selective in helping children notice common patterns in spelling (-tion, -able, -ed, -ing, etc.).

_____   _____   9. If children are allowed to experiment with written language, conventions begin to surface in their writings.

_____   _____   10. Children need to be exposed to a variety of forms (genres) of writing.

_____   _____   11. We need to provide children with many demonstrations of our own involvement in writing for a variety of purposes.

_____   _____   12. We need to teach writing skills with textbooks, rather than leave the acquisition of skills to chance.

_____   _____   13. We cannot write about something for which we lack prior knowledge.

My questions:

Learning to Write Is Like (#1)

- designing a bridge

- learning to swim

- the Suzuki method of learning the violin

- dancing with an invisible partner

Learning to Write Is Like (#2)

- making a cake

- building a tower of blocks

- learning to ride a bike

- dancing

Discussion Questions on Writing

1. How did you learn to write?

2. What kinds of things do you write?

3. What kinds of things would you LIKE to write, but don't? Why?

4. Have your writing habits changed over the years? If so, how and why?

5. How do you feel about yourself as a writer? Why do you feel that way?

How Adults Facilitate Writing Acquisition

1. By calling children's attention to print in the environment and reading it to and with them.

2. By modeling what it means to be a writer: letting children see you write.

3. By encouraging children's experimentations with writing and responding positively to their efforts and products.

4. By providing an emotionally safe environment for risk-taking.

5. By supporting children's engagement in the writing process.

6. By expecting children to eventually learn to write like an adult.

Reed: Phonics Room

RB·ihɑ b ɑig ɑ g.

ihɑcdɑd.

ihɑɑɔɑt.

I had a gag.

I had a dad.

I had a cat.

Jeffrey and Amy: Skills Room

Jeffrey H)

Bill can run.
Jill can run.
Jeff can run.
I can run.

Amy S
Jill Bill I am Lad
Bill I am Jill
Lad I am Bill
I am Jill Bill
I am Lad Bill
Jill I am Bill Jill
I k Ro
I Bik

Creating Support for Effective Literacy Education by C. Weaver, L. Gillmeister-Krause, & G. Vento-Zogby, © 1996. Portsmouth, NH: Heinemann. May be copied for transparency use only.
From Diane De Ford, Literacy: Reading, writing, and other essentials. *Language Arts, 58*, 652–658. ©1981 by the National Council of Teachers of English. Reprinted by permission.

Jason: Whole-Language Room

Iran is fighting U.S. 19 bombers ne down. 14 fighters. we olny have. 3 bombers down 6 fighters. we have droped 9 bombs over iran the hostges have been ther so Long. How we head twards them I try Like a game of Cheecers. We have distrojed iran Singing out jason

T7.6   *Whole Language Classroom*   *Creating Support for Effective Literacy Education* by C. Weaver, L. Gillmeister-Krause, & G. Vento-Zogby, © 1996. Portsmouth, NH: Heinemann. May be copied for transparency use only.

From Diane De Ford, Literacy: Reading, writing, and other essentials. *Language Arts, 58,* 652–658. ©1981 by the National Council of Teachers of English. Reprinted by permission.

M ρ 9 9 A ⌐ R B

I M P S

T7.7   *Emergent Spelling: Incipient and Developing Stages (Cory)*   *Creating Support for*
Effective Literacy Education by C. Weaver, L. Gillmeister-Krause, & G. Vento-Zogby, © 1996. Portsmouth, NH: Heinemann. May be copied for transparency use only.
From *Teaching grammar in context* by Constance Weaver. Portsmouth, NH: Boynton/Cook, 1996.

I WNT TIK
r t w mt
frn .

I WNT to go to the
noRT Pol and Bak
hom befor Crsmas
moring.

T7.9   *Emergent Spelling: Approximate Stage (#2) (Cory)*   *Creating Support for Effective Literacy*
Education by C. Weaver, L. Gillmeister-Krause, & G. Vento-Zogby, © 1996. Portsmouth, NH: Heinemann. May
be copied for transparency use only.
From *Teaching grammar in context* by Constance Weaver. Portsmouth, NH: Boynton/Cook, 1996.

Last nit I et my hamburger and i swaloed my tooth

T7.10   *Emergent Spelling: Independent Stage (Cory)*   *Creating Support for Effective Literacy Education* by C. Weaver, L. Gillmeister-Krause, & G. Vento-Zogby, © 1996. Portsmouth, NH: Heinemann. May be copied for transparency use only.

From *Teaching grammar in context* by Constance Weaver. Portsmouth, NH: Boynton/Cook, 1996.

Ways of Teaching Spelling (#1)

- posting lists of commonly used words in the classroom, for children to use in editing their writing

- encouraging children to notice and circle words that may not be spelled correctly

- helping children develop and learn to use an individualized collection (list or index cards) of words they write often but haven't learned to spell with certainty

- teaching minilessons in which children are helped to develop lists and charts of words with the same spelling for the onset or rime (word families)

- teaching various other kinds of minilessons, such as lessons contrasting different spellings for words that sound the same

- helping children develop an increasing repertoire of strategies for correcting their spellings

T7.11   *Ways of Teaching Spelling (#1)*   *Creating Support for Effective Literacy Education* by C. Weaver, L. Gillmeister-Krause, & G. Vento-Zogby, © 1996. Portsmouth, NH: Heinemann. May be copied for transparency use only.

Critique on " Frozen Fire"
~ Houston

sentenses - sentences

loge - long

to - too

exsiting - exciting

biging - beginning

whith - with

ic strimly - extremely

beter - better

becos - because

geting - getting

JD

Creating Support for Effective Literacy Education by
C. Weaver, L. Gillmeister-Krause, & G. Vento-Zogby, © 1996. Portsmouth, NH: Heinemann. May be copied for
transparency use only.

Oct 17 Tuesday

YESTRDAY I HAD
A SPELLING BOX AND
I AM HAPPY.
I am so glad you like
your Spelling Box.

yesterday

saturday we HAD
A FESTEVAL

October 19 1995.

Thursday

What a fun day it was.
The Harvest Festival

Strategies for Correcting Spelling

- Circle words that might not be spelled correctly

- "Have a go" at the spelling: Write the word two or three different ways and see which looks better

- Locate the spelling in a familiar text or somewhere in the environment

- Ask someone

- Use an individualized list or set of words (a personal dictionary)

- Use a regular or class-made dictionary

- Use a spelling checker on the computer or a hand-held spelling checker

T7.15 *Strategies for Correcting Spelling*   *Creating Support for Effective Literacy Education* by C. Weaver, L. Gillmeister-Krause, & G. Vento-Zogby, © 1996. Portsmouth, NH: Heinemann. May be copied for transparency use only.

MY MOM AND.
DED AND.
B .SK.

T7.16   *Errors as Signs of Progress (#1): Placement of Periods (Rachel)*   *Creating Support for*
Effective Literacy Education by C. Weaver, L. Gillmeister-Krause, & G. Vento-Zogby, © 1996. Portsmouth, NH:
Heinemann. May be copied for transparency use only.
From *Teaching grammar in context* by Constance Weaver. Portsmouth, NH: Boynton/Cook, 1996.

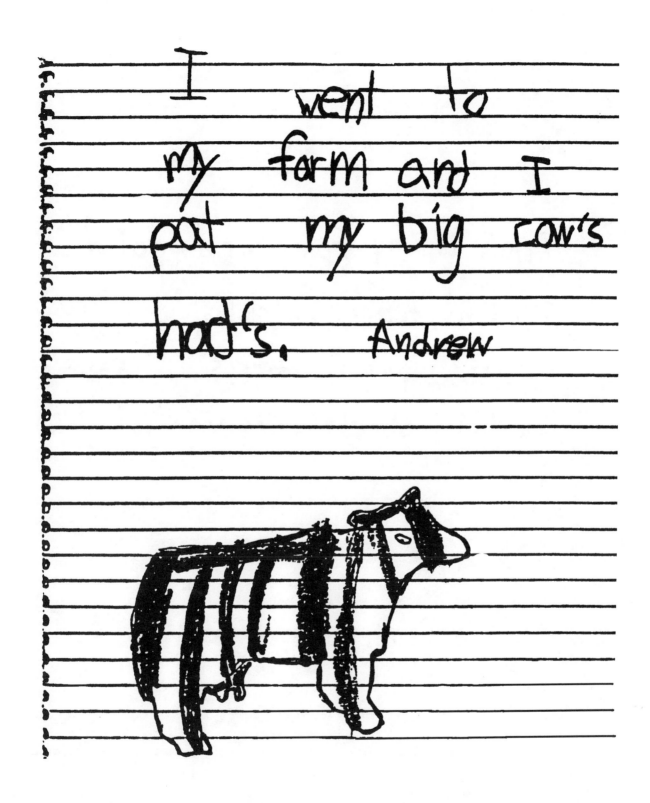

I went to
my farm and I
pat my big cow's
had's. Andrew

T7.17 *Errors as Signs of Progress (#2): Overgeneralization of apostrophe (Andrew)*
Creating Support for Effective Literacy Education by C. Weaver, L. Gillmeister-Krause, & G. Vento-Zogby, © 1996.
Portsmouth, NH: Heinemann. May be copied for transparency use only.

Pink is my favorite color.

Pink is fengrnael polish' shirts' swetrs' papr' dresis' crans' harts' shorts' earsengs'

T7.18   *Errors as Signs of Progress (#3): Placement of Commas*   *Creating Support for Effective*
Literacy Education by C. Weaver, L. Gillmeister-Krause, & G. Vento-Zogby, © 1996. Portsmouth, NH:
Heinemann. May be copied for transparency use only.
From *Teaching grammar in context* by Constance Weaver. Portsmouth, NH: Boynton/Cook, 1996.

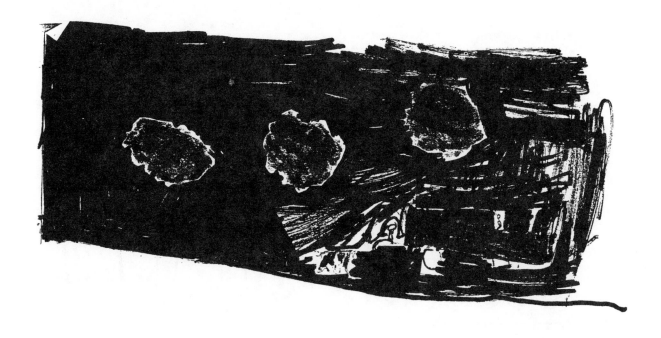

Oct 16

I HaVe a PUPPY.WeaAegoINgForaruN

I have a puppy. We are going
for a run.

Who runs who?
You run her?
She runs you?

T7.19   *From Observation to Teaching (#1): No Spaces Between Words (Danielle)*

Oct 20

Misty had a swollen
eye last night.

Poor little Misty.

What happened?

T7.20   *From Observation to Teaching (#2): Beginning to Use Spaces (Danielle)*
Creating Support for Effective Literacy Education by C. Weaver, L. Gillmeister-Krause, & G. Vento-Zogby, © 1996.
Portsmouth, NH: Heinemann. May be copied for transparency use only.

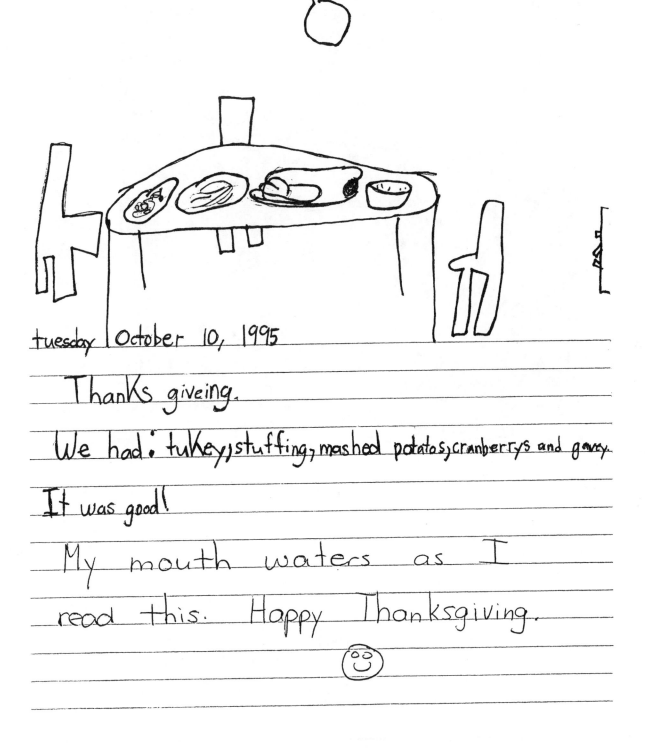

tuesday October 10, 1995

Thanks giveing.

We had: tuKey, stuffing, mashed potatos, cranberrys and gavy.

It was good!

My mouth waters as I

read this. Happy Thanksgiving.

T7.22   *Examining and Guiding Progress Over Time (#1): Name Written Backwards (Robbie)*   *Creating Support for Effective Literacy Education* by C. Weaver, L. Gillmeister-Krause, & G. Vento-Zogby, © 1996. Portsmouth, NH: Heinemann. May be copied for transparency use only.

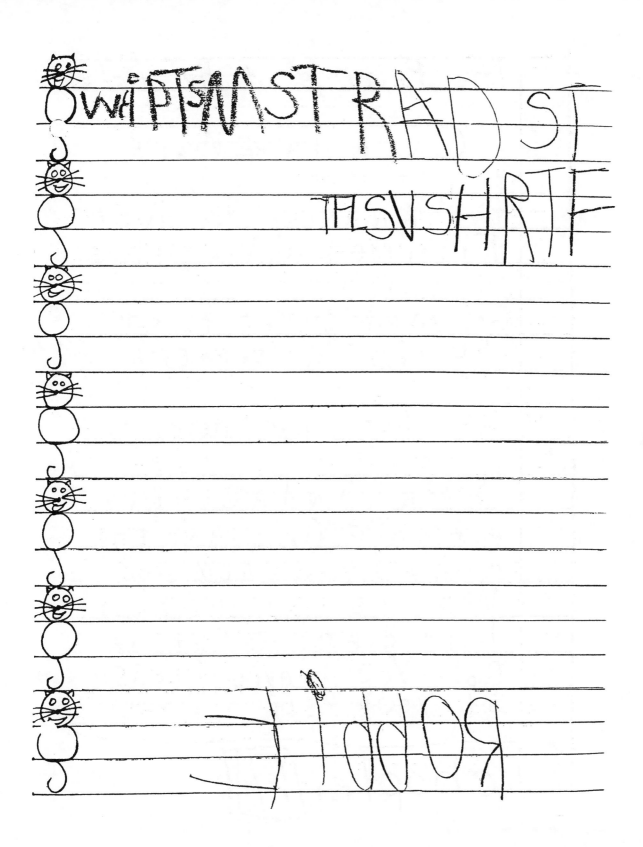

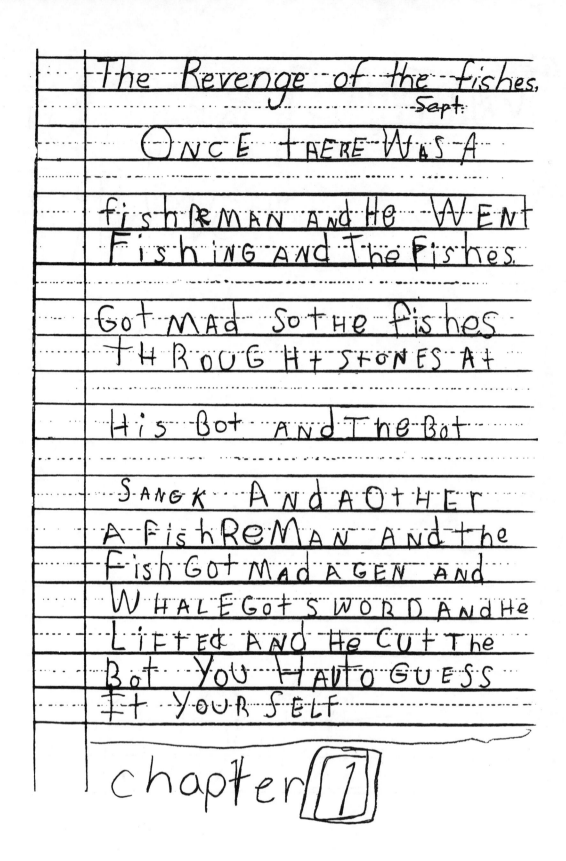

The Revenge of the fishes.
Sept.

ONCE tHERE WAS A

fishRMAN AND He WENt
Fishing and The fishes.

Got MAd soTHe fishes
THROUGHt StoNES At

His Bot AND The Bot

SANGK AND A OTHEr
A fish REMAN AND the
Fish Got MAd A GEN and
WHALE Got SWORD AND He
Liftéd AND He Cut The
Bot YOU HAuto GUESS
It YOUR SELF

chapter 1

T7.24   *Examining and Guiding Progress Over Time (#3): Independent Writing, First Grade (Robbie)*   Creating Support for *Effective Literacy Education* by C. Weaver, L. Gillmeister-Krause, & G. Vento-Zogby, © 1996. Portsmouth, NH: Heinemann. May be copied for transparency use only.

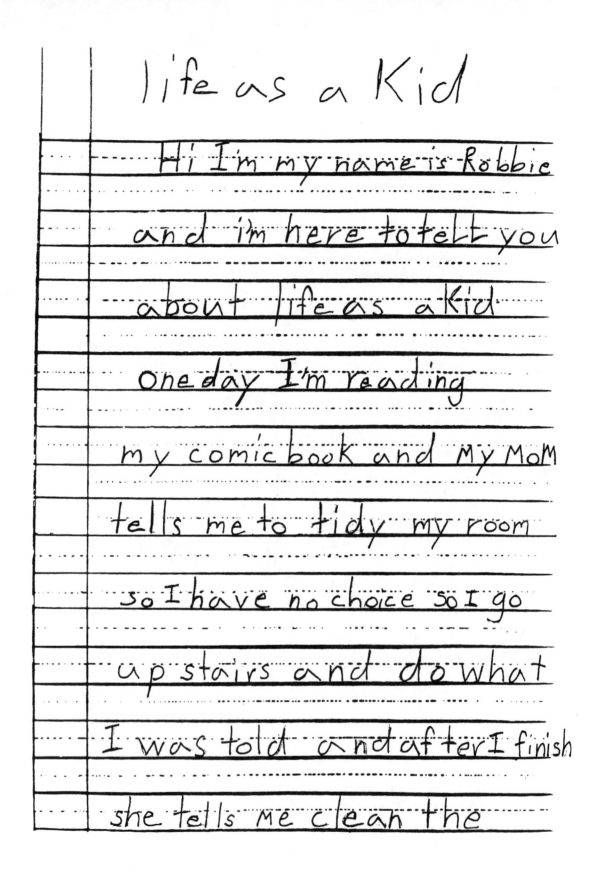

life as a Kid

Hi I'm my name is Robbie

and I'm here to tell you

about life as a kid

one day I'm reading

my comic book and My Mom

tells me to tidy my room

so I have no choice so I go

up stairs and do what

I was told and after I finish

she tells me clean the

T7.26a   *Examining and Guiding Progress Over Time (#5): Second Grade Writing Sample*
(Robbie)   *Creating Support for Effective Literacy Education* by C. Weaver, L. Gillmeister-Krause, &
G. Vento-Zogby, © 1996. Portsmouth, NH: Heinemann. May be copied for transparency use only.

bath room what a day that
was. Next day was saturday
and i was just going to
turn the tv on for my cartoons,
But as alwas My MoM
agian, She tells me thoch
that Knob or die i'm going
to wacth My soapopra.
well i had nothing
to do

But get a snak but my mom
said you just had
lunch which i had 2 hours
ago, so thats all
I think i hear my mom
calling me so long.

The end

T7.26c *Examining and Guiding Progress Over Time (#5) (continuation)*   *Creating Support*
for Effective Literacy Education by C. Weaver, L. Gillmeister-Krause, & G. Vento-Zogby, © 1996. Portsmouth, NH:
Heinemann. May be copied for transparency use only.

Sixth Grader's First Draft

There was a guy by the name of George. George was in high school and he loved to run track. He was very fast. George was so fast that he was eight tenths of a second off the world record and two tenths of a second off the United States record. George could of had a free scholarship to collage. A few guys said he didn't have to worry about work all they wanted him for was track. George didn't go instead he stoped running track and went to the marines. They had found out that George was deaf in one ear so he couldn't be in the marines. When he got home he decided to get married and have a healthy family.

T7.27 *Sixth Grader's First Draft* *Creating Support for Effective Literacy Education* by C. Weaver, L. Gillmeister-Krause, & G. Vento-Zogby, © 1996. Portsmouth, NH: Heinemann. May be copied for transparency use only.

Sixth Grader's Second Draft

There was a guy by the name of Micky Walker. He was a very good runner in his time. Micky ran for Sauquoit Valley Central School. He used to know when track started and would start running about a month early to get in shape.

While riding the team bus to the other team's track, Mickey could feel his excitement inside of him. Just before his race, his heart pounding, being very nervous, he walks out to the track. Very tensely he gets in the starting blocks, waiting for the gun to go off, it seems like a hundred meters. His heart was beating faster, sweat was dropping off of him. He sees the finish line he never looks back. He's going, he's going, he wins!

People from the college came out on the track and tried to get Micky to go to their college on a free scholarship for track. They started to come more when he started to become a better runner. He was eight tenths of a second off the WORLD record and two tenths of a second off the UNITED STATES record. He was only in high school at that time too.

Micky didn't take the scholarship. Instead, he tried to make it in the Marines. Micky couldn't because when he took his physical they found out he was deaf in one ear from hitting someone real hard in football.

So Micky went home and started a new life. He got married and had four kids. I was one of them and I hope someday I follow in his footsteps.

Sixth Grader's Third Draft

There was a guy by the name of Micky Walker. He was a very good runner in his time. Micky ran for Sauquoit Valley Central School. You would know when the track season was about to start because you could see Micky running about a month early to get in shape.

While riding the team bus to the other team's track, Micky would feel his excitement inside of him. Just before his race, his heart would begin pounding. Being very nervous, he would walk out to the track. Very tensely he would get in the starting blocks and wait anxiously for the gun to go off. At the sound of the gun, Micky would concentrate on the track, it would seem like a hundred meters. His heart would beat faster, sweat would drip off of him. He concentrated on reaching the finish line and he would never look back as he was the first to cross it.

People from the college came out on the track and tried to get Micky to go to their college on a track scholarship. They started to come more often when he started to become a better runner and win more races. He was eight tenths of a second off the world record and two tenths of a second off the United States record.

Micky didn't take the scholarship. Instead, he tried to make it in the Marines. Micky couldn't because when he took his physical they found out he was deaf in one ear because of a football injury.

So Micky went home and started a new life. He got married and had four kids. I was one of them and I hope someday I follow in his footsteps.

Things I can do when I write:

1 I can rit my Nam.
2 I can Pot a Perd at the END.
3 I can lev spqs.
4 I can yous cd,ln g,er.
5 I can yous ?,!.

 Creating Support for Effective Literacy Education by C. Weaver, L. Gillmeister-Krause, & G. Vento-Zogby, © 1996. Portsmouth, NH: Heinemann. May be copied for transparency use only.

ASSESSMENT

An anticipation guide on assessment precedes the transparency pages in this section. It should be noted that the writing samples are all from average or lower-ability students, not the top writers in the class.

Assessment Is/Should Be Like: Transparency 8.1

Transparency 8.1 parallels transparency 2.1 on learning the language, transparency 3.1 on learning to read, and transparencies 7.1 and 7.2, on learning to write. Participants can be invited to respond to any item that catches their interest. We think traditional forms of assessment, tests and particularly standardized tests, can be a lot like dancing a ballet in rubber boots. When children are taught isolated reading and writing skills before they engage in reading and writing, and when they are then tested on these skills, assessment can be a lot like taking a test on the rules of the road when you haven't been behind the wheel, or taking a test on the history and components of the ballpoint pen before actually trying to write. In fact, trying to assess component skills in isolation can be about as ridiculous as assigning a number grade to the *Mona Lisa*. The other two analogies contrast traditional assessment with authentic portfolio assessment. That is, assessment via tests and especially the periodically administered standardized tests is like a series of snapshots taken over a relatively long period of time and hung on a clothesline. In contrast, the ongoing nature of assessment in whole lan-

guage classrooms is more like a videotape of performance over time, wherein it is not only the product but the processes that are recorded. (For this comparison, we are indebted to Kathryn Mitchell Pierce.)

Discussion Questions on Assessment: Transparency 8.2

In preparation for whole-group discussion of responses to the questions in **transparency 8.2**, you can use the "think/pair/share" procedure. That is, invite participants to think about their responses and jot some of them down, then turn to a partner nearby and share reflections.

In discussing their responses to these questions, workshop participants may reveal that when they were in school, they were typically assessed by means that did not adequately reflect their knowledge and abilities (tests of isolated skills, one-draft-only samples of their writing, questions that demanded recall of minute details, multiple-choice questions with more than one good answer, timed tests that pressured them into choosing wrong answers, etc.). If this point does indeed emerge, the participants should be prepared to understand the validity of alternative means of assessment.

Pitfalls of Traditional Assessment: Transparencies 8.3 and 8.4

Taken from Connie's *Understanding Whole Language* (1990), **transparency 8.3** is an attempt to demonstrate the absurdity—and sometimes the unintended difficulty—of the kinds of comprehension questions that have traditionally characterized standardized tests of reading. In the first set of pictures, would children necessarily realize that steam is supposed to be rising from the bowl of food, that they are to circle the object for which both of the statements are true, and that only the bowl of food is meant to meet both these criteria? Would they necessarily realize from the second set of pictures that the cat is supposed to be jumping?

Notice, too, that most of the items require much more emphasis on reading individual words than is normally required in authentic reading. In other words, these comprehension questions might more accurately be called picture and/or word identification questions. The last kind of item requires not so much comprehension but locating words in sentences. (This is the kind of situation where the test-wise student first reads the questions and then looks for the answers in the text.)

Also drawn from Connie's *Understanding Whole Language*, **transparency 8.4** lists six key reasons for downplaying the results of standardized tests in assessing children's abilities and achievement. One reason is that norm-referenced standardized tests are given for the purpose of rank-ordering students—and thereby also ranking teachers, schools and school districts, and states. Such tests are constructed so that a representative sampling of the population taking the test will produce scores that generate the bell curve. Therefore, half of the students are statistically consigned to be "below average," regardless of the actual quality of their learning, abilities, or performance. Criterion-referenced tests may be better, but they share some of the other pitfalls of standardized tests. In particular, they too may consign children to "death at an early age"—or at least to a life sentence of lower "ability" groups and lower tracks, where they will receive a less challenging education that fulfills the initial prophecy.

Assessment as Collaboration: Transparency 8.5

As **transparency 8.5** implies, authentic assessment involves collaboration among parents, children, and teachers. They need to mutually establish goals and support one another through the planning and the process.

Some teachers help the children prepare for the traditional parent conference, write letters of invitation to their parents, and conduct the conference with their parents, a procedure that makes it possible for more than one conference to occur at the same time—though of course the teacher is available to listen and respond to the parents, too (Anthony, Johnson, Mickelson, and Preece, 1991).

Some teachers Grace works with at Sauquoit invite children to participate in the parent-teacher conference. Approximately a week before the conference, each parent receives a letter outlining possible topics for discussion. Another possibility is to send home a note that includes positive encouraging statements regarding the child's progress in school. The parents can be asked to respond with positive statements regarding the child's work, interests, concerns, and so forth. The children can also be encouraged to provide feedback about their successes, concerns, and/or questions pertaining to school. During the conference, the parent, teacher, and child review the child's progress and discuss any questions and concerns, then set goals for the immediate future.

Students are often asked to write self-evaluations of their reading and writing and of the accomplishments they have made during the marking period. The child is asked to include behavior and academic goals for the next semester. Such self-evaluations are also shared during the conference with the parents. At first it is difficult for children to evaluate their own progress, so it can be helpful for the children to create (with guidance, of course) a rubric or set of guidelines to serve as indicators of progress. Having children actively involved in their assessment and evaluation typically encourages greater commitment to school.

Every two weeks, the same teachers at Sauquoit write an encouraging entry in a journal to each student. The student, in turn, writes to his or her parents commenting on current class issues, such as goals, projects enjoyed and/or completed, literature read, and so forth. The parent responds to the child. The journal is then returned to school for the teacher to review and provide any follow-up information that may be helpful to the parent or child.

In addition to this bimonthly communication, many Sauquoit teachers send home fliers, letters, or brochures, such as those included in Part Two of this book. Some teachers send home student-written newsletters informing parents of class activities, evaluation procedures, goals, and so forth.

Questions to Guide Assessment: Transparencies 8.6 and 8.7

In assessing students' growth, teachers need to become excellent observers of children, guided by knowledge of how children develop literacy. We need to know what to look for. What can the child do? Where does the child need help? In the section on writing, several of the sets of transparencies would also be helpful in demonstrating how teachers observe children's work and assess their needs, determining what they are ready for next.

Transparency 8.6 includes questions that we might want to include in authentic, comprehensive, "portfolio" assessment of reading, while **transparency 8.7** includes similar questions about writing. These two transparencies may be used to explore the possibilities for monitoring children's progress in reading and writing—both formally and informally.

Reading assessment may include listening to children read and/or conducting a running record or miscue analysis periodically (and perhaps tape-recording the readings to help demonstrate progress over time). Such means of assessment can help us determine the strategies a child uses when reading, and whether the child demonstrates understanding of stories read. The results should help the teacher

choose and recommend reading materials that will help the child progress as a reader.

In addition to the "formal" assessment that a running record or miscue analysis can provide, teachers—and parents—can document the child's reading progress through careful, thoughtful monitoring and observation. Many of the questions on this transparency revolve around teachers observing the child and being sensitive "kidwatchers." Notes taken regarding reading behavior, interests, and attitudes can be shared with parents, along with the conclusions from more formal assessments.

Writing assessment may include observations that focus on attitudes and interests. The questions on transparency 8.7—or similar ones—can be used when observing children. Notes can be recorded on an index card or a form devised for the purpose. The notes can be used in conjunction with periodic writing samples and writing checklists indicating what the child has attained and what new goals need to be met. Individual children can develop writing checklists, and/or the whole class can collaborate in determining criteria for good writing and even in developing a rubric defining different levels of competence based on the criteria. This process gives children a stake in assessment in a way that no adult-imposed criteria or rubric could possibly do.

Children should be encouraged to comment on the stories they read and write. With guidance, they can learn to evaluate their progress as readers and writers and to set new goals for themselves. Teachers can promote such evaluation by focusing on what children are able to do and encouraging them to think about what they could learn to do next. For example, children should be able to verbalize the strategies they use when encountering a word they don't know while reading, as well as the skills they are able to use as a writer.

Kinds of Data for Assessment: Transparency 8.8

Whole language assessment involves the continuous collection of information in authentic contexts and looks at process as well as product. It reflects the teacher's beliefs about learning and involves the student and sometimes the parent(s) as well as the teacher. The result of data collection and evaluation may support changes in the types of strategies and activities used with the child, the kinds of learning materials, and the types of groupings used. In other words, the data is detailed and pertinent to making instructional decisions. Because of the diversity of data collected, such assessment leads to charting progress rather than labeling children as deficient.

Portfolio assessment is not merely a collection of students' work over the course of a semester or school year. Assessment should involve reflection on the part of the student, constructive suggestions from the teacher, and perhaps mutual goal-setting for the future—not merely number or letter grades.

Transparency 8.8 lists some of the kinds of data that might be used for literacy assessment in whole language classrooms. Sharing some of the following information in a workshop setting may be useful. The resources in the final bibliography will help teachers in developing their own assessment tools.

• *Periodic Performance Samples*
A literacy and learning portfolio can include periodically collected samples of children's reading and writing. For example, the portfolio might include periodic miscue analyses (typically in simplified form; see Y. Goodman, Watson, & Burke, 1987) or running records (Clay, 1993), focusing on reading strategies rather than the quantity of miscues. As Ken Goodman has noted, miscues provide a window into the reading process—a process of making meaning, not merely of sounding out or identifying words. Children's reading can be taped about three times a year. The child may select a book to read as a "warm-up" before being asked to read a new selection. It is important to have the child retell and discuss the selection after reading it, because one can easily draw inaccurate inferences about the child's comprehension by listening to the oral reading alone.

Through miscue analysis or running records, the knowledgeable teacher can assess the reader's strategies: whether, for example, the child adequately predicts, monitors comprehension, and corrects or tries to correct miscues that don't fit the context. The teacher and child can listen to these tapes together, note strategies used and strategies needing work, and formulate goals that can be written and included in the portfolio. The tapes and the accompanying written data, including information on the child's retellings and discussion of the selections, can also be shared with parents during conferences and may become part of a child's portfolio, following him or her throughout the grades.

Periodic writing samples may be selected by the child to be placed in a folder. The pieces should be reflective of his or her growth in writing, and key pieces can be accompanied by a written reflection (by the child and/or by the teacher) explaining how the piece represented a breakthrough in the child's writing. Other criteria for selection and reflection may be used, too. For instance, children might be invited to choose one of their weakest pieces of writing and explain why the piece is not strong. Such reflection shows the child's growth in understanding the qualities of good writing.

• *Think-alouds*
In a think-aloud, the child reflects aloud as to how he or she is going about the process of reading or writing. While reading silently, the reader is asked to make comments upon his or her own reading: how the reader tackles unknown words, what connections are made to other texts or experiences, what the reader is confused about, and so forth. The teacher needs to model this process for the children. Think-alouds may be tape-recorded for the teacher to listen to later, and/or for permanent record-keeping. If the teacher and student listen to the tape together during a reading conference, this activity may serve as a springboard for evaluation and goal-setting.

Similarly, children can be invited to think

aloud while writing, and to tape-record their thinking aloud for later replaying and reflection.

• *Recorded Observations*

These reflect what Yetta Goodman called "kid-watching" (1978). Knowledgeable teachers become enlightened observers, taking notes as children engage in daily activities. Teachers watch to see what the children know and can do, not merely what they cannot do, though the latter is important too in helping teachers make instructional decisions.

Some teachers keep a binder containing one section for each child. Some find it helpful to jot down their observations on sheets of adhesive-backed labels (perhaps with children's names already added via a computerized address label program), and later to put these labels on a sheet of paper in the child's section of the notebook. Notes are kept on observations the teacher has made while the child is involved in reading or writing, carrying out a project, working collaboratively with others, and so forth. For example, the teacher can note the child's processes, choices and interests, work habits and social behaviors. Finished products thus become only a small part of what is assessed.

It is important that observations be recorded systematically and not just anecdotally, for otherwise the teacher is likely to note only the highs and lows, not the everyday activities and learning of the child. Some questions to keep in mind when observing children:

What is the learner attempting to do?

Is the learner collaborating with others?

Does the learner ask for help? If so, what kind and from whom?

What does the learner attend to? What does he or she ignore?

Does the learner take time to reflect? Can the learner reflect thoughtfully on what he or she is doing and has done?

• *Conferences and Interviews*

Some teachers hold a conference with parents and the child near the end of the summer, before school begins. In such conferences they can learn a lot about children's reading and writing interests and abilities, about literacy in the home, and about ways they can work with the children's parents to support their literacy development. Parents can be invited to come to the classroom and participate in literature discussions, too (which can alleviate their concern about the content of particular books and how the teacher handles it, their concern about skills and how strategies and skills are taught in context, and so forth). During the year, meeting individually with students can provide valuable insights into how the child views himself or herself as a learner, how the child understands the reading and writing process, what strategies are used and neglected while reading and writing, the child's developing interests, and so forth.

• *Inventories and Questionnaires*

We have found that the reading inventory in Y. Goodman, Watson, & Burke (1987) and a writing interview with parallel questions provide us with valuable insights into students' perceptions of reading and writing. Responses are usually solicited in a conference situation, in which the teacher can ask follow-up questions as appropriate; the teacher may write or tape-record the child's responses. The interview questions may alternatively be given to a group of students at once, allowing them to respond in writing to the questions. Teachers often create their own inventories and questionnaires, based on what they are interested in learning about the students as readers, writers, and learners, and being sensitive to the background of their students and the values of the community.

• *Dialogue Journals and Literature Logs*

Journals may take on several forms, such as:

a dialogue journal between students, with reflections and reactions to literature read a learning log: that is, a journal kept by students in response to a content area subject such as math or science

a literature log, in which the focus is primarily on a literary work; the journal entries are often used as a catalyst for responding in literature discussion groups

The information obtained from the journals provides data for assessing what and how students are reading (strategies, procedures); their sophistication in making connections between texts and in discussing literary elements; and so forth. Such journals also provide material that can spark discussion during a conference with a student.

• Lists and Record Cards or Sheets

Students are often asked to keep lists of books they have read. We have had our students develop class record sheets listing title/author/dates/comments about the book. Often a form will be developed when a need arises. For example, a child may need help in organizing time to read. In that case, a form that includes a weekly calendar may be helpful.

With the advent of computer technology, we have found it useful to have students keep a database on books read. The fields include: title, author, date the book was started and completed, and comments. A field can be created to allow the student to evaluate his or her process of reading the text, too. A printout of the books read may be made to share with parents during conference time.

• Projects Across the Curriculum

In *Theme Exploration: A Voyage of Discovery* (Weaver, Chaston, & Peterson, 1993), the authors share how they and classes of first graders and fourth graders each explored a topic of interest over a period of months. *Theme Immersion* (Manning, Manning, & Long, 1995) likewise demonstrates ways of engaging in theme immersion, while *Creating Classrooms for Authors and Inquirers* (Harste & Short with Burke, 1995) emphasizes the process of inquiry.

There is no prepackaged or predetermined unit: the theme study or inquiry evolves as teachers and students negotiate the curriculum. Themes and projects reflect students' interests and ownership while, at the same time, demonstrating the development of important concepts and the application of skills. Assessment includes student and teacher evaluation of the products, but it is at least as important to record the students' processes as they work, so recorded observation becomes critical during theme study as students' projects draw upon language, literacy, and literature to explore various topics.

• Other Media

Readers' understanding of a text can be evaluated through other media, such as drawings, drama, music, and so forth. Children can be asked to illustrate and discuss the part of a story they liked best. They can choose to act out a scene of a book that they found particularly compelling. They may choose to create a documentary video on a topic of study. However, worthwhile projects will be valuable in their own right and will maintain the integrity of the literature; they will not be merely cute, "fun" activities. Rather, such extensions of the literature should offer students the opportunity to reflect upon the reading and to share their understanding and appreciation of the text.

Determining Children's Spelling and Writing Growth: Transparencies 8.9 and 8.10

Of course, the most important way of determining a child's spelling growth is simply to save writing samples over time and compare them. Another way is to give a child the same list of words at different intervals, perhaps adding to the later assessments some new words that the child is not likely to "know," in order to see the patterns in the emergent writer's approximate spellings.

Another kind of evidence can be provided by dictating a child's earlier writing to him or her. For example, **transparency 8.9** shows Cory's original writing sample on October 28 of his first-grade year, compared with the same piece dictated to him at the end of the school year. By the time of the dictation, Cory had learned to spell several of these words conventionally, and his invented spellings were more sophisticated, too. We even see an overgeneralization of the apostrophe to an ordinary plural noun, which is not uncommon as writers are beginning to learn to use the apostrophe in possessives. **Transparency 8.10** shows a similar comparison between a writing sample from November 1 and the same piece dictated at the end of the year. We see essentially the same differences—and again the overgeneralized use of the apostrophe in an ordinary plural!

Documenting Stages in Spelling and Writing Development: Transparencies 8.11 Through 8.15

Transparencies 8.11 through 8.15 show the writing development of one child who is currently a first grader. Teachers typically document such growth through pieces from the children's writing portfolios.

Transparency 8.11: As a kindergartner, Ivan's writing was represented by scribbling and letter-like shapes, reflecting his understanding that writing is symbolic. Ivan's letter-like shapes were meant to say "I am a cowboy." At first he was able to "read" the scrawls, but he was unable to reread them over time. This writing sample would fall into what we have called the *incipient* stage.

Transparency 8.12: As an entering first grader, Ivan began to write letters that were strung together. At this point, the letters had no phonemic resemblance to the words (and therefore this writing sample also falls within the incipient stage). Ivan's illustrations helped maintain meaning, though, so he was able to "read" back his piece over time. It says "Firemen put out fires."

Transparency 8.13: As Ivan entered the phonemic stage, in which letters represent sounds, each word was represented by one or two letters, usually the first consonant and the last consonant. He was able to write some words correctly. His illustrations continued to help him maintain his ability to read back his story over time. It says "I like to play soccer." This is an early example of what we have called the *approximate* stage. (Apparently Ivan skipped the *developing* stage, an observation that nicely illustrates the fact that children don't necessarily go through all these stages or go through them exactly as might be expected.)

Transparency 8.14: As Ivan's phonemic writing became more sophisticated, he was able to represent more than just one or two sounds in the word. Vowel sounds were represented along with consonant sounds. His sentences tended to be repetitive in nature. He was aware of words in his environment and used them in his writing. He was able to read his piece back over time. It says "I went to the football and I got a trophy."

Transparency 8.15: As Ivan was exposed to more and more quality literature and to many demonstrations and minilessons involving writing, he became more independent (our *independent* writer stage). He now uses both approximated and conventional spellings. His writer's voice emerges as he strives to communicate his ideas.

Writers' Hints—Children's Criteria for Good Writing: Transparencies 8.16a and 8.16b

These transparencies may be helpful in providing examples of students creating their own guidelines for good writing.

A fifth-grade class was introduced to the book *Aunt Isabel Tells a Good One*, by Kate Duke. The book discusses the elements of a story. After sharing the book, the students were asked to think about a favorite book, one they would like to read again. They brainstormed what made the book a favorite. They then created a list of pointers for writing good fiction. Taking their pointers one step further, the class decided the list needed to be interesting to read. Therefore, they included an advertising "jingle" after each pointer—a mnemonic device to help them remember the hints. The list was displayed in the classroom and each student placed a copy in his or her writing folder.

Sources

BARRS, M., ELLIS, S., TESTER, H., & THOMAS, A. (1989). [Center for Language in Primary Education.] *The primary language record: A handbook for teachers.* Portsmouth, NH: Heinemann.

CLAY, M. M. (1993). *Reading recovery: A guidebook for teachers in training.* Portsmouth, NH: Heinemann.

DUKE, K. (1992). *Aunt Isabel tells a good one.* New York: Dutton.

EDUCATION DEPARTMENT OF SOUTH AUSTRALIA. (1991). *Literacy assessment in practice.* Distributed in the U.S. by the National Council of Teachers of English.

GOODMAN, Y. M. (1978). Kidwatching: An alternative to testing. *National Elementary Principal, 57* (June), 41–45.

GOODMAN, Y. M., WATSON, D. J., & BURKE, C. (1987). *Reading miscue inventory: Alternative procedures.* Katonah, NY: Richard C. Owen.

HARSTE, J., SHORT, K., WITH BURKE, C. (1995). *Creating classrooms for authors and inquirers* (2nd ed.). Portsmouth, NH: Heinemann.

IRA/NCTE JOINT TASK FORCE ON ASSESSMENT. (1994). *Standards for the assessment of reading and writing.* Newark, DE: International Reading Association, and Urbana, IL: National Council of Teachers of English.

MANNING, M., MANNING, G., & LONG, R. *Theme immersion: Inquiry-based curriculum in elementary and middle schools.* (1994). Portsmouth, NH: Heinemann.

WEAVER, C. (1990). *Understanding whole language: From principles to practice.* Portsmouth, NH: Heinemann.

WEAVER, C. (1994). *Reading process and practice: From socio-psycholinguistics to whole language* (2nd ed.). Portsmouth, NH: Heinemann.

WEAVER, C., CHASTON, J., & PETERSON, S. (1993). *Theme exploration: A voyage of discovery.* Richmond Hill, Ontario: Scholastic. Distributed in the U.S. by Heinemann.

Resources

ANTHONY, R. J., JOHNSON, T., MICKELSON, N., & PREECE, A. (1991). *Evaluating literacy: A perspective for change.* Portsmouth, NH: Heinemann. This practical handbook for teachers involves parents and students as well as the teacher in the collection of data for assessment. A key chapter demonstrates how students can prepare for and lead conferences with their parents. Sample letters and forms are included.

AUSTIN, T. (1994). *Changing the view: Student-led parent conferences.* Portsmouth, NH: Heinemann. By demonstrating how she led her sixth graders to take responsibility for assessment and for conferences with parents, Austin offers a valuable model for other teachers.

AZWELL, T., & SCHMAR, E. (1995). *Report card on report cards: Alternatives to consider.* Portsmouth, NH: Heinemann. A collection of writings by educators, this book deals with creating reporting systems that are aligned with the curriculum. Numerous examples of alternative reporting methods are given.

BARRS, M., ELLIS, S., TESTER, H., & THOMAS, A. (1989). [Center for Language in Primary Education.] *The primary language record: A handbook for teachers.* Portsmouth, NH: Heinemann. Includes a wealth of practical ideas and forms used for literacy assessment in London.

BIRD, L. B., GOODMAN, K. S., & GOODMAN, Y. M. (1994). *The whole language catalog: Forms for authentic assessment.* Chicago: SRA/Macmillan–McGraw Hill. This book contains authentic assessment forms and strategies that were developed by educators. As a companion to *The whole language catalog: Supplement on authentic assessment*, this resource contains reproducible forms. Each one includes a description of who the form should be used for, why it was created, and how it was intended to be used.

BIRD, L. B., GOODMAN, K. S., & GOODMAN, Y. M. (1994). *The whole language catalog: Supplement on authentic assessment.* Chicago: SRA/Macmillan–McGraw Hill. This supplement to *The whole language catalog* follows the same format. It contains essays, book notes, language stories, resources, and forms, all centering around authentic assessment. It is especially useful for those making a shift from more traditional approaches to assessment and evaluation.

EDUCATION DEPARTMENT OF SOUTH AUSTRALIA. (1991). *Literacy assessment in practice.* Distributed in the U.S. by the National Council of Teachers of English. Includes theoretical background on what to assess, plus a wealth of practical ideas, forms, and examples.

GOODMAN, K. S., GOODMAN, Y. M., & HOOD, W. J. (Eds.). (1989). *The whole language evaluation book.* Portsmouth, NH: Heinemann. This collection of articles by whole language educators contains vignettes and descriptions of classrooms involved in evaluation of students' growth in literacy.

GOODMAN, Y. M., WATSON, D. J., & BURKE, C. (1987). *Reading miscue inventory: Alternative procedures.* Katonah, NY: Richard C. Owen. A must for teachers using miscue analysis to assess a reader's strategies while reading authentic text.

HARP, B. (Ed.). (1994). *Assessment and evaluation for student centered learning* (2nd ed.). Norwood, MA: Christopher-Gordon. This update of the first edition deals with principles of whole language instruction, assessment, and evaluation as well as data collection and interpretation.

IRA/NCTE JOINT TASK FORCE ON ASSESSMENT. (1994). *Standards for the assessment of reading and writing.* Newark, DE: International Reading Association, and Urbana, IL: National Council of Teachers of English. Describes in detail eleven guidelines for the development and uses of assessment in literacy.

KEMP, M. (1990). *Watching children read and write: Observational records for children with special needs.* Portsmouth, NH: Heinemann. Demonstrates with procedures and record forms and examples the observation that children with special needs can be assessed in the same ways as other children.

RHODES, L. (Ed.). (1993). *Literacy assessment: A handbook of instruments.* A companion to *Windows into literacy*, this book contains all the assessment instruments discussed in that book; it can be especially useful for teachers developing their own assessment instruments.

RHODES, L., & SHANKLIN, N. (1993). *Windows into literacy: Assessing learners K–8.* Portsmouth, NH: Heinemann. Provides a comprehensive view of literacy assessment. Chapters deal with assessment and its guiding principles, assessment of reading and writing, and using a wide variety of instruments.

The following anticipation guide is designed to raise questions. Please begin by indicating your response in the "Before" column. You may use the following key: SA for "strongly agree"; A for "agree"; U for "uncertain"; D for "disagree"; and SD for "strongly disagree."

When you have finished, please circle three or four items you particularly want to have clarified by today's workshop, and/or list some other questions that you have generated.

Before   After

_____   _____   1. When assessing writing, we should consider clarity of content, organization, voice and style, appropriateness for audience and purpose, and writing mechanics.

_____   _____   2. Writing assessment should focus on a writer's growth.

_____   _____   3. We should expect children to master and demonstrate basic writing skills before expecting them to write something interesting.

_____   _____   4. Assessing a child's writing with a single, timed writing task is an appropriate way to measure the child's writing ability.

_____   _____   5. Asking a child to "bubble in" answers on a machine-scorable sheet can create either an unrealistically negative or an unrealistically positive impression of the child's knowledge or ability.

_____   _____   6. The class time used for testing and for practice-before-the-test drilling eats up much precious learning time.

_____   _____   7. Timed tests are a good way to measure children's ability.

_____   _____   8. Measuring reading skills (phonics, word identification, comprehension skills like cause-effect relationships) is a good way to determine whether a child can read well.

_____   _____   9. In order to determine who reads well and who doesn't, it is important to have tests that are designed to result in scores that resemble the bell curve.

_____   _____   10. Children who score below average and therefore "below grade level" on norm-referenced standardized tests may nevertheless be good readers.

_____   _____   11. When assessing children's reading, we should have them read and then discuss selections for which they have some interest and prior knowledge.

_____   _____   12. We should assess the strategies a reader uses or doesn't use effectively for processing texts, rather than basing reading assessment on word identification.

_____   _____   13. Schools should assess reading and writing in ways that reflect the meaningful reading and writing that children engage in daily.

My questions:

Anticipation Guide on Assessment   *Creating Support for Effective Literacy Education* by C. Weaver, L. Gillmeister-Krause, & G. Vento-Zogby, © 1996. Portsmouth, NH: Heinemann. May be copied for transparency use only.

Assessment Is/Should Be Like

- taking a test on the rules of the road when you haven't been behind the wheel

- dancing a ballet in rubber boots

- assigning a number grade to the *Mona Lisa*

- a series of snapshots hung on a clothesline

- taking a test on the history and components of the ballpoint pen before actually trying to write

- a videotape of process and performance over time

Discussion Questions on Assessment

1. Do you remember studying for a test, only to forget much of the information several days after taking it?

2. Do you remember taking timed tests containing isolated, trivial facts?

3. Do you remember when working cooperatively with someone on solving a problem was considered cheating?

4. Do you remember receiving a numerical grade and not knowing how the teacher determined the grade?

5. How do you think standardized tests and test scores affect children?

It is hot.

It tastes good.

The cat is

○ running   ○ flying   ○ jumping

The cat is in a box on the floor.

We like to play in the

     ○ ripe   ○ rope   ○ rain   ○ risk

The children wanted to have a party for Billy. Sally made cookies.
Jimmy got some ice cream. Mother had milk for them to drink. The party
was fun!

Who made cookies?   Who got some ice cream?   What else did they have?
○ Billy   ○ Sally   ○ cookies
○ Sally   ○ Jimmy   ○ cake
○ Mother   ○ Billy   ○ milk

T8.3   *Kinds of Comprehension Questions*   *Creating Support for Effective Literacy Education* by
C. Weaver, L. Gillmeister-Krause, & G. Vento-Zogby, © 1996. Portsmouth, NH: Heinemann. May be copied for
transparency use only.
From *Understanding whole language* by Constance Weaver. Portsmouth, NH: Heinemann, 1990.

Why Downplay Standardized Tests

1. The purpose of standardized tests is to rank-order students.

2. Such tests give a false impression of objectivity and consequently of equal opportunity and fairness.

3. These tests tend to focus everyone's attention on what students do not know and cannot do, in situations unlike daily life. At the same time, they do not tell us what we really need to know in order to foster individual students' learning.

4. Such tests tend to discourage effective teaching and engaged learning, by encouraging teaching to the test.

5. Furthermore, standardized tests don't tell teachers much that's useful in helping children become better readers.

6. For many young children, standardized tests result in death at an early age—or at least a life sentence.

T8.4   *Why Downplay Standardized Tests*   *Creating Support for Effective Literacy Education* by C. Weaver, L. Gillmeister-Krause, & G. Vento-Zogby, © 1996. Portsmouth, NH: Heinemann. May be copied for transparency use only.

From *Understanding whole language* by Constance Weaver. Portsmouth, NH: Heinemann, 1990.

Assessment as Collaboration Among

- parents

- children

- teachers

Questions About a Child's Reading

- Does the reader show an interest in books?

- Does the reader read for meaning?

- Does the reader demonstrate curiosity about words?

- What reading strategies has the reader been observed to use?

- Does the reader spontaneously comment about books read?

- Does the reader spontaneously make connections between books, authors and illustrators, and/or between books and real life?

- Does the reader frequently choose to read, when given a choice of activities?

- Does the reader demonstrate interest in an expanding range of genres?

- Does the reader demonstrate the ability to describe his or her own strengths as a reader and to set goals as a reader?

T8.6 *Questions About a Child's Reading*   *Creating Support for Effective Literacy Education* by C. Weaver, L. Gillmeister-Krause, & G. Vento-Zogby, © 1996. Portsmouth, NH: Heinemann. May be copied for transparency use only.

Questions About a Child's Writing

- Does the writer show an interest in writing?

- Does the writer write about topics that are meaningful to him or her?

- Does the writer experiment with words?

- What writing and spelling strategies has the writer been observed to use?

- Does the writer spontaneously share writings?

- Does the writer spontaneously make connections between different pieces and/or drafts of writing, and/or between books and his or her own writing?

- Does the writer frequently choose to write, when given a choice of activities?

- Does the writer demonstrate an expanding range of genres in his or her writing?

- Does the writer demonstrate the ability to describe his or her own strengths as a writer and to set goals as a writer?

Kinds of Data for Assessment

- periodic performance samples

- think-alouds

- recorded observations

- conferences and interviews

- inventories and questionnaires

- dialogue journals and literature logs

- lists and record cards or sheets

- projects across the curriculum

- other media

T8.8 *Kinds of Data for Assessment*   *Creating Support for Effective Literacy Education* by C. Weaver, L. Gillmeister-Krause, & G. Vento-Zogby, © 1996. Portsmouth, NH: Heinemann. May be copied for transparency use only.
From *Understanding whole language* by Constance Weaver. Portsmouth, NH: Heinemann, 1990.

I WNT TIK
r t w mr
frn .

I went trik or tring
with my frendes.

T8.9   *Child's Spelling Growth (#1, Cory, Dictation)*   *Creating Support for Effective Literacy*
Education by C. Weaver, L. Gillmeister-Krause, & G. Vento-Zogby, © 1996. Portsmouth, NH: Heinemann. May
be copied for transparency use only.
From *Teaching grammar in context* by Constance Weaver. Portsmouth, NH: Boynton/Cook, 1996.

my dad s

hrs   d fs tet

my dad sos horses
and fis teth.

T8.10 *Child's Spelling Growth (#2, Cory, Dictation)* *Creating Support for Effective Literacy Education* by C. Weaver, L. Gillmeister-Krause, & G. Vento-Zogby, © 1996. Portsmouth, NH: Heinemann. May be copied for transparency use only.

T8.11   *Emergent Writing: Incipient Stage (#1)*   *Creating Support for Effective Literacy Education*
by C. Weaver, L. Gillmeister-Krause, & G. Vento-Zogby, © 1996. Portsmouth, NH: Heinemann. May be copied
for transparency use only.

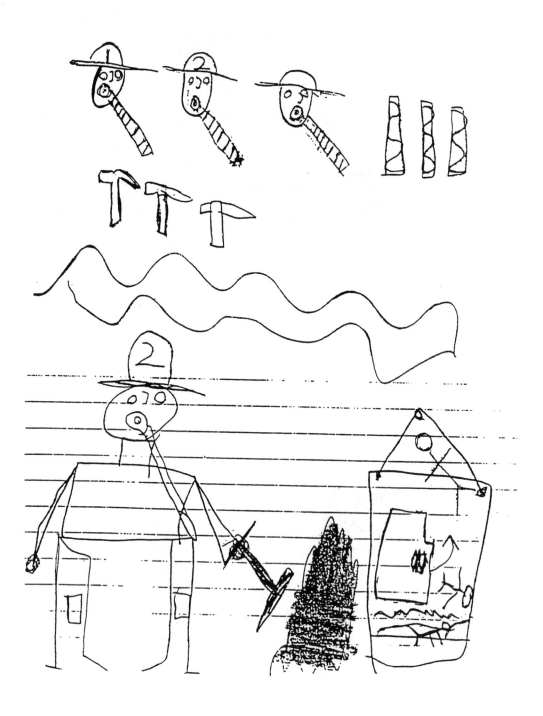

119.5 MOK.8SRS.9065

T8.12   *Emergent Writing: Incipient Stage (#2)*   *Creating Support for Effective Literacy Education*
by C. Weaver, L. Gillmeister-Krause, & G. Vento-Zogby, © 1996. Portsmouth, NH: Heinemann. May be copied
for transparency use only.

T8.13 *Emergent Writing: Approximate Stage (#3)*   *Creating Support for Effective Literacy*

I read good books
evry day.
I redd with my
techer.
I am d very good
readr.

Education by C. Weaver, L. Gillmeister-Krause, & G. Vento-Zogby, © 1996. Portsmouth, NH: Heinemann. May be copied for transparency use only.

Writers' Hints

1. To make the reader want to read on, you must have an interesting lead that "grabs" the reader: "... 'cause you never get a second chance to make a first impression."

2. Use vivid language. Show, don't tell. Have the reader feel the emotion. "It doesn't get any better than this."

3. Describe the character(s) so the reader will know him or her well. "100%, UH HUH."

4. Create a problem. "It does a body (of writing) good."

5. Keep the reader in suspense by using cliffhangers. "Gotta have it."

6. Twist the plot. Sometimes reality isn't everything. "MM, MM, Good!"

7. Use dialogue. "Just do it!"

8. Use real actions to make the readers feel like the story is happening around them. They're "in" the piece. "If it's out there, it's in here."

9. Use your imagination. "When you believe in magic, and I hope you do, you'll always have a friend with big red shoes."

10. Have a good conclusion. "That's all, folks!"

11. Proofread your story for content and mechanical errors: "... makin' it great!!!"

12. Use run on sentences ... NOT! "They just keep going and going."

13. When you finish a piece, get moving on a new one: "... 'cause no one can write just one."

We love to write and it shows!

T8.16 *Writers' Hints* *Creating Support for Effective Literacy Education* by C. Weaver, L. Gillmeister-Krause, & G. Vento-Zogby, © 1996. Portsmouth, NH: Heinemann. May be copied for transparency use only. Written by Ms. LaFache's fifth graders, Sauquoit Valley Elementary

Fliers, Letters, Brochures, and Fact Sheets

Part Two contains fliers, letters, and brochures that are especially designed for sharing with parents. The brochures and fact sheets should help not only parents but colleagues, administrators, and the public understand the nature and the values of an emergent literacy approach to reading and writing.

In some cases there is considerable overlap. For example, a flier on one side of a sheet of paper may include approximately the same material as a two-sided brochure on the same topic. In some instances, there are more detailed and simpler versions of the same brochure. We realize that even the simpler materials will be too detailed for some audiences. You might find it useful to record just a few points on a tape and to loan the tape and tape recorder to some parents. Feel free also to develop your own fliers, letters, and brochures by drawing upon what we have developed. A credit line would be appreciated, though, if you've drawn significantly from our materials. We would welcome any contributions you might offer for a possible second edition of this book.

Because the materials in Part Two were intended to be copied and distributed as needed, they are not paginated.

Fliers

This section contains six fliers that can be copied on one side of a sheet and shared with parents. The fliers are:

Readers' rights

Writers' rights

Hints for getting your child to read

How to help your child learn phonics

Observing and guiding your child's reading growth

How to help your child become a writer

The fliers on helping your child learn phonics and on helping your child become a writer are almost identical to brochures included here; it's mostly the format that differs.

Letters

The sample letters are as follows:

On teaching children to read

On teaching children to write

On spelling for parents of primary children

On spelling for parents of intermediate children

The letter on reading is a generic letter reflecting some of the literacy-related activities that occur in many primary-grade classrooms, especially kindergarten and first grade. The letter on teaching children to write was drafted by Lorraine, who based it on her own teaching in her one-room schoolhouse, Soulanges Elementary. It describes many activities that help children become writers, even in the primary grades. The letters on spelling were drafted by Grace, who has described some practices current in her elementary school, Sauquoit Valley Elementary. (You'll notice a significant difference between Lorraine's individualized approach to spelling and the word lists that were developed at Sauquoit; however, the results should be much the same.) Feel free to copy and share these letters if they suit your needs, or to draw from them in drafting your own.

Brochures

The brochures were designed to be copied onto two sides of a sheet and folded into a tri-fold. These brochures can be shared with parents, administrators and school board members, colleagues and preservice teachers; however, they were drafted with parents particularly in mind. The brochures are as follows:

Helping children learn to talk, read, and write

How to help your child become a reader (longer version)

How to help your child become a reader (shorter version)

How to help your child learn phonics (longer version)

How to help your child learn phonics (shorter version)

How will my child learn phonics, spelling, and grammar?

How to help your child become a writer

Why whole language for my child?

Why alternative forms of assessment?

Basal readers and the state of American reading instruction: A call for action (Commission on Reading of the National Council of Teachers of English, 1988–89)

NCTE's position on the teaching of English: Assumptions and practices (NCTE, 1988–89)

Fact sheets

The fact sheets were designed with administrators, school board members, and politicians especially in mind—but of course they can be shared with anyone. Like the brochures, they can be copied onto both sides of a single sheet. The fact sheets are as follows:

On teaching skills in context

On research on the teaching of phonics

On the teaching of phonics

On the teaching of spelling

On the teaching of grammar

On the nature of whole language education

On myths about whole language education

On phonics in whole language classrooms

On research on whole language education

On standardized tests and assessment alternatives

On student achievement in our public schools

On student achievement in our public schools: SAT scores revisited

Readers' Rights

As Readers, Children Should Have the Right

- to choose kinds of reading material that interest them

- to choose something of interest even if it's relatively difficult

- to read a book without afterwards having to create a diorama, mural, summary, sequel, story web, or other project

- not to write a journal entry after each and every day's reading

- not to finish a book if it doesn't hold their interest

- to read a book again and again and again

- to read a book for their own purposes, in their own way

- not to look up vocabulary words before they begin reading

- to skip words and go on reading for meaning

- to share with others a book they're excited about

- to check out an unlimited number of books from the library

- to read for the love of it

Creating Support for Effective Literacy Education by C. Weaver, L. Gillmeister-Krause, & G. Vento-Zogby, © 1996. Portsmouth, NH: Heinemann. May be copied.

Writers' Rights

As Writers, Children Should Have the Right

- to write about topics that interest them

- to abandon a piece if it doesn't hold their interest

- to return to a piece again and again and again

- to write for their own purposes, in their own way

- to write in genres other than the narrative

- not to have to "get it right" in the first draft

- not to have their writing marked up with corrections but to have help revising and editing pieces they want to publish

- not to have to write "spelling words" ten times

- to collaborate with other writers

- to share with others a piece they're excited about

- to write for the love of it

Creating Support for Effective Literacy Education by C. Weaver, L. Gillmeister-Krause, & G. Vento-Zogby, © 1996. Portsmouth, NH: Heinemann. May be copied.

Hints for Getting Your Child to Read

- Read aloud, even to older children.

- Read aloud *with* your child, taking turns.

- Take your child to the library to obtain a card. Then, make regular visits to the library.

- Don't let anyone convince you that your child needs an expensive program to learn to read. No program is a quick fix, and many commercial programs and most workbooks can bore children and turn them off to reading.

- If you want to help your child learn letter/sound relationships, you might, for instance, read Dr. Seuss books with your child and notice some of the letter/sound clusters as you enjoy the books together.

- Consider obtaining books on tape (book-tape combinations)—from the library, a bookstore, or a children's book club.

- Don't assume that books put onto a computer program will necessarily help your child read, because some are only trivially interactive and debase the literature. If possible, preview before you buy.

- Encourage your child to watch television programs based on children's books, and to compare them with the books. PBS has several such programs.

- Invite your child to tell you about what he or she is reading, but don't grill your child on the content. Encourage informal sharing instead.

- Get caught reading. Let your child see *you* reading something for enjoyment.

- Share what you yourself are reading for pleasure or information.

- Don't ask your child if a book he or she has selected is too hard, and don't worry about the child not being able to read all the words. You might, however, volunteer to read part of the book to or with the child.

- Don't insist that your child read aloud if the child is uncomfortable doing so.

- Have a go-to-bed-with-a-book policy. Let the child read for half an hour after going to bed. If there isn't a light near your child's bed, provide a special reading light.

- Don't bribe a child to read, or reward a child for the number of books he or she has read; reading should be its own reward.

- Don't punish your child or remove privileges if your child does not read. Reading should be associated with pleasure, not punishment.

Creating Support for Effective Literacy Education by C. Weaver, L. Gillmeister-Krause, & G. Vento-Zogby, © 1996. Portsmouth, NH: Heinemann. May be copied.

How to Help Your Child Learn Phonics

- Read and reread favorite nursery rhymes to reinforce the sound patterns of the language. Enjoy tongue twisters and other forms of language play together.

- Read aloud to your child every day. This is perhaps the most important thing you can do to help your child become a reader. Rereading and discussing the child's favorite books is especially helpful.

- When your child is already familiar with whatever you are reading aloud, you can run your hand or finger under the words, to help your child associate spoken words with their written forms.

- Read and discuss alphabet books together, and make alphabet books of your own.

- Part of the time, read stories, poems, rhymes, and songs with repeated sounds at the beginnings of words (alliteration) and/or at the ends of words (rhyme). Children may especially enjoy words that sound like what they describe (for instance, *purr, crackle, splash*). They may especially enjoy the book *Noisy Poems*, edited by Jill Bennett.

- When sharing literature that has some interesting sound elements and patterns, discuss them. Focus on consonants at the beginnings of words, and on vowel + consonant combinations, like *-ate, -an, -ast, -est, -ing, -ish, -ight, -ound, -old, -ook*). Together, you and your child might want to make charts of words with the same sound pattern.

- If you and your child put words with the same beginning or ending sound patterns onto strips of paper or cards, your child may enjoy sorting them according to patterns the child notices. These patterns may include but not be limited to the beginning and ending letters and their sounds.

- You can put different beginnings of words on strips of paper or cards, and different endings too (one strip or card for each beginning and ending). Your child may enjoy putting different beginnings and endings together to make words. Be sure to appreciate the nonsense words your child creates, as well as the real words!

- When your child is reading, help your child "think what would make sense here" and then use the first letter or letters of the next word to make a prediction. You can then confirm or correct the word together by looking at the rest of the word.

- Write while your child is watching, and talk about some of the letters and sounds. When your child's own attempts at writing show that he or she is trying to represent sounds, help your child do so. At first, though, don't expect your child to write more than the first sound of most of the words. Be patient and supportive!

Observing and Guiding Your Child's Reading Growth

- Notice whether your child enjoys being read to. **You can help by** informally discussing the words and pictures with the child as you read.

- Notice whether your child reads first and foremost to get meaning. **You can help by** inviting the child to informally tell you about what he or she has read.

- With a beginning reader, notice whether your child is starting to use both meaning and letter/sound knowledge as cues for getting words. **You can help by** first asking "What would make sense?" when your child stops at or struggles with a word, then by helping the child notice especially the first letter(s).

- Notice whether your child has several ways of dealing with problem words, such as checking the picture, thinking what would make sense, looking at letters and parts of words, starting the sentence over and rereading, reading to the end of the sentence and coming back, putting in something else that fits, or just going on. **You can help by** sometimes prompting your child to do one or more of these things, as appropriate.

- Notice if your child's reading has a natural flow. Does it sound like talking, rather than word-calling? **You can help by** reading expressively when you read aloud to your child. Or, you might obtain children's books on tape—from your local library, from a bookstore, or from a children's book club. Your child can listen to a tape while following along in the book.

- Notice if your child will attempt to read a book of interest, even though the book contains many difficult words. **You can help by** encouraging your child to read for meaning, rather than to identify all the words. Most of our vocabulary is learned gradually, by repeatedly encountering words in context.

- Notice whether your child spontaneously talks about books, and notice whether the child seems to understand what he or she has read. **You can help by** asking thoughtful questions.

- Notice whether your child likes to read with and to you. **You can help by** volunteering to read with your child or to listen to the child read—while praising your child's efforts to get words and meaning independently.

- Recognize that your child may have difficulty reading something he or she knows little about. Through discussion, **you can help by** providing background knowledge.

- Notice if your child is reading longer and harder books, and new kinds of books. **You can help by** introducing your child to new kinds of books, while not discouraging current interests.

- Recognize that new kinds of books present new challenges, so your child may at first seem to read less well than before. A step forward in one thing may mean a step backward in something else. **You can help by** praising your child's attempts to grow as a reader.

A great resource for parents is the 1995 edition of Jim Trelease's *The New Read-Aloud Handbook* (New York: Penguin).

Creating Support for Effective Literacy Education by C. Weaver, L. Gillmeister-Krause, & G. Vento-Zogby, © 1996. Portsmouth, NH: Heinemann. May be copied.

How to Help Your Child Become a Writer

- Encourage a young child's scribbles and letterlike symbols, knowing that these demonstrate the beginnings of writing. Just as your child babbled and spoke one-word sentences in the process of becoming a talker, so your child needs to experiment with language in the process of becoming a writer.

- Celebrate your child's efforts. Display your child's writing on the refrigerator; share it with relatives and friends.

- Provide materials for writing, such as pens, markers, crayons, chalkboard and chalk, and various kinds of paper. For older students, provide such aids as a desk lamp, stationery and stamps, a dictionary and thesaurus. Children of all ages may appreciate their own space for writing.

- Help your child notice various forms of writing within the environment: signs, labels, cereal boxes and cookie packages, TV guides, catalogs, newspapers, telephone books, and magazines, as well as books.

- Let your child see you writing frequently: lists, reminders, notes, letters, and the other things you write in your daily life.

- Let your child play with magnetic letters on the refrigerator, making sure the letters are at the child's eye level.

- Encourage friends and relatives to write to your child, and invite and (if needed) help your child to write back.

- Find authentic reasons for your child to write. For example, letters to friends and relatives, thank-you notes, invitations, postcards, lists, and reminders.

- Put notes in your child's lunchbox, in book bags, under pillows, in pockets, on bikes, on the TV, and in other surprising places.

- Talk with your child as he or she prepares to write. Help your child tap into what he or she already knows about the topic.

- Talk with your child about his or her writing, focusing on meaning rather than correctness. Remember that writing is not merely copying. It takes time to become a writer. Meanwhile, focus on what your child *can* do.

- Accept your child's best efforts at writing and spelling.

- Don't make your child "correct" or recopy something he or she has written just for pleasure.

- Spelling and grammar *are* important. However, even professional writers often do not worry about these conventions until they have written down their ideas and played with content and organization. Children need to be allowed to experiment as they attempt to spell and to use words whose spelling they haven't yet mastered. With frequent opportunities to read and with help in developing spelling strategies, your child will become a better and better speller as well as a more fluent writer. With frequent help in revising and editing writing, your child will become a proficient writer who has increasing command of the conventions of writing, too.

Creating Support for Effective Literacy Education by C. Weaver, L. Gillmeister-Krause, & G. Vento-Zogby, © 1996. Portsmouth, NH: Heinemann. May be copied.

Sample Letter on Teaching Children to Read

Dear Parents,

In our classroom, I follow and build upon many of the ways parents have helped children learn to read before coming to school. These and other practices provide a comprehensive reading and writing program. Each of the following activities has many benefits:

- immersing the children in "environmental print," such as signs, labels, notes, written directions, lists of the children's names, morning message, notices, letters, lists, stories, poems, and reports we have composed together
- reading aloud every day; discussing authors and illustrators along with the stories
- listening to books on tape and following along in the text
- shared reading experiences with Big Books and charts, including books and charts the children have composed together
- pointing to words while rereading Big Books and charts together (this helps children learn how print works in English and helps them begin to make associations between spoken words and written words and also between letters and sounds)
- discussing words and letter/sound patterns as part of the shared reading experience
- collaborative activities such as making charts of common words or sound patterns encountered in our reading
- reading and making alphabet books
- oral language play with nursery rhymes, songs, poetry, tongue twisters, and so forth
- independent reading and looking through books (may be done with a partner)
- explicit teaching of reading strategies and skills through demonstrations and other minilessons, usually integrated with daily reading and writing
- guided writing, wherein I help the children compose together (and thereby demonstrate letter/sound correspondences, spelling, conventions of print and punctuation, and the writing process itself)
- encouragement to use approximated spellings as needed to get their ideas down, when writing independently (this promotes phonics knowledge)
- individual opportunities to read to me and to get help with reading strategies as needed

In order to become readers, children need to learn various things, such as how books are read (from front to back, left to right in English); the nature of book language; sight vocabulary; letter/sound relationships; word attack skills; strategies for processing texts; conventions of punctuation and intonation patterns in reading aloud; new grammatical structures and common ways texts are structured; how to draw inferences, analyze meanings, think critically about texts, and so forth. In addition, children benefit from exposure to a variety of genres: songs, poetry, pattern books and other predictable books, folktales, biographies, and informational texts of various kinds. Most important, in order to become good readers, children need to find pleasure and satisfaction in reading. The various reading and writing activities in my classroom contribute to all these goals. Children's progress is documented through observation, periodic analysis of their reading strategies, and records of their reading interests and what they have read.

If you would like to know more about my reading and writing program, please feel free to contact me at any time.

Sincerely,

Creating Support for Effective Literacy Education by C. Weaver, L. Gillmeister-Krause, & G. Vento-Zogby, © 1996. Portsmouth, NH: Heinemann. May be copied.

Sample Letter on Teaching Children to Write

Dear Parents,

The following should help you understand how I teach writing. In our classroom children are engaged in many experiences that enable them to learn the art and craft of writing—experiences that enable them to become writers.

First, children are taught the natural uses of writing: that writing is simply another way of communicating with one another. As the children come into the classroom each day, they sign in on a sheet that is posted for that purpose. This encourages them to write their name and experiment with various sign systems. Sometimes they print, sometimes they draw, sometimes they experiment with cursive writing, but always they use writing to announce that they are in the school.

The children are encouraged to use writing in all facets of record keeping and communicating. For example, they run their own library. When checking out books, the children write their name and the titles of books signed out, then file the card in a given place. All books read are then recorded daily in their personal reading log. Another writing task they do during the morning routine is to fill in an agenda of the work they will be required to do that day; this is updated throughout the day. The children who might find this task too difficult for them are helped by other students in the class. It is amazing how quickly each child masters the art of filling in his or her reading log and daily agenda.

My formal writing program is very closely linked to the reading that we do in the classroom and therefore touches upon various genres: for example, lists, notes, signs, letters, cards, poetry, research, and narratives. Initially, the children write in their journal on a daily basis, usually describing or commenting on something that happened to them that day or the day before; these journal entries (or alternative kinds of writing, if parents prefer) are typically shared with the class. Writing for an audience is emphasized and demonstrated right from the beginning. The first rule that we have about writing is that when you have an idea about something that you want to write, we say "Don't get it right: Get it written, *then* get it right." So often when we have wonderful ideas that we want to write about, we become so tied up with getting it right that we forget what it was that we were trying to write! This classroom motto puts content first, without ignoring the conventions of writing.

I encourage children to take risks in their writing with content, spelling, and form. If they show reluctance, I encourage them to try and sometimes to "pretend" they can write. It is amazing what children can do when they try, and they often surprise even themselves when they "pretend." The children have their own computer disks on which they type their writing. What I have found is that when children use this technology, their editing skills develop at an amazing rate and they become very conscious of the importance of editing their writing. Using the computer facilitates editing to such a degree that it actually becomes an enjoyable task for the children, as opposed to the frustrating and time-consuming chore of editing hand-written texts which then must be rewritten in their entirety.

Obviously, spelling is an integral part of this writing program. Each child is responsible for developing his or her own word list throughout the year. Specifically, I supply each child with a recipe box, alphabetized dividers, and blank 3 x 5 index cards on which the children record the words that they want to spell conventionally. The process begins with the child *trying* to write the word on this card. If difficulty is encountered, the rule in the classroom is "Ask three, then ask me."

If none of the three classmates knows for certain how to spell the word, then all four children come to me and we discover together how the word is spelled. At this point, the word goes on a card for each of the four children and is filed in their spelling boxes. This word is also added to the list of spelling words that is kept on their computer disks for further use. Each of the four children is then responsible for spelling this word correctly each time it is used in the child's writing. It's amazing how many words are accumulated by each child in the class. This personal word list is used for spelling tests.

Children are encouraged to use writing in all aspects of their daily activity in the classroom. As this use expands, we work on phonics and grammar too, in the context of writing for meaning. Often, I will teach minilessons to groups of students who have exhibited the need for a particular convention or structural feature of the language. Groups change daily, depending upon the needs of the children. I also encourage students to help other students. This not only helps the student asking for assistance but also helps the students giving assistance. Again and again, I see the truth of the old adage, "You learn it best when you teach it."

In addition to keeping their writing on a computer disk, children keep their writing organized in a writing portfolio that they have personally made from colored cardboard or other material and library mending tape. These portfolios have three pockets that children use in whatever manner suits them best, as long as they can explain their filing system to me. These portfolios are also used by the students to examine the breadth and depth of the writing samples enclosed, as well as other aspects of their growth as writers.

Together we examine various genres of writing and I encourage and insist that over time, children write in as many genres as possible. For keeping track of children's expanding range of genres, even unfinished pieces are kept for reference. In many cases, children will go back and finish an abandoned piece. We say, "Throwing away any writing is like throwing away a piece of one's own history." Therefore, children keep even their tentative and abandoned drafts.

As stated earlier, writing is an integral part of the learning activities in our classroom. Although this brief overview discusses only writing, it is impossible to separate reading, writing, speaking, and listening in the communication process. The focus of the entire curriculum is to continue to learn language by using language to learn.

Sincerely,

Creating Support for Effective Literacy Education by C. Weaver, L. Gillmeister-Krause, & G. Vento-Zogby, © 1996. Portsmouth, NH: Heinemann. May be copied.

Sample Letter on Spelling for Parents of Primary Children

Dear Parents,

This letter is to provide you with information regarding children's spelling development and how I help children in my class develop as spellers. Standard spelling is valued in our society and therefore is an important goal in my classroom.

When children first become aware of the link between letters and sounds, I encourage them to write the sounds they hear. Every day I provide meaningful demonstrations and minilessons involving writing and spelling strategies. As a class we write and spell together, notice spelling patterns in words, develop lists of words we use often in writing, and start using strategies for correcting spelling. With time and guidance and exposure to class poetry, class charts and stories, and literature, children's initial approximate spellings give way more and more to standard spellings, along with approximate spellings of more sophisticated words. I work with each child to encourage continued development as a reader and writer, focusing on spelling in that context.

Research shows that just as children go through stages in learning how to walk and talk, they may go through stages in learning how to spell—particularly if they are encouraged even from the preschool years or kindergarten to write as best they can. Each child is unique in learning to spell, but some landmarks are common:

At the beginning of children's development in spelling, they use letters to represent words, but the letters may not yet represent sounds.

M P g g A ⊦ R ⋈

I am pushing my tractor.

When the child begins to write letters to represent sounds, usually the first sound of each word is represented (mostly consonants).The child may or may not space between words or include other letters.

I M P S

I am playing soccer.

As children become more sophisticated in their spelling development, they may begin representing at least three of the sounds in longer words, including a vowel.

I WNT ⊦IK
r ⊦ W m
frn .

I went trick or treating with my friends.

As children progress still more, their spellings include overgeneralizations of spelling patterns, more sophisticated approximate spellings, and the use of some conventionally spelled words.

Lはsะ n⋅ſ 1
eT my hamburg
cr ม⋅ ⋅Sw੧l o d
my tooth

Last night I ate my hamburger and I swallowed my tooth.

Children in these early stages of spelling development need to be exposed to a wide variety of print. Young children especially benefit from reading favorite selections again and again. Children are greatly influenced by the authors they read. What they read will have a direct impact on what they write—and how they spell.

If you should have any questions, please feel free to contact me at any time.

Sincerely,

Creating Support for Effective Literacy Education by C. Weaver, L. Gillmeister-Krause, & G. Vento-Zogby, © 1996. Portsmouth, NH: Heinemann. May be copied.

Sample Letter on Spelling for Parents of Intermediate Children

Dear Parents,

I would like to share some information regarding your child's spelling program this year.

Spelling is more than the ability to memorize a list of words for Friday's test. We all know someone who could get 100% on a test, only to forget some words by Monday and not be able to spell them correctly on daily writing assignments. Although your child will be required to learn 50 core spelling words during the school year, he or she will also be given many opportunities to practice the process of spelling through daily writing.

Teachers at each grade level have reviewed the 500 most frequently used words in writing. From this list, each grade level has been assigned 30–50 words for the class to learn by the end of the school year. These words are posted in the classroom and are selected for attention when they are misspelled.

In addition to the core list, my spelling program includes:

- Developing in children a respect for conventional spelling and a willingness to spell correctly when the writing is to "go public." I encourage children to first make an attempt at spelling the word, based on their knowledge of phonics and spelling patterns, and with the understanding that they can correct the spelling on their final draft.

- Helping children understand that spelling is a process requiring a range of strategies—and of course helping them develop and use such strategies.

- Helping children develop an interest in and a curiosity about words and their meanings. My students are given opportunities to spell and discuss words in math, science, social studies, and so forth. The class participates in minilessons involving spelling patterns and strategies, including the strategy of using the meanings of some Latin and Greek elements to read and spell words.

- Having my students write on a daily basis in a variety of ways, thus using their spelling skills in authentic situations.

- Helping each student view himself or herself as a speller. Spelling should not be embarrassing or intimidating to a child. I adjust my expectations of correct spelling to the child's level of development. Because spelling is developmental, some children are not able to spell as accurately as others. Therefore, I may ask children to correct only a percentage of the misspelled words in a piece of writing. When a child feels overwhelmed by having to correct every error, the child may simply use less sophisticated vocabulary or, worse, develop negative attitudes toward writing and have no motivation to spell correctly.

If you should have any questions, please feel free to contact me at any time.

Sincerely,

Creating Support for Effective Literacy Education by C. Weaver, L. Gillmeister-Krause, & G. Vento-Zogby, © 1996. Portsmouth, NH: Heinemann. May be copied.

Helping Children Learn to Talk, Read, and Write

Have you ever thought about how we "teach" babies and toddlers to speak? We adults do not directly teach our babies and toddlers the structure of our language, but we do various things that help. We can help children learn to read and write in similar ways.

Learning to talk

Of course, learning to talk involves more than just learning words. It involves learning the grammar and the sound system of the language, learning various functions of language, and learning language appropriate to various situations and listeners. Yet few of these things are taught directly.

Here are some of the ways we adults help youngsters learn their native language.

- We model adult language. Most of the time we do not utter isolated sounds, or words that are not clear from context. Usually we use meaningful, "whole" language when we speak to or in the presence of our children.

- We provide an emotionally safe environment for taking risks. That is, we don't scold or punish youngsters for not yet

- We expect the child to eventually succeed at writing like an adult, and therefore we don't worry prematurely about adult correctness. For instance, we know that with help in developing spelling competence and strategies, most children will learn to spell reasonably well and to correct their misspellings as needed. Similarly, and with help in learning to edit their writing, most children will eventually be able to write and to edit their writing according to accepted conventions.

Resources on learning to read and write

Barron, M. 1990. *I learn to read and write the way I learn to talk: A very first book about whole language.* Richard C. Owen. Also available in Spanish.

Clay, M. M. 1987. *Writing begins at home.* Heinemann.

Doake, D. 1988. *Reading begins at birth.* Scholastic.

Fields, M. F. 1988. Talking and writing: Explaining the whole language approach to parents. *The Reading Teacher,* May 1988.

Laminack, L. 1991. *Learning with Zachary.* Scholastic.

Newman, J. M. 1984. *The craft of children's writing.* Scholastic Canada & Heinemann.

Villiers, U. 1989. *Luk Mume luk Dade I kan rite.* Scholastic. Also available in Spanish.

Prepared for the Michigan English Language Arts Framework project and © 1995 by Constance Weaver. In C. Weaver, L. Gillmeister-Krause, & G. Vento-Zogby, *Creating Support for Effective Literacy Education* (Heinemann, 1996). May be copied for distribution.

speaking like adults. In fact, we often greet children's early efforts with great joy and excitement.

- We typically respond to the child's meaning instead of correcting the emergent speaker's pronunciation or grammar.

- We "teach" the language partly by naming objects, but mostly by speaking. We respond to what the child says, and we may expand the child's utterances. If the child says "More" we may ask, "You want more? Sure, you can have more juice." We demonstrate how to make the meaning clear with words alone.

- We expect that children will eventually learn to talk like adults. Because we assume that "of course" our children will learn to talk, we don't worry about childish grammar and pronunciation or bother correcting them—unless the child's language development seems delayed well beyond that of most peers.

- Basically, we give children the time and the opportunity to learn the rules of the language for themselves, based on what they hear and the context that clarifies what we adults say.

In short, we support children in their efforts to communicate, and most of them learn to speak like adults without any direct instruction, other than the naming of objects.

Learning to read

Of course, a child who can already communicate through spoken language does not necessarily have the same need and drive for learning to read and write as the child had for learning to talk. We adults can help create that drive, though. And, as research has clearly demonstrated, we can help children learn to read and write in ways similar to how we helped them learn to talk. Here are some of the ways we adults help children learn to read.

- We read in children's presence, thereby modeling what it is to be a reader.

- We read to children—sometimes even before they are born.

- We read books with whole, natural language. Many of these books may have simple but patterned language.

- We respond positively to the children's early attempts. At first, a child may retell a favorite story from the pictures and remembered words. Or, the child may "read" a story mostly from memory, rather than by looking at the print. We help children on their reading journey by encouraging and praising such efforts, rather than by dismissing them as "not really reading."

- We provide an emotionally safe environment for taking risks. For example, we respond positively to the child's efforts to make meaning, instead of trying to get the child to identify all the words on the page.

- We support the child in reading. For example, we help the child figure out words and demonstrate ways of dealing with problem words independently.

- We expect the child to succeed at reading, rather than to fail.

Learning to write

In similar ways, we adults help children learn to write.

- We write in the children's presence: by making lists, writing notes and memos and letters, and so forth. By so doing, we model what it is to be a writer.

- We provide an emotionally safe environment for taking risks as a writer. For instance, we encourage children's scribbles, their attempts to communicate by making letter-like shapes, their use of just some of the letters to represent the sounds they hear in words, and so forth.

- We support children in their writing. For instance, we can help beginning writers decide what letters to use to represent the sounds they hear in words.

How to Help Your Child Become a Reader

When we suggest helping your child become a reader, we mean helping your child become not only someone who *can* read, but also someone who *likes* to read and who *does* read, for his or her own purposes and pleasure. We mean a lifetime reader.

Many of these suggestions are relevant for children of all ages and reading ability. Others are particularly relevant for the emergent reader.

1. Let your child see you reading and writing, every day. When you yourself are a reader and writer, you provide a powerful model for your child.

2. Read aloud to your child every day. Point to pictures and ask "What's this?" Invite your child to predict what's going to happen next. Discuss the meanings of the story. Reading and discussing books together is one of the most important things you can do for your child. With children who are not yet confident readers, you can take turns reading every other page. With more proficient readers, you can both read the book and simply discuss it together. Sharing books creates a bond—between parent and child, and between children and books.

3. Take your child to the library often, and/or buy books for your child if you can.

Readings & resources for parents

Laminack, Lester. 1991. *Learning with Zachary.* Scholastic. A wonderfully insightful book for parents of preschoolers and primary-grade children.

Kobrin, Beverly. 1988. *Eyeopeners! How to choose and use children's books about real people, places, and things.* Penguin.

Oppenheim, J., Brenner, B., & Boegehold, B. D. 1986. *Choosing books for kids: How to choose the right book for the right child at the right time.* Annotated bibliographies. Ballantine.

Trelease, Jim. 1995. *The new read-aloud handbook* (2nd ed.). Penguin. Includes annotated bibliographies.

Prepared for the Michigan English Language Arts Framework project and © 1995. In C. Weaver, L. Gillmeister-Krause, & G. Vento-Zogby, *Creating Support for Effective Literacy Education* (Heinemann, 1996). May be copied for distribution.

14. When the child makes a lot of miscues that don't make sense in context, it may help to stop the child occasionally at the end of the paragraph or sentence, recall the error, and ask "Did that make sense?" (Or, if the miscue made the sentence ungrammatical, ask "Did that sound right?") Letting the child first read to the end of the sentence or the paragraph allows the child to notice miscues independently, while going back to a meaningless and/or ungrammatical miscue helps the child develop an important reading strategy. But you shouldn't do this with every miscue, since that may convince the child that he or she can't read without someone present to help.

15. Especially with independent readers, it can be helpful to reflect upon the strategies you yourself use in dealing with problem words, and to share these strategies with your child. Do you use context and meaningful word parts? Do you reread, or read on? Do you skip words that don't seem critical to the meaning? Sharing your own strategies with your child can significantly help him or her become more proficient as a reader.

16. To help an emergent reader become an independent reader, it is important to encourage the child to read by himself or herself, every day—without anyone listening. Of course, daily reading is very important for independent readers, too.

17. Surround your child with reading materials—not only books, but also magazines, newspapers, and catalogs. Help your child learn to use reference materials, such as telephone books.

18. Writing promotes reading too, so encourage your child not only to read but to WRITE.

19. Don't pressure your child about reading, because you may turn the child off to reading. Make sure the experience of reading together is enjoyable for you both.

Your emergent reader will benefit from listening to a book on tape and following along with the text, so purchase or create such tapes if possible. Independent readers will often enjoy such tape-plus-book combinations, too.

4. Help an emergent reader notice the print in your environment—lists, logos, signs, labels, and so forth. If your child does not yet recognize letters, encourage him or her simply to "read" such labels and signs by telling what they might mean. Later, when appropriate, help your child use context and initial letters to begin to read words (for example, to read *Women* and *Men* on restroom doors).

5. When your emergent reader is familiar with a book or other text you are reading, you can encourage the child to "read" the story by turning the pages and using the pictures and memory to retell the story. With unfamiliar books, invite your child to predict the story from the pictures.

6. To help your emergent reader associate spoken words with written words, you can point out some of the more interesting words and begin asking "What's this word?" after you have read and enjoyed the selection together. You can also run your hand or finger under the words as you reread familiar texts.

7. Look through a new picture book with your child. Discuss the story line and illustrations before having your child read it the first time. Your child will be more successful if you preview the book and/or read it to your child first.

8. Part of the time, make sure you read stories, poems, rhymes, and songs with repeated sounds at the beginnings of the words (alliteration) and/or at the ends of words (rhyme). Invite your child to notice these patterns. You might even make lists of some words that begin or end the same, or put such words on slips of paper or cards that can be resorted by the child.

9. Some discussion of letter/sound patterns and activities involving them may be useful to a child who has already learned that print provides enjoyment and information. (See the related brochure "How to Help Your Child Learn Phonics.") However, keep in mind that the most important part of reading is making sense. If you focus too much on phonics, your child may think that reading means sounding out words rather than enjoying and getting meaning from texts.

10. Help your child develop the important reading strategy of predicting, and focus on phonics at the same time. In a text you've read together, find a word that is especially predictable. Cover the word (your finger or a Post-It should do nicely) and invite your child to predict what word(s) would fit there. Then uncover the first letter(s) of that word, and ask your child which word(s) would fit now. Finally, uncover the whole word and examine it together, to confirm (or correct) the child's prediction.

11. Remember to praise what your child can do. Accept his or her errors. When your child makes an error (a "miscue") in reading, allow your child to continue reading to see if he or she corrects the miscue without your help. When the miscue doesn't change the meaning significantly, it is often best to let the child continue without interrupting.

12. In any case, don't be too quick to supply the word when your child miscues. If the context looks helpful, ask the child what would make sense there. *Then* you might help your child sound out the word—not letter-by-letter, but in pronounceable chunks. This will help your child develop important reading strategies.

13. When your child comes to an unknown word and stops, try using prompts that will teach the child good reading strategies. The first three prompts below are intended to be used in order, one after the other.

- Look at the picture and see if that helps. (*For beginning readers.*)

- Think, what would make sense here?

- *For beginning readers . . .*
  Look at the first letter (or letters).
  What word would fit here?

  For independent readers . . .
  Try to sound out the word in chunks.
  And/or
  See if you can figure out what the parts of the word mean.

- Back up to here (*point with your finger*) and try it again.

- Read to the end of the sentence and see if that gives you a clue.

- Does the sentence make sense without the word? If it does, then just go on.

- Put in a word that makes sense, and go on.

It is important to help your child develop good reading strategies by offering such prompts—sometimes. But don't make your child struggle to correct every miscue that disrupts meaning. Just supply the word and let the reader go on.

How to Help Your Child Become a Reader

When we suggest helping your child become a reader, we mean helping your child become not only someone who *can* read, but also someone who *likes* to read and who *does* read, for his or her own purposes and pleasure.

Many of these suggestions are relevant for children of all ages and reading ability. Others are particularly relevant for the emergent reader.

1. Let your child see you reading and writing, every day. When you yourself are a reader and writer, you provide a powerful model for your child.

2. Read aloud to your child every day. Point to pictures and ask "What's this?" Invite your child to predict what's going to happen next. Discuss the meanings of the story. Reading and discussing books together is one of the most important things you can do for your child. With children who are not yet confident readers, you can take turns reading every other page. With more proficient readers, you can both read the book and simply discuss it together.

you reread, or read on? Do you skip words that don't seem critical to the meaning? Sharing your own strategies with your child can significantly help him or her become more proficient as a reader.

16. To help an emergent reader become an independent reader, it is important to encourage the child to read by himself or herself, every day—without anyone listening. Of course, daily reading is very important for independent readers, too.

17. Surround your child with reading materials—not only books, but also magazines, newspapers, and catalogs. Help your child learn to use reference materials, such as telephone books.

18. Writing promotes reading too, so encourage your child not only to read but to WRITE.

19. Don't pressure your child about reading, because you may turn the child off to reading. Make sure the experience of reading together is enjoyable for you both.

Readings & resources for parents

Laminack, Lester. 1991. *Learning with Zachary*. Scholastic. A wonderfully insightful book for parents of preschoolers and primary grade children.

Kobrin, Beverly. 1988. *Eyeopeners! How to choose and use children's books about real people, places, and things*. Penguin.

Oppenheim, J., Brenner, B., & Boegehold, B. D. 1986. *Choosing books for kids: How to choose the right book for the right child at the right time*. Annotated bibliographies. Ballantine.

Trelease, Jim. 1995. *The new read-aloud handbook* (2nd ed.). Penguin. Includes annotated bibliographies.

Prepared for the Michigan English Language Arts Framework project and © 1995. In C. Weaver, L. Gillmeister-Krause, & G. Vento-Zogby, *Creating Support for Effective Literacy Education* (Heinemann, 1996). May be copied for distribution.

Sharing books creates a bond—between parent and child, and between children and books.

3. Take your child to the library often, and/or buy books for your child if you can. Your emergent reader will benefit from listening to a book on tape and following along with the text, so purchase or create such tapes if possible. Independent readers will often enjoy such tape-plus-book combinations, too.

4. Help an emergent reader notice the print in your environment—lists, logos, signs, labels, and so forth. If your child does not yet recognize letters, encourage him or her simply to "read" such labels and signs by telling what they might mean. Later, when appropriate, help your child use context and initial letters to begin to read words (for example, to read *Women* and *Men* on restroom doors).

5. When your emergent reader is familiar with a book or other text you are reading, you can encourage the child to "read" the story by turning the pages and using the pictures and memory to retell the story. With unfamiliar books, invite your child to predict the story from the pictures.

6. To help your emergent reader associate spoken words with written words, you can point out some of the more interesting words and begin asking "What's this word?" after you have read and enjoyed the selection together. You can also run your hand or finger under the words as you reread familiar texts.

7. Look through a new picture book with your child. Discuss the story line and illustrations before having your child read it the first time. Your child will be more successful if you preview the book and/or read it to your child first.

8. Part of the time, make sure you read stories, poems, rhymes, and songs with repeated sounds at the beginnings of the words (alliteration) and/or at the ends of words (rhyme). Invite your child to notice these patterns. You might even make lists together of some words that begin or end the same, or put such words on slips of paper or cards that can be resorted by the child.

9. Keep in mind that the most important part of reading is making sense. If you focus too much on phonics, your child may think that reading means sounding out words rather than enjoying and getting meaning from texts.

10. Help your child develop the important reading strategy of predicting, and focus on phonics at the same time. In a text you've read together, find a word that is especially predictable. Cover the word (your finger or a Post-It should do nicely) and invite your child to predict what word(s) would fit there. Then uncover the first letter(s) of that word, and ask your child which word(s) would fit now. Finally, uncover the whole word and examine it together, to confirm (or correct) the child's prediction.

11. Remember to praise what your child can do. Accept his or her errors. When your child makes an error (a "miscue") in reading, allow your child to continue reading to see if he or she corrects the miscue without your help. When the miscue doesn't change the meaning significantly, it is often best to let the child continue without interrupting.

12. In any case, don't be too quick to supply the word when your child miscues. If the context looks helpful, ask the child what would make sense there. *Then* you might help your child sound out the word—not letter-by-letter, but in pronounceable chunks. This will help your child develop important reading strategies.

13. On the other hand, don't make your child struggle to correct *every* miscue that disrupts meaning. Just supply the word and let the reader go on.

14. When the child makes a lot of miscues that don't make sense in context, it may help to stop the child occasionally at the end of the paragraph or sentence, recall the error, and ask, "Did that make sense?" (Or, if the miscue made the sentence ungrammatical, "Did that sound right?") But you shouldn't do this with every miscue, since that may convince the child that he or she can't read without someone present to help.

15. Especially with independent readers, it can be helpful to reflect upon the strategies you yourself use in dealing with problem words, and to share these strategies with your child. Do you use context and meaningful word parts? Do

How to Help Your Child Learn Phonics

Recent research shows that children do not need a phonics program in order to learn phonics. What they need is adults who will help them make connections between letters and sounds, as they are reading and writing enjoyable, whole texts.

You can help your child by employing some of the same techniques that your child's teacher may be using. Here are some suggestions:

1. Read aloud to your child every day. This is perhaps the most important thing you can do to help your child become a reader. Rereading the child's favorite books is especially helpful.

2. Read and reread favorite nursery rhymes to reinforce the sound patterns of the language. Enjoy tongue twisters and other forms of language play together.

3. When your child is already familiar with a selection you are reading, you can run your hand or finger under the words, to help your child associate spoken words with their written forms.

4. Read and discuss alphabet books together, and make alphabet books of your own. This is extremely valuable in helping your child make the breakthrough to hearing individual sounds.

Books that emphasize sound

Aardema, Verna. 1981. *Bringing the rain to Kapiti plain.* Illus. Beatriz Vidal. Dial.

Bennett, Jill, editor. 1987. *Noisy poems.* Illus. Nick Sharratt. Oxford Univ. Press.

Brown, Marc. 1985. *Hand rhymes.* Puffin.

Cameron, Polly. 1961. *"I can't" said the ant.* Scholastic.

Dunrea, Olivier. 1989. *Deep down underground.* Macmillan.

Lee, Dennis. 1983. *Jelly belly: Original nursery rhymes.* Illus. Juan Wijngaard. Bedrick/ Blackie.

McMillan, Bruce. 1990. *One sun: A book of terse verse.* Holiday House.

Obligado, Lilian. 1983. *Faint frogs feeling feverish, and other terrifically tantalyzing tongue twisters.* Puffin.

Many of the poems by Jack Prelutsky and by Shel Silverstein.

Books by Dr. Seuss.

Prepared for the Michigan English Language Arts Framework project and © 1995 by Constance Weaver. In C. Weaver, L. Gillmeister-Krause, & G. Vento-Zogby, *Creating Support for Effective Literacy Education* (Heinemann, 1996). May be copied for distribution.

Alphabet books: A sampling

Anno, Mitsumasa. 1975. *Anno's alphabet: An adventure in imagination.* Harper.

Base, Graeme. 1986. *Animalia.* Harry Abrams.

Boynton, Sandra. 1987. *A is for angry: An animal and adjective alphabet.* 2nd ed. Workman.

Ehlert, Lois. 1989. *Eating the alphabet: Fruits & vegetables from A to Z.* Harcourt.

Feelings, Muriel. 1974. *Jambo means hello: Swahili alphabet book.* Illus. Tom Feelings. Dial.

Lear, Edward. *Edward Lear's ABC: Alphabet rhymes for children.* Illus. Carol Pike. Salem House.

Lobel, Arnold. 1981. *On Market Street.* Illus. Anita Lobel. Mulberry Books.

Pallotta, Jerry. 1986. *The icky bug alphabet book.* Illus. Ralph Masiello. Charlesbridge.

Van Allsburg, Chris. 1987. *The Z was zapped: A play in twenty-six acts.* Houghton Mifflin.

Wood, Jakki. 1993. *Animal parade.* Bradbury.

For parents

Laminack, Lester. 1991. *Learning with Zachary.* Scholastic.

5. Part of the time, make sure you read stories, poems, rhymes, and songs with repeated sounds at the beginnings of words (alliteration) and/or at the ends of words (rhyme). Children may especially enjoy words that sound like what they describe (for instance, *purr, crackle, splash*).

6. When sharing literature that has some interesting sound elements, discuss them. Research shows that at first, it is much more difficult for children to hear all the separate sounds in words than to hear, as units, the beginning of syllables (the "onsets") and also the middle-plus-end of syllables (the "rimes"). Examples of onsets: *s-* as in *sit*, but also *spl-* as in *split*. Examples of rimes: *-ate, -an, -ast, -est, -ing, -ish, -ist, -ight, -ound, -old, -ook*). It's easier for the child if you do not focus on vowel sounds by themselves.

7. When discussing onsets and rimes, you might invite your child first to tell what he or she notices about the sounds in the text, before sharing what you have noticed. Ask questions like "What do you notice about the sounds in this poem (or, on this page)?"

8. You and your child may want to make charts of words with the same sound pattern—the same onset, for instance, or the same rime. If you write these words on strips of paper or cards, your child may enjoy reclassifying them according to various principles, including beginning and ending sounds.

9. You can put different onsets and rimes on strips of paper or cards and see if your child enjoys putting different combinations together to make words—real words, and nonsense words, too!

10. Help your child develop the important reading strategy of predicting, and focus on phonics at the same time. In a text you've read together, find a word that is especially predictable. Cover the word (your finger or a Post-It should do nicely) and invite your child to predict what words would fit there. Then uncover the first letter(s) of that word, and ask your child which word(s) would fit now. Finally, uncover the whole word and examine it together, to confirm (or correct) the child's prediction.

11. Write grocery lists, messages, or reminders to your child and other family members—while the child is watching. Talk about the letters and sounds as you write and review what you've written.

12. Encourage your child to write the best he or she can—even if your child's early writing consists of scribbles or random marks and letters. When your child's writing shows that he or she is trying to represent sounds, help your child do so. At first, don't expect your child to write more than the first sound of words. Next, your child will likely write the first and last sounds. Gradually, as your child becomes more and more familiar with print, more of the sounds in a word will be represented, including vowel sounds. Writing the sounds they hear helps children learn phonics.

13. Write the names of family members and friends on strips of paper or cards and do various activities with them. For instance, examine a set of names like *Joey, Jennifer, Jean*. They have the same first letter, but what about the second letters? The third?

14. Call your child's attention to print in stores, on street signs—everywhere. Help your child use beginning letters as cues to meaning (in words like *women, men*).

15. If possible, provide tape recordings of some books your child has, so that the child can listen to a tape and read along in the book. This helps your child internalize many letter/sound patterns unconsciously, just as your child learned to use the grammar of our language without direct instruction in the rules.

16. Keep in mind that the most important part of reading is making sense. If you read with your child daily and keep attention focused on enjoying the text, some attention to phonics is likely to help your child become an independent reader. But if you only try to teach phonics, your child may think that reading means sounding out words rather than enjoying and getting meaning from texts.

17. When your child makes an error in reading, don't be too quick to supply the word. If the context looks helpful, ask the child what would make sense there. *Then* help your child sound out the word, not letter-by-letter but in pronounceable chunks. This helps your child develop an important strategy for reading.

How to Help
Your Child Learn
Phonics

- Read aloud to your child every day. This is perhaps the most important thing you can do to help your child become a reader. Rereading the child's favorite books is especially helpful.

- Read and reread favorite nursery rhymes to reinforce sound patterns of the language. Enjoy tongue twisters and other forms of language play together.

- When your child is already familiar with whatever you are reading aloud, you can run your hand or finger under the words, to help your child associate spoken words with their written forms.

- Read and discuss alphabet books together, and make alphabet books of your own.

- Part of the time, read stories, poems, rhymes, and songs with repeated sounds

Books that emphasize sound

Aardema, Verna. 1981. *Bringing the rain to Kapiti plain*. Illus. Beatriz Vidal. Dial.

Bennett, Jill, editor. 1987. *Noisy poems*. Illus. Nick Sharratt. Oxford Univ. Press.

Brown, Marc. 1985. *Hand rhymes*. Puffin.

Cameron, Polly. 1961. *"I can't" said the ant*. Scholastic.

Dunrea, Olivier. 1989. *Deep down underground*. Macmillan.

Lee, Dennis. 1983. *Jelly belly: Original nursery rhymes*. Illus. Juan Wijngaard. Bedrick/Blackie.

McMillan, Bruce. 1990. *One sun: A book of terse verse*. Holiday House.

Obligado, Lilian. 1983. *Faint frogs feeling feverish, and other terrifically tantalizing tongue twisters*. Puffin.

Many of the poems by Jack Prelutsky and by Shel Silverstein.

Books by Dr. Seuss.

Prepared for the Michigan English Language Arts Framework project and © 1995 by Constance Weaver. In C. Weaver, L. Gillmeister-Krause, & G. Vento-Zogby, *Creating Support for Effective Literacy Education* (Heinemann, 1996). May be copied for distribution.

- at the beginnings of words (alliteration) and/or at the ends of words (rhyme). Children may especially enjoy words that sound like what they describe (for instance, *purr, crackle, splash*).

- When sharing literature that has some interesting sound elements and patterns, discuss them. Focus on consonants at the beginnings of words, and on vowel + consonant combinations, like *-ate, -an, -ast, -est, -ing, -ish, -ight, -ound, -old, -ook*).

- You and your child might want to make charts of words with the same sound pattern—the same consonant beginnings, for instance, or the same vowel + consonant combinations at the end.

- If you and your child put words with the same beginning or ending sound patterns onto strips of paper or cards, your child may enjoy sorting them according to patterns the child notices. These patterns may include but not be limited to the beginning and ending letters and their sounds.

- You can put different beginnings of words on strips of paper or cards, and different endings too (one strip or card for each beginning and ending). Your child may enjoy putting different beginnings and endings together to make words. Be sure to appreciate the nonsense words your child creates, as well as the real words!

- When your child is reading, help your child "think what would make sense here" and then use the first letter or letters of the next word to make a prediction. You can then confirm or correct the word together by looking at the rest of the word.

- Write while your child is watching, and talk about some of the letters and sounds. When your child's own attempts at writing show that he or she is trying to represent sounds, help your child do so. At first, though, don't expect your child to write more than the first sound of most of the words. Be patient and supportive!

Alphabet books: A sampling

Anno, Mitsumasa. 1975. *Anno's alphabet: An adventure in imagination.* Harper.

Base, Graeme. 1986. *Animalia.* Harry Abrams.

Boynton, Sandra. 1987. *A is for angry: An animal and adjective alphabet.* 2nd ed. Workman.

Ehlert, Lois. 1989. *Eating the alphabet: Fruits & vegetables from A to Z.* Harcourt.

Feelings, Muriel. 1974. *Jambo means hello: Swahili alphabet book.* Illus. Tom Feelings. Dial.

Lear, Edward. *Edward Lear's ABC: Alphabet rhymes for children.* Illus. Carol Pike. Salem House.

Lobel, Arnold. 1981. *On Market Street.* Illus. Anita Lobel. Mulberry Books.

Pallotta, Jerry. 1986. *The icky bug alphabet book.* Illus. Ralph Masiello. Charlesbridge.

Van Allsburg, Chris. 1987. *The Z was zapped: A play in twenty-six acts.* Houghton Mifflin.

Wood, Jakki. 1993. *Animal parade.* Bradbury.

For parents

Laminack, Lester. 1991. *Learning with Zachary.* Scholastic.

How Will My Child Learn Phonics, Spelling, and Grammar?

In an increasing number of today's classrooms, teachers are no longer using separate programs in phonics, spelling, and grammar. Why? Because research shows that for most students, skills taught in isolation do not transfer very well to reading and writing situations. Or in other words, much of the time spent teaching skills in isolation is wasted. Skills are learned and applied better when taught in context.

So how will your child be taught, and learn, skills like phonics, spelling, and grammar? Mostly in conjunction with the reading and writing of whole, authentic, interesting texts.

Phonics

1. In the primary grades especially, your child's teacher will probably read to the class every day. Rereading favorite books, songs, poems, and rhymes is an excellent way to help children learn to read, when the teacher uses texts large enough for all the children in the group or class to see the print. Just running a pointer or finger under the text helps children begin to make associations between spoken words and written words, and even between letter patterns and sound patterns.

7. If spelling tests are given, the words usually include at least some that the children have chosen—especially words from their own writing and reading. The lists may be individualized with and by each child, and children may work in pairs to help each other review and test themselves on the words.

Grammar

Research suggests that by the time your child has entered first grade, he or she will probably be using almost all of the grammatical constructions that adults use in speech—though in simple form, of course. Your child does not need to be taught the rules of grammar in order to use the grammar of the language. On the other hand, teachers can enhance children's command of grammar, particularly as they help the children revise and edit their writing.

1. As children are doing final revisions of their writing, teachers can show them how to combine, expand, and rearrange sentences and sentence elements.

2. As children are editing their writing, teachers can help them learn how to use conventional punctuation, spelling, and grammar appropriate for their audience and purpose.

3. Many teachers will also facilitate children's learning of revision and editing skills through whole class minilessons on selected topics. In addition, teachers give students further help individually or in small groups.

4. Teachers may also engage students in doing sentence-expansion and sentence-revision activities. (Research shows this to be effective, but it may not be any more effective or even as effective as the combination of minilessons and conferences in which the teacher helps children expand and revise their own sentences.)

Phonics, Spelling, and Grammar

Research indicates that one of the best ways you and your child's teacher can foster the learning of phonics, spelling, and more sophisticated aspects of grammar is by providing plenty of materials to read, and plenty of time and encouragement for reading them. Writing is important, too.

Resources for teachers and parents

Mills, Heidi, Tim O'Keefe, & Diane Stephens. 1992. *Looking closely: Exploring the role of phonics in one whole language classroom.* National Council of Teachers of English.

Powell, Debbie, & David Hornsby. 1993. *Learning phonics and spelling in a whole language classroom.* Scholastic. Routman, Regie, & Andrea Butler. 1995. Why talk about phonics? *School Talk, 1* (November). National Council of Teachers of English.

Routman, Regie, & Andrea Butler. 1995. Why talk about phonics? *School Talk, 1* (November). National Council of Teachers of English.

Wagstaff, J. n.d. *Phonics that work! New strategies for the reading/writing classroom.* New York: Scholastic.

Weaver, Constance. 1994. *Reading process and practice: From socio-psycholinguistics to whole language.* Heinemann. (Phonics).

Weaver, Constance. 1996. *Teaching grammar in context.* Boynton/Cook.

Wilde, Sandra. 1992. *You kan red this! Spelling and punctuation for whole language classrooms, K–6.* Heinemann.

Prepared for the Michigan English Language Arts Framework project and © 1995 by Constance Weaver. In C. Weaver, L. Gillmeister-Krause, & G. Vento-Zogby, *Creating Support for Effective Literacy Education* (Heinemann, 1996). May be copied for distribution.

2. To promote the learning of phonics, the teacher may choose some good quality stories, songs, poems, and rhymes that have words beginning and/or ending the same (words that alliterate and/or rhyme). The teacher may invite children to comment on what they notice about the sounds in the text. Together, they may make lists of words that begin the same and words that have the same ending (last and words that have the same ending (last vowel sound plus anything that follows).

3. Various activities may be done with such words. For example, the teacher can write them on strips of paper or cards for the children to sort according to various principles, including beginning and ending sounds. The teacher can also make strips or cards of common beginnings of words (like *s-, st-, str-, ch-, fl-, ph-*) and common endings (like *-ate, -an, -ast, -est, -ing, ish, -ight, -old, -ound, -ook*). Putting beginnings with different endings can be an an enjoyable way for children to typically focus on letter/sound patterns—particularly if nonsense words are acceptable and if the children are allowed to work together.

4. Together the teacher and children may read and discuss alphabet books—and make their own.

5. The teacher may help children simultaneously predict as they read, and use phonics too. One way to do this is to choose a fairly predictable word in a text, cover it, and invite children to predict what words would fit there. Then the first letter or letters are uncovered, and children are asked which words will fit now. Finally, the whole word is uncovered and examined, to confirm (or correct) the predictions.

6. Another important way of helping children learn phonics is through writing. When children's early efforts to write show that they are trying to represent sounds, the teacher will help them learn to do so. At first children usually represent only the first sound of words, then the first and last sounds. Gradually, they represent more and more of the sounds. These sound-spellings give way to conventional spellings as children gain more experience with reading, and as they receive guidance in editing their writing for spelling and in developing spelling strategies and an ever-growing repertoire of words they can spell correctly.

Spelling

1. Your child's teacher will probably encourage children to spell as best they can in first drafts. Not to worry: research shows that children who are encouraged to spell words the best they can when they write typically score as well or better on standardized tests of spelling *by the end of first grade* than children who are allowed to use only correct spellings in first drafts.

2. To encourage children to use all the big and interesting words in their oral vocabularies when they write, the teacher will probably continue to encourage children to "spell the best you can" as they are getting their ideas down on paper. However, teachers help children revise and edit the pieces of writing that they want to have "go public." In this case, the teacher may help the child correct all the spellings, or correct them in a next-to-final draft, as an editor would.

3. In some schools, children are not expected to correct their spelling on final drafts until third or fourth grade. They continue, however, to learn to spell more and more words conventionally.

4. As soon as children's reading has led them to spell a number of words conventionally or almost conventionally, the teacher may begin spelling instruction. The teacher's first concern may be to generate an interest in spelling, and a concern for learning to spell conventionally. For example, the teacher might invite a child to circle two or three words in his or her own writing for which the child would like to be given the conventional spelling. Children may be asked to keep their own filebox of such words, for easy reference and learning.

5. Teachers may teach different kinds of minilessons on spelling. For instance, they may help children brainstorm for words that end the same (like *light, sight, fight, might, night, right*). Or, with older children, they may help the children brainstorm for words with the same Latin or Greek root (for example, the words *manual, manual, manipulative,* and *manuscript* all have the Latin root *manu-,* which means "hand.")

6. In addition to minilessons on spelling itself, the teacher may offer such lessons on *strategies* for spelling and correcting their spellings. Such strategies include: (1) writing the word two or three different ways and deciding which one "looks right"; (2) locating the spelling in a familiar text or in print displayed in the classroom; (3) asking someone, consulting their own word file or dictionary, or using a computer software program or hand-held electronic speller.

How to Help Your Child Become a Writer

Whether your child is just beginning to make marks on paper or is more experienced at writing, there are many things you can help your child develop as a writer. The following list includes several examples.

1. Encourage a young child's scribbles and letterlike symbols, knowing that these demonstrate the beginnings of writing. Just as your child babbled and spoke one-word sentences in the process of becoming a talker, so your child needs to experiment with written language in the process of becoming a writer.

2. Celebrate your child's efforts. Display your child's writing on the refrigerator; share it with relatives and friends.

3. Provide materials for writing, such as pens, markers, crayons, chalkboard

How will I know when my child is making progress at writing?

The following are some questions you might ask as you observe your child and your child's writing:

• Does my child show an interest in writing?

• Does my child write about topics that are meaningful to him or her?

• Does my child experiment with words?

• Does my child enjoy sharing what he or she has written?

• Does my child make connections between books and his or her own writing? Between different pieces of writing? Different drafts of the same piece?

• Does my child frequently choose to write, when given a choice of activities?

• Is my child learning to write in an increasing variety of forms (personal experience, notes, letters, stories, lists, and so forth)?

• Can my child tell me what he or she does well as a writer? Is my child trying to do and learn to do new things as a writer?

References and resources

Barron, Marlene. 1990. *I learn to read and write the way I learn to talk: A very first book about whole language.* Katonah, NY: Richard C. Owen. Also available in Spanish. Illustrates and explains children's early literacy development.

Clay, Marie M. 1987. *Writing begins at home.* Portsmouth, NH: Heinemann. Explains and illustrates children's early writing development.

Laminack, Lester. 1991. *Learning with Zachary.* Richmond Hill, Ontario: Scholastic. Helps parents understand reading and writing development by documenting and discussing Zachary's progress prior to formal schooling.

Villiers, U. 1989. *Luk Mume luk Dade I kan rite.* New York: Scholastic. Also available in a Spanish edition. Illustrates children's writing development in the primary grades.

Prepared for the Michigan English Language Arts Framework project and © 1995. In C. Weaver, L. Gillmeister-Krause, & G. Vento-Zogby, *Creating Support for Effective Literacy Education* (Heinemann, 1996). May be copied for distribution.

and chalk, and various kinds of paper. For older students, provide such aids as a desk lamp, stationery and stamps, a dictionary and thesaurus. Children of all ages may appreciate their own space for writing.

4. Help your child notice various forms of writing within the environment: signs, labels, cereal boxes, cookie packages and candy wrappers, TV guides, catalogs, newspapers, telephone books, and magazines, as well as books.

5. Let your child see you writing frequently: lists, reminders, notes, letters, and the other things you write in your daily life.

6. Let your child see your own struggles with writing: with getting down your ideas, making changes, correcting what you've written.

7. You can sometimes write down what your child wants to say: perhaps a phrase or sentence to go with a picture. Encourage your child to read it back, but remember that at first your child may "read" from memory, and that's okay, for now. Don't let your serving as a secretary become a substitute for your child's writing independently, though, even if the child can only write in scribbles or letterlike marks.

8. You can also write stories featuring your child in the experiences you've shared. Your child can illustrate and you can write the captions. You can accompany photographs with "speech bubbles" for what people say.

9. Let your child play with magnetic letters on the refrigerator, making sure the letters are at the child's eye level.

10. To help a child just beginning to make letter-sound connections, together you can sort pictures of objects that begin with the same letter. Focus on just two letters at a time, perhaps letters in your child's name.

11. Encourage friends and relatives to write to your child. Invite and, if needed, *help* your child to write back.

12. Find authentic reasons for your child to write. For example, letters to friends and relatives, thank-you notes, invitations, postcards, lists, and reminders.

13. Put notes in your child's lunchbox, in book bags, under pillows, in pockets, on bikes, on the TV, and in other surprising places.

14. Talk with your child as he or she prepares to write. Help your child tap into what he or she already knows about the topic.

15. Talk with your child about his or her writing, focusing on meaning rather than correctness. Remember that writing is not merely copying. It takes time to become a writer. Meanwhile, focus on what your child *can* do.

16. Accept your child's best efforts at writing and spelling.

17. Don't make your child "correct" or recopy something he or she has written just for pleasure.

18. Spelling and grammar *are* important. However, even professional writers often do not worry about these conventions until they have written down their ideas and played with content and organization. Children need to be allowed to experiment as they attempt to spell and to use words whose spelling they haven't yet mastered. With frequent opportunities to read and with help in developing spelling strategies, your child will become a better and better speller as well as a more fluent writer. With frequent help in revising and editing writing, your child will become a proficient writer who has increasing command of the conventions of writing, too.

Why Whole Language for My Child?

And what if my child has special needs and/or talents?

Parents who have heard of whole language education may wonder, "Why whole language? What is it, and how could my child benefit?"

Whole language teachers help children read, write, and learn in many of the same ways we as parents helped our children learn to talk. We didn't expect adult perfection right away, but encouraged all their efforts—from babbling to putting words together to make sentences. While ignoring their immature pronunciation and grammar, we guided them by modeling the use of language ourselves, and by responding positively to their efforts to communicate. Sometimes we corrected them for *what* they said, but usually not for how they said it. We knew, intuitively, that our children would achieve adult competence if we continued to model adult language and to encourage them to use language.

Whole language teachers take their cue from how parents have succeeded in helping their children learn to talk. Such teachers try to make learning as meaningful and natural in school as it is outside of school.

learning and success for students of varying needs, abilities, and accomplishments. Theme exploration, especially, promotes collaboration yet allows for individual projects and differences.

11. Thus, children labeled as "gifted" are not held back by having to teach their peers, yet they serve their classmates as wonderful models as they pursue their own projects and learning. Of course, children labeled as "at risk" or "learning disabled" are especially likely to benefit from this modeling. But all children have interests and strengths they can share with one another, in the supportive, collaborative atmosphere of a whole language classroom.

References for teachers and parents

Five, Cora Lee. 1991. *Special voices.* Heinemann.

Goodman, Kenneth. 1986. *What's whole in whole language?* Scholastic in Canada, Heinemann in the U.S.

Lang, Greg, and Chris Berberich. 1995. *All children are special: Creating an inclusive classroom.* Stenhouse.

Routman, R. 1991. *Invitations: Changing as teachers and learners K–12.* Heinemann. Ch. 14 deals with learning disabled students.

Stires, S. , ed. 1991. *With promise: Redefining reading and writing for "special" students.* Heinemann.

Weaver, C. 1990. *Understanding whole language.* Heinemann.

Weaver, C., ed. 1994. *Success at last! Helping students with Attention Deficit (Hyperactivity) Disorders achieve their potential.* Heinemann.

Prepared for the Michigan English Language Framework project and copyright © 1995 by Constance Weaver. In C. Weaver, L. Gillmeister-Krause, & G. Vento-Zogby, *Creating Support for Effective Literacy Education* (Heinemann, 1996). May be copied for distribution.

How else will your child benefit from whole language education?

1. Whole language teachers accept children as they are. This means not only that they accept children who come from different cultural or socioeconomic backgrounds from theirs, but that they do not see labels like "learning disabled" or "at risk" as impediments to learning in their classrooms.

2. Whole language teachers take charge of the curriculum in their classrooms. They deal with the essentials in the curriculum guide, but they make curricular decisions for and with the children. This enables them to build from children's strengths and encourage them to explore their interests.

3. In whole language classrooms, there is flexibility within structure. Instead of having children do one brief activity or worksheet after another, whole language teachers organize the day in larger blocks of time—for readers' and writers' workshop, for example, or for theme study that may continue for several weeks, during at least part of the school day. With larger time blocks, children can pursue bigger, more meaningful projects—with the teacher's guidance and support, of course.

4. Children are expected to succeed in reading and writing whole texts, not in doing skills work on worksheets or in workbooks. It may take children who have not experienced success in school at least a month, or even several months, to write and revise entire pieces, to read entire

books that they have chosen, and to engage in research and in sharing with the class. However, whole language teachers have found that given the *gift of time*, almost all children will succeed in really reading and writing and learning.

5. Skills are taught as they are needed to do real reading, writing, math, science, and so forth. For example, phonics, spelling, and grammar skills are taught mainly in conjunction with the texts that children are reading and writing.

6. In whole language classrooms, the teacher and the children often engage in exploring themes, or topics. Reading and writing and math become a natural part of learning as children pursue topics from social studies and science. The arts are important ways of learning, enabling children to express and share what they have learned.

7. In creating a supportive classroom community, many whole language teachers help children develop skills for interacting with each other, solving interpersonal conflicts and problems, and supporting one another in learning. At the same time, teachers guide children in making the kinds of choices that build character, responsibility, and acceptance of others.

8. Whole language teachers provide "scaffolding" for learning. That is, they teach children how to learn and to do new things, partly by helping and working with them. For example, primary grade teachers may read Big Books and charts to and with children, again and again, thus enabling the

children to read whole texts before they can read independently. By providing such scaffolding for children today, teachers enable them to do things independently tomorrow. Furthermore, the children provide similar support for one another as they collaborate on projects and share their different strengths to help one another.

9. Authentic or "portfolio" assessment is critical in whole language classrooms. While whole language teachers may still have to give standardized tests, they know that these test scores tell little about what and how children are really learning. Therefore, they focus their assessment on what children are doing and learning daily. They document learning through children's projects and other products, but also through recorded observations of their learning processes. They draw upon notes from individual conferences and literature logs. They typically involve children in assessing their learning and growth, and in setting goals for continued progress. Parents may also be involved in assessment. Individual growth and strengths are emphasized, along with progress in meeting agreed-upon goals and predetermined criteria.

10. Whole language teachers work to fit the curriculum to the children. The larger time blocks, with children often working together or independently, free up more time for teachers to attend to children with special needs. The fact that skills are taught in context rather than in isolation, the gift of time to complete significant projects, the scaffolding and the supportive classroom community—all promote

Why Alternative Forms of Assessment?

Parents have always known that tests do not necessarily reveal their children's abilities in their best light. A test is like a snapshot, reflecting what the child did at one moment in time. Even several such snapshots are not as complete a picture as a video: as a portfolio that includes information regarding children's interests, learning processes, and growth, as well as the products that demonstrate achievement.

Though students' work may indeed be kept in a portfolio (or box or other storage item), the key to "portfolio" assessment is the concepts behind it. In addition to providing a broader and deeper collection of data, portfolio or "alternative" assessment reflects other principles. It is ongoing and derives from what is occurring daily in the classroom, instead of being a one-shot assessment on unnatural kinds of tasks. Furthermore, it involves more perspectives: the learner's, the teacher's, and often that of the parents as well.

Teacher-made tests and standardized tests may still be part of the learner's portfolio, but they constitute only a small part of the data assembled and analyzed for each

Teachers may also initiate conferences in which parents are invited to share their own observations about their child's literacy development and needs.

• **Inventories and questionnaires.** These sources of information can help teachers learn about such things as children's interests, their reading and writing habits, how they perceive themselves as readers and writers, what they've read recently, what they've written about, and so forth. Of course, parents may also be invited to respond to questionnaires or to write letters that will help the teacher understand their child.

• **Dialogue journals and literature logs.** Many teachers invite children to write to their teacher or classmates, who then reply in writing. In some instances these dialogue journals are focused on particular topics, such as observations from a science activity or experiment, or a math activity. When such journals deal particularly with literature, they are sometimes called literature logs.

• **Lists and record cards or sheets.** Children may keep lists of books read, or a record sheet on a book they're currently reading—perhaps with each date when they read in the book, and the pages read. Lists of possible topics for writing are also useful, for a teacher conferring with children as well as for the children themselves.

• **Projects across the curriculum.** When children are doing projects to learn about topics from social studies and science and math, there are many opportunities to note the children's progress, the processes by which they work, and so forth—in addition to the final products themselves. (Such projects may not fit conveniently into an actual portfolio, but notes on the products and various aspects of their production can be part of a portfolio file.)

• **Other media.** Sometimes teachers may invite children to demonstrate their understanding of, or reaction to, something they've read. Writing is one way of responding, but so are various forms of art, such as murals, drama, music, and painting. Sometimes teachers may invite students to express something in a totally different symbol system: for example, to characterize an emotion through mathematical symbols or drawings. Often, using other media offers students an opportunity to make connections and to take advantage of different learning strengths, too.

Reference for teachers and parents

Anthony, R. J., Johnson, T. D., Mickelson, N. I., & Preece, A. (1991). *Evaluating literacy: A perspective for change.* Heinemann.

Prepared for the Michigan English Language Arts Framework project and © 1995 by Constance Weaver. In C. Weaver, L. Gillmeister-Krause, & G. Vento-Zogby, *Creating Support for Effective Literacy Education* (Heinemann, 1996). May be copied for distribution.

child. Furthermore, grade placement decisions are based upon a wide range of data, not upon standardized test scores alone.

With respect to literacy, here are some of the questions teachers might ask about a child's development as a reader—questions that in turn will guide the teacher's collection of data for assessment and evaluation:

• Does the reader show an interest in books?

• Does the reader read for meaning?

• Does the reader demonstrate curiosity about words?

• What reading strategies has the reader been observed to use?

• Does the reader spontaneously comment about books read?

• Does the reader spontaneously make connections between books, authors and illustrators, and/or between books and real life?

• Does the reader frequently choose to read, when given a choice of activities?

• Does the reader demonstrate interest in an expanding range of genres?

• Does the reader demonstrate the ability to describe his or her own strengths as a reader and to set goals as a reader?

Of course the teacher may gather other data in addition or instead, but these are some of the kinds of questions common in alternative or "portfolio" assessment.

With respect to writing, here are some similar questions a teacher might ask about a child's development as a writer:

• Does the writer show an interest in writing?

• Does the writer write about topics that are meaningful to him or her?

• Does the writer experiment with words?

• What writing and spelling strategies has the writer been observed to use?

• Does the writer spontaneously share writings?

• Does the writer spontaneously make connections between different pieces and/or drafts of writing, and/or between books and his or her own writing?

• Does the writer frequently choose to write, when given a choice of activities?

• Does the writer demonstrate an expanding range of genres in his or her own writing?

• Does the writer demonstrate the ability to describe his or her own strengths as a writer and to set goals as a writer?

The following are some of the sources that teachers can draw upon in answering questions like these.

• **Periodic performance samples.** For example, this might include periodic tape recordings of the child's reading, with written comments or a detailed analysis. It would surely include samples of the child's writing, too: not only final drafts, but at least some multiple drafts of the same piece. To accompany these samples, both the teacher and the child might include an analysis of the child's strengths and growth, then suggest future goals for reading and writing.

• **Think-alouds.** Some teachers make tape recordings of children talking their way through something they are reading or writing. Listening to the recordings can help teachers and parents understand what strategies the child is using effectively and what strategies the child might need to develop further.

• **Recorded observations.** Records of observations are a critical aspect of authentic or portfolio assessment. The teacher will jot down anything unusual or particularly noteworthy, such as a child suddenly grasping an important concept. In addition to such anecdotal records, teachers systematically observe each child's work at regular intervals and record the observations.

• **Conferences and interviews.** An individual conference can be an opportunity for a teacher to listen to a child read and help the child develop an important reading strategy, or help a child learn an editing concept needed for the child's writing. Conferences and interviews are also valuable for gathering many of the kinds of data listed.

A Statement of the Commission on Reading, National Council of Teachers of English

Basal Readers and the State of American Reading Instruction: A Call to Action

The Problem

As various national studies suggest, the problem of illiteracy, semi-literacy, and aliteracy in the United States appears to be growing, due at least in part to escalating standards of literacy in the workplace and in the civic arena. And at a time when our information-age society demands increased literacy from all citizens, reading instruction is locked into a technology that is more than half a century out-of-date.

Basals: Part of the Problem

There is a significant gap between how reading is learned and how it is taught and assessed in the vast majority of our classrooms today. This gap is perpetuated by the basal reading series that dominate reading instruction in roughly 90 percent of the elementary classrooms in the United States. Such textbook series are often viewed as complete systems for teaching reading, for they include not only a graded series of books for the students to read but teachers'

—provide time for teachers to work with one another to set up innovative programs

• Give teachers the opportunity to demonstrate that standardized test scores will generally not be adversely affected by using alternatives to basal readers, and may in fact be enhanced.

• Provide incentives for teachers to develop and use alternative methods of reading assessment, based upon their understanding of reading and learning to read.

• Allow/encourage teachers to take charge of their own reading instruction, according to their informed professional judgment.

For Policymakers:

• Change laws and regulations that favor or require use of basals, so that

—state funds may be used for nonbasal materials

—schools may use programs that do not have traditional basal components

—teachers cannot be forced to use material they find professionally objectionable.

• Provide incentives to local districts to experiment with alternatives to basals, by

—developing state-level policies that permit districts to use alternatives to basals

—changing teacher education and certification requirements so as to require teachers to demonstrate an understanding of how people read, of how children learn to read, and of ways of developing a reading curriculum without as well as with basals

—mandating periodic curriculum review and revision based upon current theory and research as to how people read and how children learn to read

—developing, or encouraging local districts to develop, alternative means of testing and assessment that are supported by current theory and research in how people read and how children learn to read

—funding experimental programs, research, and methods of assessment based upon current theory and research on reading and learning to read.

Prepared for the Commission on Reading of the National Council of Teachers of English by the present and immediate past directors of the Commission, Connie Weaver and Dorothy Watson, and based on the *Report Card on Basal Readers*, written by Kenneth S. Goodman, Patrick Shannon, Yvonne Freeman, and Sharon Murphy and published by Richard C. Owen, Publishers, 1988. See also the Commission on Reading's Position Statement "Report on Basal Readers"; one copy is free upon request from the National Council of Teachers of English if a self-addressed and stamped envelope is sent with the request. Write NCTE, 1111 Kenyon Road, Urbana, IL 61801.

manuals telling teachers what and how to teach, workbooks and dittos for the students to complete, sets of tests to assess reading skills, and often various supplementary aids. Because of their comprehensiveness, basal reading systems leave very little room for other kinds of reading activities in the schools where they have been adopted. This is all the more unfortunate because current theory and research strongly support such conclusions as the following:

• Basal reading series typically reflect and promote the misconception that reading is necessarily learned from smaller to larger parts.

• The sequencing of skills in a basal reading series exists not because this is how children learn to read but simply because of the logistics of developing a series of lessons that can be taught sequentially, day after day, week after week, year after year.

• Students are typically tested for ability to master the bits and pieces of reading, such as phonics and other word-identification skills, and even comprehension skills. However, there is no evidence that mastering such skills in isolation guarantees the ability to comprehend connected text, or that students who cannot give evidence of such skills in isolation are necessarily unable to comprehend connected text.

• Thus for many if not most children, the typical basal reading series may actually make learning to read more difficult than it needs to be.

• So much time is typically taken up by "instructional" activities (including activities with workbooks and skill sheets) that only a very slight amount of time is spent in actual reading—despite the overwhelming evidence that extensive reading and writing are crucial to the development of literacy.

• Basal reading series typically reflect and promote the widespread misconception that the ability to verbalize an answer, orally or in writing, is evidence of understanding and learning. Thus even students who appear to be learning from a basal reading series are being severely short-changed, for they are being systematically encouraged not to think.

• Basal reading series typically tell teachers exactly what they should do and say while teaching a lesson, thus depriving teachers of the responsibility and authority to make informed professional judgments.

• "Going through the paces" thus becomes the measure of both teaching and learning. The teachers are assumed to have taught well if and only if they have taught the lesson. Students are assumed to have learned if and only if they have given "right" answers.

• *The result of such misconceptions about learning and such rigid control of teacher and student activities is to discourage both teachers and students from thinking, and particularly to discourage students from developing and exercising critical literacy and thinking skills needed to participate fully in a technologically advanced democratic society.*

Recommended Actions for Local Administrators and for Policymakers

For Local Administrators:

• Provide continual district inservice for teachers to help them develop a solid understanding of how people read and how children learn to read and how reading is related to writing and learning to write.

• Provide time and opportunities for teachers to mentor with peers who are trying innovative materials and strategies.

• Support teachers in attending local, regional, state, and national conferences to improve their knowledge base, and support continued college coursework for teachers in reading and writing.

• Allow/encourage teachers to use alternatives to basal readers or to use basal readers flexibly, eliminating whatever their professional judgment deems unnecessary or inappropriate; for example,

—encourage innovation at a school level, offering teachers a choice of basals, portions of basals, or no basal, using assessment measures that match their choice

—discuss at a school level which portions of the basal need not be used, and use the time saved for reading and discussion of real literature

NCTE'S POSITION ON THE TEACHING OF ENGLISH: ASSUMPTIONS AND PRACTICES

Working Paper Developed by the Elementary, Secondary, and College Sections, 1988–89, for Planning and Articulation by Council Constituencies

ENGLISH/LANGUAGE ARTS PRACTICES

In the English/language arts curriculum, students should have guidance and frequent opportunities to:

1. read whole texts in their original versions, sharing written and oral meanings, not simply supplying workbook answers or responses to predetermined questions

2. read texts by authors of diverse backgrounds: e.g., ethnic, racial, gender, age

3. bring their own cultural values, languages, and knowledge to their classroom reading and writing

4. collaborate in writing many whole texts, not answers to exercises

5. read and write different kinds of texts for different readers: personal essays, informative writing, literature, and persuasive writing

6. learn grammar and usage by studying how their own language works in context

7. work with teachers and other students as a community of learners, observing their teachers as readers and writers

8. experience the interaction of reading, speaking, listening, and writing as reasoning and communicating acts

9. have their work assessed by many measures:
   a. portfolios of their writing
   b. extended oral and written responses to reading
   c. essay tests with sufficient time for planning and revising, scored by a variety of means: holistic, primary trait, analytic
   d. records of reading in class and outside class
   e. one-to-one or small group conferences

10. encounter and critique a diversity of print materials—books, signs, posters, brochures, and so forth

11. have their own work shared, displayed, or published

These statements of NCTE's position on the teaching of English are published for planning and articulation by Council constituencies.

Single copies of this statement are free upon request, and may be copied without permission from NCTE. Multiple copies are available at a bulk rate of U.S. $7 per 100, prepaid only. Stock #50837. Send request to NCTE Order Department, 1111 Kenyon Road, Urbana, IL 61801

Knowledge is not information, yet it requires information. Because the world's diverse information base is expanding at a rapid rate, teachers cannot limit their classes to narrow lists of information or sets of readings. Although students use certain resources, they also know that a much larger body of resources exists and that they can gain access to these resources. Individualized, learner-based pedagogy requires that students have access to a variety of texts through libraries and other sources.

Knowledge is more than a mastery of facts and processes. It includes an understanding and use of these facts and processes in historical, social, political, and personal contexts. Students bring substantial knowledge to the classroom. Teachers build on that information.

ASSUMPTIONS ABOUT LANGUAGE

Language is a vital medium for creating individual and social identities. Through language, students make meaning and come to understand and define themselves. Through language, they communicate their sense of the world, function with others, and get things done. Through language, they exercise power over the world.

Students' language is valued and used as a means of learning, change, and growth within the classroom. Students' use of language is a major source of content for the study of language in the classroom. What students write, read, speak, and listen to is what is studied. Paying attention to students' talk about what they are learning, thinking, and feeling, teachers analyze what students can do with language in order to help them learn. Teachers validate students' experiences as sources of language.

The power of language and the rules that it follows are discovered, not invoked. Students know about the power of language to influence. They are able to recognize powerful language and to use it in some contexts. They learn about how language works through systematic analysis of what is said and written. Language instruction is developmental rather than remedial.

Literacy has a wide range of genres and functions, which are important to teachers and learners.

Every person is a learner. It is the nature of everyone to learn: to grow and change through interacting with others and responding to experiences. Learning is not confined to school times. It is ongoing and limited only by the sensory and reflective powers of the learner.

Teachers and students are a community of learners. Learning is a collaborative effort. Teachers are learners—from self and others. Learners are teachers—of self and others. Through genuine interaction, teacher-learners grow and change. Students and teachers build predictable yet fluid structures for interaction. Teachers listen to and observe students, collecting data from and about them, and use a variety of strategies to engage them in learning.

Teachers respond to students in ways that enable them to explore options, make choices, and participate in meaning-making experiences. Teachers not only bring their expertise and authority to interactions with students, they also precipitate change by nudging and questioning to stimulate thinking and enable students to ask their own questions and seek answers.

Learners are aware of the uniqueness of each other's backgrounds, and value this uniqueness. Learners have diverse backgrounds, which reflect a mosaic of cultural heritages. They bring to their classrooms their different language proficiencies, their learning styles, and their own authority and expertise. The community of learners appreciates these diversities of cultural heritage and socioeconomic background, validating and challenging learners' representations of the world. Every language, culture, and experience is a resource in the classroom.

The community of learners values experience as the stimulus for growth and change. Learning comes from active response, evaluation of ideas and events, interactions with texts, discussion with others, and construction of knowledge. In a learning environment, students are given time to articulate and revise what they know. Teachers structure classrooms so that experiences address their interests as well as students' interests. They orchestrate experiences within or outside the classroom so that students can call upon these as sources of language use.

Language is the primary medium for teaching, growth, and change. The learning event is a social interaction with language. By communicating, learners articulate and make of learning something that can be reflected upon, becoming conscious and critical about the change in their knowledge.

Teachers and learners assume many roles, often shared, often overlapping, always interdependent and interactive. They respect each other in these roles. Teachers have a repertoire of roles with reflective, authentic stances: mediator, facilitator, and participant. They delicately balance the roles of manager/director and enabler/interactor with individuals, small groups, and the whole class. Teachers provide information and direction, respond thoughtfully to students' efforts, demonstrate appropriate actions and attitudes, and systematically observe students to assess their progress toward desired ends. Teachers are authorities on learning and pedagogy. They are also researchers, working both theoretically and practically. Teachers plan, organize, choose materials and teaching strategies, and set up structured learning environments to foster desired academic and social interactions.

Teachers are reflective practitioners, aware of the theoretical bases from which they operate, making informed judgments for which they are accountable. In charge of their classroom, they are professionals responsible for planning, implementing, and evaluating the process of learning.

Learners are problem solvers and decision makers. Students develop as active learners by participating in planned activities, thinking and questioning, creating, exploring, experimenting, and making choices and decisions.

Learning entails making mistakes in a climate of trust. Students make mistakes in the process of acquiring knowledge and skill. In a climate of trust, learners are valued as those who have much to give, demonstrate, and teach others, thus permitting them to take responsibility for and maintain ownership of their learning. A trusted individual becomes a risk taker. Support for risk taking requires acceptance of error as a part of learning.

The classroom is an extended community. It includes parents, other faculty, staff, specialists, other students, community members, experts, and resource people. It involves the neighborhood and the other overlapping communities to which students belong. The extended classroom—as well as the additional roles students play—yields a vast resource of information and interaction.

The classroom setting contributes to the climate of the learning. The class schedule provides opportunity to reflect on personal and community actions, allowing students and teachers to engage in language activities for real purposes. Uninterrupted time blocks allow for learning, not "just covering." Freedom to use time in a flexible way helps students to become committed to the tasks at hand. The pace of the classroom is determined partly in response to the development and inquiry of the students.

The variety of materials available reflects the diversity of the students. Students have easy access to learning materials of all types, which are organized and accessible to entice and accommodate students. Students are free to choose materials and texts, work in a variety of situations, and interact with all class members in an environment that is predictable but not static, exciting but not chaotic, disciplined but not restrictive.

Assessment reflects what is valued in education. The community of learners uses diverse kinds of assessment, including self-assessment, as opportunities for reflection on individual growth and change. Beyond simple recall of facts, assessment, which is always limited, grows naturally from classroom learning and is an extension of that learning.

ASSUMPTIONS ABOUT KNOWLEDGE

Knowing is active and ongoing, a process of interactive learning. The classroom is a place where knowledge is socially constructed through interaction among teachers, students, and materials. Knowledge is not neutral, but political, enabling the knower to make choices among conflicting sources.

Facts

On teaching skills in context

Basic skills belong in context.—Lucy McCormick Calkins, 1980

Background

Teachers, researchers, parents, and the public agree that children need to develop and use what are sometimes called "basic skills," such as the ability to use phonics knowledge in reading, the ability to spell conventionally, and the ability to use grammatical constructions effectively and according to the norms of the communities with which they want to communicate. What many people do not realize, however, is that the ability to *use* these skills is best fostered by teaching them in the context of their use. Research demonstrates that skills taught, practiced, and tested in isolation are not used as consistently or effectively as skills taught when children are actually reading and writing.

Phonics

• Recent research demonstrates that in classrooms where phonics is taught in the context of rereading favorite stories, songs, and poems, children develop *and use* phonics knowledge better than in classrooms where skills are taught in isolation. Similarly, phonics knowledge is developed by encouraging and helping emergent writers to spell by writing appropriate letters for the sounds they hear in words (for a summary, see Weaver, 1994b).

• Effective phonics instruction focuses children's attention on noticing the letter/sound patterns in initial consonants and consonant clusters and in rimes (the vowel of a syllable, plus any consonants that might follow, such as -ake, -ent, -ish, -ook). Focusing on rimes rather than on vowels alone is particularly important in helping children learn to decode words (for a summary, see Adams, 1990).

• Effective reading instruction helps children learn to use phonics knowledge *along with* their prior knowledge and context, rather than in isolation. For example, children can be encouraged to predict words by using prior knowledge and context along with initial consonants, then look at the rest of the word to confirm or correct their prediction.

• Both teachers and parents can do various things to help children gain phonics knowledge in the context of reading and writing. For example: (1) read and reread favorite nursery rhymes to reinforce the patterns of the language, and enjoy tongue twisters and other forms of language play together; (2) reread favorite poems, songs, and stories and discuss alliteration and rhyme within them; (3) read alphabet books to and with children, and make alphabet books together; (4) discuss words and make lists, word banks, or books of words that share interesting spelling/sound patterns; (5) discuss similar sounds and letter/sound patterns in children's names; (6) emphasize selected letter/sound relationships while writing with, for, or in front of children; (7) help children write the sounds they hear in words, once the children have begun to hear some separate sounds; (8) when reading together, help children predict and confirm as explained above (Mills et al., 1992; Powell & Hornsby, 1993; Wagstaff, n.d.; Griffith & Olson, 1992; Weaver, 1994a and b).

Spelling

• Children who are encouraged to spell words as best they can when they write typically score as well or better on standardized tests of spelling by the end of first grade than children allowed to use only correct spellings in first drafts. Meanwhile, the children encouraged to spell by writing the sounds they hear in words seem to develop word recognition and phonics skills sooner (Clarke, 1988). They also use a greater variety of words in their writing.

• At least in grades 3–6, it is not clear that spelling instruction has much of an effect beyond what is learned through reading alone, if children are reading extensively (Krashen, 1991).

• Emergent writers benefit from help in writing the sounds they hear in words. Gradually, with extensive writing experience, their early invented spellings will give way to more sophisticated invented spellings and to conventional spellings.

• Extensive exposure to print and reading helps children internalize not only the spellings of particular words, but spelling patterns (Moustafa, 1996). Just as children learn the patterns of the spoken language from hearing it, children learn patterns of the written language from reading and rereading favorite texts. Texts with regular patterns like "Nan can fan Dan" are not necessary, however, nor are they even as readable as texts written in natural language patterns.

- In the long run, teaching children strategies for correcting their spelling is far more important than giving them the correct spelling of any particular word. Such strategies include: (1) writing the word two or three different ways and deciding which one "looks right"; (2) locating the spelling in a familiar text or in print displayed in the classroom; (3) asking someone, consulting a dictionary, or using a computer software program or a hand-held electronic speller (Wilde, 1992).

- Discussing spelling patterns and drawing spelling generalizations as a class will also help children develop an ever-growing repertoire of words they can spell correctly in first drafts. Such interactive, thought-engaging lessons are likely to be more productive than spelling lists and tests (e.g. Wilde, 1992; Wagstaff, n.d.; Cunningham, 1995; Buchanan, 1989).

Grammar

- Decades of research demonstrate that teaching grammar as a school subject does not improve most students' writing, nor even the "correctness" of their writing (Hillocks and Smith, 1991). What works better is teaching selected aspects of grammar (including sentence variety and style, punctuation, and usage) in the context of students' writing—that is, when they are revising and editing their writing (Calkins, 1980; DiStefano & Killion, 1984; see summary in Weaver, 1996).

- For improving editing skills, it is most effective and efficient to teach only the grammatical concepts that are critically needed for editing writing, and to teach these concepts and their terms mostly through minilessons and writing conferences, particularly while helping students edit their writing.

- Research shows that systematic practice in combining and expanding sentences may increase students' repertoire of syntactic structures and may also improve the quality of their sentences, when stylistic effects are discussed as well (Hillocks and Smith, 1991; Strong, 1986). Thus sentence combining and expansion may be taught as a means of improving sentence variety and style. However, isolated activities are not necessarily any more effective than minilessons and writing conferences in which teachers help students rearrange, combine, and expand their sentences for greater effectiveness.

REFERENCES AND RESOURCES

Adams, M. J. (1990). *Beginning to read: Thinking and learning about print.* Cambridge: Harvard University Press.
Bolton, F., & Snowball, D. (1993). *Teaching spelling: A practical resource.* Portsmouth, NH: Heinemann.
Buchanan, E. (1989). *Spelling for whole language classrooms.* Katonah, NY: Richard C. Owen.
Calkins, L. M. (1980). When children want to punctuate: Basic skills belong in context. *Language Arts, 57,* 567–73.
Clarke, L. K. (1988). Invented versus traditional spelling in first graders' writings: Effects on learning to spell and read. *Research in the Teaching of English, 22,* 281–309.
Cunningham, P. M. (1995). *Phonics they use: Words for reading and writing* (2nd ed.). New York: HarperCollins College Publishers.
DiStefano, P., & Killion, J. (1984). Assessing writing skills through a process approach. *English Education, 16* (4), 203–207.
Freppon, P. A., & Dahl, K. L. (1991). Learning about phonics in a whole language classroom. *Language Arts, 68,* 190–197.
Griffith, P. L., & Olson, M. W. (1992). Phonemic awareness helps beginning readers break the code. *The Reading Teacher, 45,* 516–25.
Hillocks, G., Jr., & Smith, M. W. (1991). Grammar and usage. In J. Flood, J. M. Jensen, D. Lapp, & J. R. Squire (Eds.), *Handbook of research on teaching the English language arts* (pp. 591–603). New York: Macmillan.
Krashen, S. D. (1991). Is spelling acquired or learned? A re-analysis of Rice (1897) and Cornman (1902). *ITL: Review of Applied Linguistics, 91–92,* 1–49.
Laminack, L. L., & Wood, K. (1996). *Spelling in use.* Urbana, IL: National Council of Teachers of English.
Mills, H., O'Keefe, T., & Stephens, D. (1992). *Looking closely: Exploring the role of phonics in one whole language classroom.* Urbana, IL: National Council of Teachers of English.
Moustafa, M. (1996). *Reconceptualizing phonics instruction in a balanced approach to reading.* Unpublished manuscript. San Jose, CA: San Jose State University.
Powell, D., & Hornsby, D. (1993). *Learning phonics and spelling in a whole language classroom.* New York: Scholastic.
Strong, W. (1986). *Creative approaches to sentence combining.* Urbana, IL: ERIC and the National Council of Teachers of English.
Tunnell, M. O., & Jacobs, J. S. (1989). Using 'real' books: Research findings on literature based reading instruction. *The Reading Teacher, 42,* 470–477.
Wagstaff, J. (n.d.). *Phonics that work! New strategies for the reading/writing classroom.* New York: Scholastic.
Weaver, C. (1994a). *Phonics in whole language classrooms.* ERIC: ED 372 375.
Weaver, C. (1994b). *Reading process and practice: From socio-psycholinguistics to whole language.* Portsmouth, NH: Heinemann.
Weaver, C. (1996). *Teaching grammar in context.* Portsmouth, NH: Boynton/Cook.
Wilde, S. (1992). *You kan red this! Spelling and punctuation for whole language classrooms, K–6.* Portsmouth, NH: Heinemann.

Prepared for the Michigan English Language Arts Framework project and © 1996 by Constance Weaver. An earlier draft was published as a SLATE Starter Sheet by the National Council of Teachers of English (1996). In C. Weaver, L. Gillmeister-Krause, & G. Vento-Zogby, *Creating Support for Effective Literacy Education* (Heinemann, 1996). May be copied.

Facts

On research on the teaching of phonics

Educators agree that children learning to read texts written in English need to learn that there are relationships between letter patterns and sound patterns in English, and that children need to develop the ability to relate letter patterns to sound patterns.—Constance Weaver, 1994

Background

Through the 1980s and the early 1990s, some prominent reading researchers have argued for the teaching of phonics intensively and systematically (e.g. Chall, 1967/1983; Adams, 1990; Stahl, 1992). Unlike these researchers, however, those advocating the teaching of phonics in the popular media (as in letters to the editor) commonly imply that phonics is all that children need in order to learn to read. Such polemics can often be traced to one of two original sources: Samuel Blumenfeld, author of *NEA: Trojan Horse in Education* and of the *Blumenfeld Education Letter*, and/or Patrick Groff, who has written several items published by the National Right to Read Foundation, which has received substantial funding from the Gateway company producing the *Hooked on Phonics* program. These sources of phonics-first propaganda buttress their arguments with references to respected researchers and their research, which is commonly thought to have demonstrated the superiority of teaching phonics intensively and systematically. However, even these researchers do not advocate phonics only, or phonics first, as a means of teaching children to read (e.g., Adams, 1990). Furthermore, even some of these prominent phonics advocates have pointed out that the alleged success of the *Hooked on Phonics* program is not substantiated by research, a charge made by the Federal Trade Commission as well. Typically, other phonics programs on the market also lack research support. In making educational decisions, it is vital that teachers and other educational decision-makers consider both the pros and cons of the actual research, broadly defined.

The oft-cited research base, considered and reconsidered

The major body of comparative research arguing for the teaching of phonics intensively and systematically is still that summarized by Jeanne Chall in 1967 and updated in 1983, with few additions other than the 1965–1966 U.S.O.E. cooperative first grade studies (Bond & Dykstra, 1967). Chall writes: "In summary, judging from the studies comparing systematic with intrinsic phonics [phonics taught more gradually, in the context of meaningful reading] we can say that systematic phonics at the very beginning tends to produce generally better reading and spelling achievement than intrinsic phonics, at least through grade three. . . . Finally, there is probably a limit to the advantage that early facility with the code gives on comprehension tested after grade 4" (Chall, 1967, 1983). In a more recent pro-phonics book, Marilyn Adams (1990) cites no further comparative studies that can validly claim to support the intensive, systematic teaching of phonics. Note, however:

• The research is said to show intensive phonics producing better reading and spelling *achievement* than traditional basal reading programs of previous decades, at least through grade three. In this context, "achievement" means scores on standardized tests, which—for reading—often contain subtests of phonics knowledge. This body of research says nothing about how children read and comprehend normal texts.

• The comparative research summarized by Chall has been examined and critiqued in minute detail by Marie Carbo (1988), who concluded that in interpreting the available but often flawed data, Chall tended to skew the data as being more favorable to systematic phonics instruction than the data actually warranted. Indeed, even Chall herself admitted (1983 edition) that several other reviewers of the U.S.O.E. data did not draw the same conclusions she did.

• To try to resolve the discrepancy between Chall's conclusions and Carbo's critique, an expert on assessment undertook to reexamine the research yet again. He excluded the vast majority of studies critiqued by Carbo, thus considering only the best research: nine randomized field experiments that compared systematic phonics with a whole word approach (NOT whole language), wherein phonics was taught intrinsically or not at all. The results? "My overall conclusion from reviewing the randomized field studies is that systematic phonics falls into that vast category of weak instructional treatments with which education is perennially plagued. Systematic phonics appears to have a slight and early advantage over a basal-reader/whole-word approach as a method of beginning reading instruction. . . . However, this difference does not last long and has no clear meaning for the acquisition of literacy" (Turner, 1989).

The research base expanded

In the last decade, one body of research has demonstrated that there is a strong correlation between phonemic awareness (awareness of the separate "sounds" in words) and reading achievement, as measured by scores on standardized tests (e.g. Adams & Bruck, 1995; Beck & Juel, 1995; Foorman, 1995). This and other research showing the opposite correlation (low phonemic awareness, low scores on standardized tests) has led to the argument that many children need explicit help in developing phonemic awareness—not merely to sound out words, but to recognize words on sight, automatically (e.g. Stanovich, 1991, 1992). However, a correlation simply means that the two go together, like bread and butter; it says nothing about whether one causes the other—for example, whether phonemic awareness leads to independent reading, whether learning to read results in phonemic awareness, or both.

Another body of research from the last decade has compared the traditional teaching of isolated reading and writing skills in the primary grades to the development of literacy in whole language classrooms. Though whole language teaching involves much more than a different approach to reading and writing, one key element of whole language classrooms is that children receive the support they need to read and write whole texts and to develop reading and writing skills within meaningful reading and writing situations. This includes explicit help in developing phonemic awareness, phonics knowledge, and decoding skills. Part of what many whole language teachers do in the primary grades is spend significant time each day reading to children from a large text that all can see, then rereading the text with the children chiming in. Repeated rereadings and calling attention to words and letter/sound patterns help the children learn words and phonics, as well as basic concepts of print. For example, extensions of such reading activities may include discussing and making charts of words that alliterate or rhyme. Examining and comparing the spellings of children's names is another way phonics may be taught. Whole language teachers also promote phonics knowledge by helping children write the sounds they hear in words. By teaching phonics through reading, minilessons, and writing, whole language teachers help children develop phonics knowledge in the context of the texts they enjoy reading and writing. The emerging body of comparative research reveals the following patterns, which deal with phonics but go beyond (Weaver, 1994b, and various research studies listed in References, all of which used diverse measures):

• Children in whole language classrooms typically show slightly greater gains on various reading tests and subtests, including subtests of phonics knowledge.

• Children in whole language classrooms develop greater ability to *use* phonics knowledge effectively in reading and writing than children in more traditional, skills-oriented classrooms.

• Children in whole language classrooms are more inclined to read for meaning than just to identify words, and they are better at retelling what they have read. They also develop more strategies for dealing with problems in reading, such as problems in identifying words.

• Children in whole language classrooms develop vocabulary, spelling, grammar, and punctuation skills as well as or better than children in more traditional classrooms.

• Children in whole language classrooms develop greater independence as readers and writers, and a stronger sense of themselves as readers and writers.

In whole language classrooms like the ones in these studies, where phonics is taught briefly but explicitly in the context of reading and writing, the concepts of phonemic awareness, phonics, and decoding skills seem to be learned at least as well as in skills emphasis classrooms (Stahl & Kuhn, 1995). Other comparisons of literature-based instruction with more traditional instruction are also relevant (Tunnell & Jacobs, 1989; Shapiro, 1990; Krashen, 1993; Smith & Elley, 1995). In addition, various naturalistic studies support the teaching and learning of phonics in the context of meaningful reading (Stephens, 1991). Moustafa's (1995) and others' research suggests a mechanism by which such learning may happen.

A recent study (Foorman et al., forthcoming) *seems* to suggest that teaching phonics in isolation may get children off to a better start in developing phonemic awareness and phonics skills and in using these skills in word identification than a program that embeds phonics into a whole literacy context, but from this report it is impossible to tell just how much time was spent focusing on letter/sound relationships in the "embedded phonics" and "whole language" treatments. The study included only one independent (multiple-choice) measure of comprehension, on which there were no significant differences among treatment groups. No other kinds of factors were measured. So the study speaks only to the early acquisition of phonemic awareness and phonics skills, not to the overall issue of becoming a competent and independent reader who *uses* such skills in the service of constructing meaning.

Toward a consensus on the teaching of phonics

There are still critical differences in how reading researchers conceptualize and characterize reading. Those who have examined the reading process through an analysis of the miscues ("errors") made by proficient readers have concluded that what most obviously characterizes proficient reading is the reader's drive to construct meaning (Goodman, 1973; Brown, Marek, & Goodman, 1994). Those who have examined word identification and correlations among test scores more than the process of reading whole texts have concluded that what most obviously characterizes proficient reading is the ability to read most words in a text automatically and fluently (e.g., Adams & Bruck, 1995; Beck & Juel, 1995; Stanovich, 1991).

The former group of researchers point out that too much attention to phonics can detract from the construction of meaning, while the latter cite correlations between tests of phonemic awareness (awareness of the "separate" sounds in a word) and scores on standardized tests as evidence that phonemic awareness and phonics must be taught early to promote reading achievement—that is, high standardized test scores. Another major difference: Researchers who have studied emergent literacy (e.g. Harste, Woodward, & Burke, 1984) point out that phonics knowledge is gained in the process of becoming a reader and writer, while those who have examined correlations between phonemic awareness and reading test scores note that phonemic awareness is a pre-requisite to becoming an *independent* reader (e.g., Beck & Juel, 1995). Note, however, that the two ideas are compatible: independent readers may have developed phonemic awareness in the process of becoming readers and writers, and in fact there is substantial evidence that this happens (Moustafa, 1995; Mann, 1986; Morais, Bertelson, Cary, and Alegria, 1986; Winner, Landerl, Linortner, & Hummer, 1991).

Considering, then, the major theoretical differences and the resulting emphases, it is particularly noteworthy that researchers and educators from various backgrounds are beginning to converge on four major points about the teaching of phonics: (1) that children should be given some explicit, direct help in developing phonemic awareness and a functional command of phonics; (2) that such direct teaching does not need to be intensive and systematic to be effective; (3) that, indeed, worksheets and mindless drills are not the best means of developing phonics knowledge (e.g. A. E. Cunningham, 1990); and (4) that phonemic awareness and phonics knowledge also develops without instruction, simply while reading and writing whole, interesting texts. As someone who once advocated systematic phonics (Stahl, 1992) now puts it, "there is little evidence that one form of phonics instruction is strongly superior to another" (Stahl, McKenna, & Pagnucco, 1994).

How has this partial convergence begun to come about? On the one hand, whole language researchers and educators have done research and written books, articles, and other documents on teaching phonics in context (McIntyre & Freppon, 1994; Mills, O'Keefe, & Stephens, 1992; Powell and Hornsby, 1993; Weaver, 1994a; Routman & Butler, 1995). On the other hand, the researchers who most adamantly insist on teaching phonemic awareness and phonics are suggesting teaching methods and materials that resemble those of the whole language educators (Adams & Brock, 1995; Beck & Juel, 1995; also P. Cunningham, 1995; Griffith & Olson, 1992). For example, some educators within both groups recommend using nursery rhymes, tongue twisters, and books like the rhymed Dr. Seuss books. Both groups recognize the importance of reading to and with children. One remaining difference, however, is that phonemic awareness researchers and educators often advocate oral language play and games in the preschool years (Yopp, 1992), while whole language educators typically are convinced this is unnecessary and that children will learn more in less time when the teacher focuses on phonemic awareness in the context of written texts (e.g., Kasten & Clarke, 1989; Richgels, Poremba, & McGee, 1996).

Overall, though, researchers and educators with different backgrounds seem to be moving toward consensus on at least some aspects of how phonemic awareness and phonics should be taught: indirectly, through extensive reading and writing; directly too, but not necessarily in great detail; not through worksheets and drill, but with guidance in examining letter/sound patterns in the meaningful texts that children read and write. Such teaching is not a panacea, as some children continue to have difficulty in developing phonemic awareness and phonics knowledge no matter how they are taught (e.g. Dahl & Freppon, 1992). However, teaching phonics in context and through discussion and collaborative activities seems to be more effective with more children than other means—and children in classrooms where skills are taught in the context of reading and writing whole texts get a better start on becoming proficient and independent readers, not mere word-callers (e.g., Dahl & Freppon, 1992; Stice & Bertrand, 1990; Kasten & Clarke, 1989).

Helping children develop phonics knowledge

Without using programs for teaching phonics intensively and systematically, parents and teachers can do various things to help children gain phonics knowledge and develop phonemic awareness in the context of meaningful reading and writing and language play. Whole language educators differ among themselves and with others as to which particular practices they adopt or recommend, but many educators and researchers advocate at least some of the following: (1) Read and reread favorite nursery rhymes and enjoy tongue twisters and other forms of language play together; (2) reread favorite poems, songs, and stories; discuss alliteration and rhyme within them; and play with sound elements (e.g. starting with *cake*, remove the *c* and consider what different sounds could be added to make other words, like *take, make, lake*); (3) read alphabet books to and with children, and make alphabet books together; (4) discuss words and make lists, word banks, or books of such words that share interesting spelling/sound patterns; (5) discuss similar sounds and letter/sound patterns in children's names; (6) emphasize selected letter/sound relationships while writing with, for, or in front of the children; (7) help children write the sounds they hear in words, once they have begun to hear some separate sounds; (8) when reading together, help children use prior knowledge and context plus initial consonants to predict what a word will be, then look at the rest of the word to confirm or correct (Mills et al., 1992; Powell & Hornsby, 1993; Freppon & Dahl, 1991; Griffith & Olson, 1992; Weaver, 1994a and b; Routman & Butler, 1995; P. Cunningham, 1995; Wagstaff, n.d.). The latter activity is especially important for helping children orchestrate prior knowledge with context and letter/sound cues in order not merely to identify words but to construct meaning from texts—which, after all, is the primary purpose of reading.

Teaching phonics and phonemic awareness in such ways helps keep them in proper perspective, but only when children spend substantially more time daily in listening to books read aloud (live, and on tape); in reading independently or with a partner (even if they still read the pictures more than the words); in discussing the literature they have heard and read; in reading classroom messages, signs, directions, and other informational print; in composing and writing together with the teacher, as a group; and in writing independently. Teaching phonics first and only, as some people urge, is a good way of separating children who can do isolated phonics from those who can't, but it is not a good way to teach children to read. Nor should we assume that children or adults who have difficulty recognizing and/or sounding out words cannot comprehend texts effectively; indeed, even "dyslexic" readers can often comprehend well (Fink, 1995/96; Weaver, 1994c), because of the redundancy of language and the knowledge they bring to texts. Thus teaching phonics directly, but in the context of reading and writing and discussing texts, is much more effective than isolated phonics and "phonics first"—effective not only in teaching phonemic awareness and phonics itself but in teaching others to comprehend texts rather than just to identify words.

REFERENCES AND RESOURCES

Adams, M. J. (1990). *Beginning to read: Thinking and learning about print.* Cambridge: Harvard University Press.

Adams, M. J., & Bruck, M. (1995). Resolving the "Great debate." *American Educator, 19* (2), 7, 10–20.

Allington, R. L., & Cunningham, P. M. (1996). *Schools that work: Where all children read and write.* New York: HarperCollins College Publishers.

Beck, I. L., & Juel, C. (1995). The role of decoding in learning to read. *American Educator, 19* (2), 8, 21–25, 39–42.

Bond, G. L., & Dykstra, R. (1967). The cooperative research program in first-grade reading instruction. *Reading Research Quarterly, 2*, 5–142.

Brown, J., Marek, A., & Goodman, K. S. (1994). *Annotated chronological miscue analysis bibliography.* Program in Language and Literacy, No. 16. Tucson: University of Arizona.

Carbo, M. (1988). Debunking the great phonics myth. *Phi Delta Kappan, 70*, 226–240.

Chall, J. (1967/1983). *Learning to read: The great debate.* New York: McGraw-Hill.

Cunningham, A. E. (1990). Explicit versus implicit instruction in phonemic awareness. *Journal of Experimental Child Psychology, 50*, 429–444.

Cunningham, P. (1995). *Phonics they use: Words for reading and writing.* New York: HarperCollins.

Dahl, K. L., & Freppon, P. A. (1992). *Learning to read and write in inner-city schools: A comparison of children's sense-making in skills-based and whole language classrooms.* Final report to the Office of Educational Research and Improvement. Washington, DC: U.S. Department of Education. (Grant No. G008720229)

Fink, R. (1995/96). Successful dyslexics: A constructionist study of passionate interest reading. *Journal of Adolescent and Adult Literacy, 39*, 268–280.

Foorman, B. R. (1995). Research on "The great debate": Code-oriented versus whole language approaches to reading instruction. *School Psychology Review, 24*, 376–392.

Foorman, B. R., Francis, D. J., Beeler, T., Winikates, D., & Fletcher, J. M. (Forthcoming). Early intervention for children with reading problems: Study designs and preliminary findings. *Learning Disabilities: A Multi-Disciplinary Journal.*

Freppon, P. A., & Dahl, K. L. (1991). Learning about phonics in a whole language classroom. *Language Arts, 68* (3), 190–197.

Goodman, K. S. (1973). *Theoretically based studies of patterns of miscues in oral reading performance.* Detroit: Wayne State University. ERIC: ED 079 708.

Goodman, Y. M., & Marek, A. M. (1996). *Retrospective miscue analysis: Revaluing readers and reading.* Katonah, NY: Richard C. Owen.

Griffith, P. L., & Olson, M. W. (1992). Phonemic awareness helps beginning readers break the code. *The Reading Teacher, 45*, 516–525.

Gunning, R. G. (1995). Word building: A strategic approach to the teaching of phonics. *The Reading Teacher, 48*, 484–488.

Harste, J. C., Woodward, V. A., & Burke, C. L. (1984). *Language stories and literacy lessons.* Portsmouth, NH: Heinemann.

Kasten, W. C., & Clarke, B. K. (1989). *Reading/writing readiness for preschool and kindergarten children: A whole language approach.* Sanibel, Florida: Educational Research and Development Council, ERIC: ED 312 041.

Krashen, S. D. (1993). *The power of reading: Insights from the research.* Englewood, CO: Libraries Unlimited.

Mann, V. (1986). Phonological awareness: The role of reading experience. *Cognition, 24*, 65–92.

Manning, M., Manning, G., & Long, R. (1989). *Effects of a whole language and a skill-oriented program on the literacy development of inner city primary children.* ERIC: ED 324 642.

McIntyre, E., & Freppon, P. A. (1994). A comparison of children's development of alphabetic knowledge in a skills-based and a whole language classroom. *Research in the Teaching of English, 28*, 391–417.

Mills, H., O'Keefe, T., & Stephens, D. (1992). *Looking closely: Exploring the role of phonics in one whole language classroom.* Urbana, IL: National Council of Teachers of English.

Morais, J., Bertelson, P., Carey, L., & Alegria, J. (1986). Literacy training and speech segmentation. *Cognition, 24*, 45–64.

Moustafa, M. (1995). Children's productive phonological recoding. *Reading Research Quarterly, 30*, 464–476.

Powell, D., & Hornsby, D. (1993). *Learning phonics and spelling in a whole language classroom.* New York: Scholastic.

Richgels, D., Poremba, K., & McGee, L. (1996). Kindergarteners talk about print: Phonemic awareness in meaningful contexts. *The Reading Teacher, 49*, 632–641.

Routman, R., & Butler, A. (1995). Why talk about phonics? *School Talk, 1* (2). (National Council of Teachers of English.)

Shapiro, J. (1990). Research perspectives on whole-language. In V. Froese (Ed.), *Whole language: Practice and theory* (pp. 313–356). Boston: Allyn & Bacon.

Smith, J. W. A., & Elley, W. B. (1995). *Learning to read in New Zealand.* Katonah, NY: Richard C. Owen.

Stahl, S. A. (1992). Saying the "p" word: Nine guidelines for exemplary phonics instruction. *The Reading Teacher, 45*, 618–625.

Stahl, S. A., & Kuhn, M. R. (1995). Does whole language or instruction matched to learning styles help children learn to read? *School Psychology Review, 24*, 393–404.

Stahl, S. A., McKenna, M. C., & Pagnucco, J. R. (1994). The effects of whole-language instruction: An update and a reappraisal. *Educational Psychologist, 29*, 175–185.

Stanovich, K. E. (1991). Word recognition: Changing perspectives. In R. Barr, M. L. Kamil, P. Mosenthal, & P. D. Pearson (Eds.), *Handbook of reading research* (Vol. 2, pp. 418–452). New York: Longman.

Stanovich, K. E. (1992). Speculations on the causes and consequences of individual differences in early reading acquisition. In P. B. Gough, L. C. Ehri, & R. Treiman (Eds.), *Reading acquisition* (pp. 307–342). Hillsdale, NJ: Erlbaum.

Stephens, D. (1991). *Research on whole language: Support for a new curriculum.* Katonah, NY: Richard C. Owen.

Stice, C. F., & Bertrand, N. P. (1990). *Whole language and the emergent literacy of at-risk children: A two-year comparative study.* Nashville: Center of Excellence: Basic Skills, Tennessee State University. ERIC: ED 324 636.

Tunnell, M. O., & Jacobs, J. S. (1989). Using 'real' books: Research findings on literature based reading instruction. *The Reading Teacher, 42*, 470–477.

Turner, R. L. (1989). The "great" debate: Can both Carbo and Chall be right? *Phi Delta Kappan, 71*, 276–283.

Wagstaff, J. (n.d.). *Phonics that work! New strategies for the reading/writing classroom.* New York: Scholastic.

Weaver, C. (1994a). *Phonics in whole language classrooms.* ERIC: ED 372 375.

Weaver, C. (1994b). *Reading process and practice: From socio-psycholinguistics to whole language.* Portsmouth, NH: Heinemann.

Weaver, C. (1994c). Reconceptualizing reading and dyslexia. *Journal of Childhood Communication Disorders, 16* (1), 23–35.

Winner, H., Landerl, K., Linortner, R., & Hummer, P. (1991). The relationship of phonemic awareness to reading acquisition: More consequence than precondition but still important. *Cognition, 40*: 219–249.

Yopp, H. (1992). Developing phonemic awareness in young children. *The Reading Teacher, 45*, 696–703.

Facts

On the teaching of phonics

Through critical attention to relevant research and careful observation of children in the reading-writing process, we teachers can intelligently decide how to teach phonics. . . . I prefer to teach phonics strategically, in the meaningful context of the predictable stories children read and write every day. In the context of written language, phonics instruction facilitates meaning making and independence.—Regie Routman, 1991

Background

Educators generally agree that children learning to read and write English need to understand that there is a relationship between letter patterns and sound patterns in English (the alphabetic principle), to internalize major relationships between letter and sound patterns, and eventually to develop an awareness of the "separate" sounds in words (phonemic awareness). In other words, educators agree that emergent readers and writers need to develop a functional command of what is commonly called *phonics*. However, this does not not necessarily mean that children should be taught phonics intensively and systematically, through special phonics programs or even through phonics lessons in basal reading books and workbooks. Indeed, various lines of research argue for helping children develop phonics knowledge in the context of reading and enjoying literature and in the context of writing, rather than through isolated skills lessons. Many of these reasons are listed below, followed by a list of ways that teachers and parents can help children learn phonics and develop phonemic awareness while reading and writing interesting texts.

Comparative and naturalistic research

• Despite extravagant claims found in the popular media, research does not strongly support the teaching of phonics intensively and systematically—and certainly not phonics *first*. At best, systematic phonics (in comparison with traditional basal-reader/whole word approaches) may produce better scores on reading comprehension tests, but only through grade 3 (Chall, 1967/1983). A recent study suggests that an approach which emphasizes phonemic awareness and phonics may get children off to an earlier start in grasping letter/sound relationships and reading words than an approach that embeds phonics in a whole literacy context, but the direct instruction, whole language, and embedded phonics groups showed no significant differences in comprehension (Foorman et al., forthcoming). Overall, "there is little evidence that one form of phonics instruction is strongly superior to another" (Stahl, McKenna, & Pagnucco, 1994) in developing phonics knowledge and phonemic awareness.

• From 1985 onward, the small body of experimental research has typically compared traditional skills instruction with whole language instruction in reading and writing, in primary grade classrooms. Though many of the differences are not large enough to be statistically significant, the children in whole language classrooms scored the same or higher on virtually every measure in every study, including standardized tests and subtests that assess phonics skills (Weaver, 1994b; Tunnell & Jacobs, 1989, present other studies comparing literature-based with skills-based reading instruction).

• Research on how children learn to read and write in the home indicates that children become literate in much the same way as they learn their first oral language, though of course the processes are not exactly the same. Just as we do not teach babies and toddlers the rules for putting words together to make grammatical sentences, so we do not need to teach children phonics rules if we give them plenty of guided opportunities to learn letter/sound patterns (Holdaway, 1979; Cambourne, 1988; Stephens, 1991; Weaver, 1994b; Smith & Elley, 1995). In short, phonics and phonemic awareness are best learned and used *in the course of* learning to read and write, *not as prerequisites* (Goodman, 1993).

• Many—indeed, most—young readers are not good at learning analytically, abstractly, or auditorily (e.g. Carbo, 1987). Therefore, for most young children, it is harder to learn phonics through part-to-whole teaching (phonics first) than through whole-to-part teaching (reading and writing first, and learning phonics from and along with the words in familiar texts).

Research on the reading process and on the effects of reading instruction

• Of course fluent readers can identify many words on sight. However, when reading texts rather than word lists, proficient readers use prior knowledge and context *along with* letter/sound knowledge as they identify words and construct meaning (e.g. Goodman, 1973, Smith, 1988). Even though readers may see all the letters of a word, it appears that they identify the word before recognizing all the letters separately.

• Many poorer readers are ones for whom phonics was overtaught, with little or no emphasis on trying to make meaning while reading (e.g. Chomsky, 1976; Carbo, 1987; Meek, 1983).

• Too much emphasis on phonics encourages children to use "sound it out" as their first and possibly only independent strategy for dealing with problem words (Applebee, Langer, & Mullis, 1988).

• Programs for teaching phonics often emphasize rules rather than patterns and focus on "separate" sounds, called phonemes. In contrast, the most effective and efficient phonics instruction focuses children's attention on noticing letter/sound patterns in the major components of syllables: that is, on noticing the letter/sound patterns in initial consonants and consonant clusters and in the rime, which consists of the vowel of a syllable plus any following consonants, such as -ake, -ent, -ish, -ook (Moustafa, 1996).

• Without using phonics programs, parents and teachers can do various things to help children gain phonics knowledge in the context of meaningful reading and writing and language play. The following are some of these: (1) read and reread favorite nursery rhymes to reinforce the patterns of the language, and enjoy tongue twisters and other forms of language play together; (2) reread favorite poems, songs, and stories and discuss alliteration and rhyme within them; (3) read alphabet books to and with children, and make alphabet books together; (4) discuss words and make lists, word banks, or books of words that share interesting spelling/sound patterns; (5) discuss similar sounds and letter/sound patterns in children's names; (6) emphasize selected letter/sound relationships while writing with, for, or in front of children; (7) help children write the sounds they hear in words, once they have begun to hear some separate sounds; (8) when reading together, help children use prior knowledge and context plus initial consonants to predict what a word will be, then look at the rest of the word to confirm or correct (Mills et al., 1992; Powell & Hornsby, 1993; Wagstaff, n.d.; Freppon & Dahl, 1991; Griffith & Olson, 1992; Weaver, 1994a and b; for other ideas, see Cunningham, 1995).

REFERENCES AND RESOURCES

Adams, M. J. (1990). *Beginning to read: Thinking and learning about print*. Cambridge: Harvard University Press.

Applebee, A. N., Langer, J. A., & Mullis, I. V. S. (1988). *Learning to be literate in America: Reading, writing and reasoning. The nation's report card*. Princeton, NJ: National Assessment of Educational Progress, Educational Testing Service.

Cambourne, B. (1988). *The whole story: Natural learning and the acquisition of literacy in the classroom*. New York: Scholastic.

Carbo, M. (1987). Reading style research: "What works" isn't always phonics. *Phi Delta Kappan, 68*, 431–35.

Chall, J. (1967/1983). *Learning to read: The great debate*. New York: McGraw-Hill.

Chomsky, C. (1976). After decoding: What? *Language Arts, 53*, 288–296, 314.

Cunningham, P. (1995). *Phonics they use: Words for reading and writing*. New York: HarperCollins.

Freppon, P. A., & Dahl, K. L. (1991). Learning about phonics in a whole language classroom. *Language Arts, 68* (3), 190–97.

Foorman, B. R., Francis, D. J., Beeler, T., Winikates, D., & Fletcher, J. M. (Forthcoming.) Early intervention for children with reading problems: Study designs and preliminary findings. *Learning Disabilities: A Multi-Disciplinary Journal*.

Goodman, K. S. (1973). *Theoretically based studies of patterns of miscues in oral reading performance*. Detroit: Wayne State University. ERIC: ED 079 708.

Goodman, K. (1993). *Phonics phacts*. Portsmouth, NH: Heinemann.

Griffith, P. L., & Olson, M. W. (1992). Phonemic awareness helps beginning readers break the code. *The Reading Teacher, 45*, 516–525.

Kasten, W. C., & Clarke, B. K. (1989). *Reading/writing readiness for preschool and kindergarten children: A whole language approach*. Sanibel, Florida: Educational Research and Development Council. ERIC: ED 312 041.

Meek, M. (1983). *Achieving literacy*. London: Routledge & Kegan Paul.

Holdaway, D. (1979). *The foundations of literacy*. Portsmouth, NH: Heinemann.

Manning, M., Manning, G., & Long, R. (1989). *Effects of a whole language and a skill-oriented program on the literacy development of inner city primary children*. ERIC: ED 324 642.

McIntyre, E., & Freppon, P. A. (1994). A comparison of children's development of alphabetic knowledge in a skills-based and a whole language classroom. *Research in the Teaching of English, 28*, 391–417.

Mills, H., O'Keefe, T., & Stephens, D. (1992). *Looking closely: Exploring the role of phonics in one whole language classroom*. Urbana, IL: National Council of Teachers of English.

Moustafa, M. (1996). *Reconceptualizing phonics instruction in a balanced approach to reading*. Unpublished manuscript. San Jose, CA: San Jose State University.

Powell, D., & Hornsby, D. (1993). *Learning phonics and spelling in a whole language classroom*. New York: Scholastic.

Richgels, D., Poremba, K., & McGee, L. (1996). Kindergarteners talk about print: Phonemic awareness in meaningful contexts. *The Reading Teacher, 49*, 632–641.

Routman, R. (1991). *Invitations: Changing as teachers and learners K–12*. Portsmouth, NH: Heinemann.

Routman, R., & Butler, A. (1995). Why talk about phonics? *School Talk, 1* (2). (National Council of Teachers of English.)

Smith, F. (1988). *Understanding reading* (4th ed.). Hillsdale, NJ: Erlbaum.

Smith, J. W. A., & Elley, W. B. (1995). *Learning to read in New Zealand*. Katonah, NY: Richard C. Owen.

Stahl, S. L., McKenna, M. C., & Pagnucco, J. R. (1994). The effects of whole-language instruction: An update and a reappraisal. *Educational Psychologist, 29*, 175–185.

Stephens, D. (1991). *Research on whole language: Support for a new curriculum*. Katonah, NY: Richard C. Owen.

Tunnell, M. O., & Jacobs, J. S. (1989). Using 'real' books: Research findings on literature based reading instruction. *The Reading Teacher, 42*, 470–477.

Wagstaff, J. (n.d.). *Phonics that work! New strategies for the reading/writing classroom*. New York: Scholastic.

Weaver, C. (1994a). *Phonics in whole language classrooms*. ERIC: ED 372 375.

Weaver, C. (1994b). *Reading process and practice: From socio-psycholinguistics to whole language* (2nd ed.). Portsmouth, NH: Heinemann.

Facts

On the teaching
of spelling

Too much that is known about how to teach spelling isn't being put into practice. I can think of no subject we teach more poorly or harbor more myths about than spelling.—Richard Gentry, 1987

Background

For decades, more people seem to have considered themselves poor spellers than good spellers, despite the fact that most of us spell correctly the vast majority of the words we write. With spelling, we seem to expect that all of us should spell one hundred percent correctly, even on first drafts, and even as young children. Perhaps it is this unrealistic expectation that leads some parents and others to object when teachers use newer methods of helping children learn to spell, such as encouraging children to "use invented spelling" in their early attempts to write. Such critics mistakenly assume that children who initially use approximate spellings will never become good spellers, or that if the time-honored method of memorizing spelling lists were used instead, every child would become a perfect speller. Neither observed experience nor research supports these assumptions.

What research demonstrates

• Young children using invented spelling employ a considerably greater variety of words in their writing than those encouraged to use only the words they can spell correctly (Gunderson & Shapiro, 1987, 1988; Clarke, 1988; Stice & Bertrand, 1990).

• By the end of first grade, children encouraged to use invented spellings typically score as well or better on standardized tests of spelling than children allowed to use only correct spellings in first drafts (Clarke, 1988; Stice & Bertrand, 1990).

• Young children encouraged to use invented spellings seem to develop word recognition and phonics skills sooner than those not encouraged to spell the sounds they hear in words (Clarke, 1988).

• At least in grades 3–6, it is not clear that spelling instruction has much of an effect beyond what is learned through reading alone, if children are reading extensively (Krashen, 1991).

What helps children learn to spell

• Learners of all ages need encouragement to write, write, write, and just to spell words the best they can in first drafts.

• As young children begin to hear separate sounds in words, they benefit from help in writing the sounds they hear: that is, from guidance in inventing spellings. Gradually, their initial invented spellings (usually one letter per word) more or less naturally give way to more complete and sophisticated invented spellings and to conventional spellings, as long as the children are reading and writing extensively.

• Extensive exposure to print helps children internalize not only the spellings of particular words, but spelling patterns. Young children especially benefit from reading favorite selections again and again. Learners of all ages need to read, read, read.

• Children benefit from guidance in developing a spelling conscience: a concern for spelling, and a sense of when something may not be spelled correctly. For instance, as a first step toward correcting their spelling, children who are already spelling many words correctly might be encouraged to circle words in their first draft that they think might be spelled incorrectly.

• Teaching children strategies for correcting spelling is far more important than giving them the correct spelling of any particular word. Such strategies include: writing the word two or three different ways and deciding which one "looks right"; locating the correct spelling in a familiar text or in print displayed in the classroom; asking someone, consulting a dictionary, or using a spelling checker on the computer or a hand-held electronic speller.

• Spelling strategies and major spelling patterns can be taught much more effectively through minilessons involving student discussion than through workbook pages or spelling tests. Children benefit especially when, as a group, they are guided in noticing spelling patterns for themselves.

• By the intermediate grades and middle school, students can benefit immensely from minilessons that help them discover the meanings of Latin and Greek roots and suffixes. Such learning is valuable for spelling and writing but perhaps even more valuable for vocabulary development and reading.

• Studying spelling lists is most useful if children each choose a limited number of words (say five a week) that they want to learn: ideally, words they are interested in, and words they use frequently in their writing but haven't yet learned to spell correctly all the time. At the end of the week, partners can test each other on the words they each have practiced during the week.

• Individualized spelling dictionaries can be helpful as children are trying to get a grasp on the spellings of words. Teachers can make each child a booklet in which the child can enter words he or she is learning to spell. File boxes with index cards, or even computer files or data bases for each child, can serve the same purpose.

REFERENCES AND RESOURCES

Bolton, F., & Snowball, D. (1993). *Teaching spelling: A practical resource*. Portsmouth, NH: Heinemann.

Buchanan, E. (1989). *Spelling for whole language classrooms*. Katonah, NY: Richard C. Owen.

Clarke, L. K. (1988). Invented versus traditional spelling in first graders' writings: Effects on learning to spell and read. *Research in the Teaching of English, 22*, 281–309.

Cunningham, P. M. (1995). *Phonics they use: Words for reading and writing* (2nd ed.). New York: HarperCollins College Pubs.

Gentry, J. Richard. (1987). *Spel . . . is a four-letter word*. Portsmouth, NH: Heinemann.

Gunderson, L., & Shapiro, J. (1987). Some findings on whole language instruction. *Reading-Canada-Lecture, 5* (1), 22–26.

Gunderson, L., & Shapiro, J. (1988). Whole language instruction: Writing in 1st grade. *The Reading Teacher, 41*, 430–437.

Laminack, L. L., & Wood, K. (1996). *Spelling in use*. Urbana, IL: National Council of Teachers of English.

McGee, L. M., & Richgels, D. J. (1990). *Literacy's beginnings: Supporting young readers and writers*. Boston: Allyn and Bacon.

Routman, R. (1991). *Invitations: Changing as teachers and learners K–12*. Portsmouth, NH: Heinemann.

Routman, R., & Maxim, D. (1996). Invented spelling: What it is and what it isn't. *School Talk, 1* (4). Urbana, IL: National Council of Teachers of English.

Stice, C. F., & Bertrand, N. P. (1990). *Whole language and the emergent literacy of at-risk children: A two-year comparative study*. Nashville: Center for Excellence, Basic Skills, Tennessee State University. ERIC: ED 324 636.

Temple, C., Nathan, R., Temple, F., & Burris, N. A. (1993). *The beginnings of writing* (3rd ed.). Boston: Allyn and Bacon.

Wilde, S. (1992). *You kan red this! Spelling and punctuation for whole language classrooms, K–6*. Portsmouth, NH: Heinemann.

Prepared for the Michigan English Language Arts Framework project and © 1996 by Constance Weaver. A similar version was published as a SLATE Starter Sheet by the National Couincil of Teachers of English (1996). In C. Weaver, L. Gillmeister-Krause, & G. Vento-Zogby, *Creating Support for Effective Literacy Education* (Heinemann, 1996). May be copied.

Facts

On the teaching of grammar

Research over a period of nearly 90 years has consistently shown that the teaching of school grammar has little or no effect on students.—George Hillocks & Michael Smith, 1991

Background

The most common reason for teaching grammar as a system for analyzing and labeling sentences has been to accomplish some practical aim or aims, typically the improvement of writing. For decades, however, research has demonstrated that the teaching of grammar rarely accomplishes such practical goals. Relatively few students learn grammar well, fewer retain it, and still fewer transfer the grammar they have learned to improving or editing their writing.

What doesn't work: The research

• "Diagraming sentences . . . teaches nothing beyond the ability to diagram" (1960 *Encyclopedia of Educational Research*).

• "The impressive fact is . . . that in all these studies . . . the results have been consistently negative so far as the value of grammar in the improvement of language expression is concerned. Surely there is no justification in the available evidence for the great expenditure of time and effort still being devoted to formal grammar in American schools" (DeBoer, 1959).

• "None of the studies reviewed for the present report provides any support for teaching grammar as a means of improving composition skills. If schools insist upon teaching the identification of parts of speech, the parsing or diagraming of sentences, or other concepts of traditional grammar (as many still do), they cannot defend it as a means of improving the quality of writing" (Hillocks, 1986).

• For most students, the systematic study of grammar is not even particularly helpful in avoiding or correcting errors (Elley et al., 1976; McQuade, 1980; Hillocks, 1986).

• "The teaching of formal grammar has a negligible or, because it usually displaces some instruction and practice in actual composition, even a harmful effect on the improvement of writing" (Braddock, Lloyd-Jones, and Schoer, 1963).

What works better: The research

• Studying formal grammar is less helpful to writers than simply discussing grammatical constructions and usage in the context of writing (Harris, 1962).

• Learning punctuation in the context of writing is much more effective than studying punctuation marks and rules for punctuation in isolation (Calkins, 1980).

• Usage, sentence variety, sentence-level punctuation, and spelling are applied more effectively in writing itself when studied and discussed in the context of writing, rather than through isolated skills instruction (DiStefano and Killion, 1984).

• Systematic practice in combining and expanding sentences can increase students' repertoire of syntactic structures and can also improve the quality of their sentences, when stylistic effects are discussed as well (Hillocks and Smith, 1991).

• For learners of English as a second language, research suggests that extensive *reading* may promote the acquisition of grammatical structures better than explicitly studying or practicing such structures (Elley, 1991).

Indeed, for both first and second language learners, extensive reading significantly promotes grammatical fluency and a command of the syntactic resources of the language (Krashen, 1993).

Implications for teaching grammar as an aid to writing

• Teach only the grammatical concepts that are critically needed for editing writing, and teach these concepts and terms mostly through minilessons and conferences, while helping students edit.

• Help students expand their syntactic repertoire and explore style by considering effective examples, then experimenting and discussing the results. Grammatical terminology can be used, but need not be taught as an end in itself.

• Have students experiment with and discuss various activities in sentence combining, expanding, and manipulating (Strong, 1986; Killgallon, 1987; Daiker, Kerek, & Morenberg, 1990).

• Give students plenty of opportunities and encouragement to write, write, write: for a variety of purposes and real audiences. Teacher response should include assistance with sentence structure and the mechanics of writing, during both revision and editing (Rosen, 1987).

• Give students plenty of opportunities and encouragement to read, read, read.

• Read aloud to students, choosing at least some selections that have more sophisticated sentence structures than the literature that the students would ordinarily read by themselves.

REFERENCES AND RESOURCES

Braddock, R., Lloyd-Jones, R., & Schoer, L. (1963). *Research in written composition.* Urbana, IL: NCTE.

Calkins, L. M. (1980). When children want to punctuate: Basic skills belong in context. *Language Arts, 57,* 567–573.

Daiker, D. A., Kerek, A., & Morenberg, M. (1990). *The writer's options: Combining to composing* (4th ed.). New York: Harper & Row.

DeBoer, J. J. (1959). Grammar in language teaching. *Elementary English, 36,* 413–421.

DiStefano, P., & Killion, J. (1984). Assessing writing skills through a process approach. *English Education, 16* (4), 203–207.

Elley, W. B. (1991). Acquiring literacy in a second language: The effect of book-based programs. *Language Learning, 41* (3), 375–411.

Elley, W. B., Barham, I. H., Lamb, H., & Wyllie, M. (1976). The role of grammar in a secondary English curriculum. *Research in the Teaching of English, 10,* 5–21.

Encyclopedia of educational research (3rd ed.). (1960). New York: Macmillan.

Harris, R. J. (1962). *An experimental inquiry into the functions and value of formal grammar in the teaching of written English to children aged twelve to fourteen.* Unpublished doctoral dissertation, University of London.

Hillocks, G., Jr. (1986). *Research on written composition: New directions for teaching.* Urbana, IL: NCTE.

Hillocks, G., Jr., & Smith, M. W. (1991). Grammar and usage. In J. Flood, J. M. Jensen, D. Lapp, & J. R. Squire (Eds.), *Handbook of research on teaching the English language arts* (pp. 591–603). New York: Macmillan.

Hunter, S., & Wallace, R. (1995). *The place of grammar in writing instruction: Past, present, future.* Portsmouth, NH: Boynton/Cook.

Killgallon, D. (1987). *Sentence composing: The complete course.* Portsmouth, NH: Boynton/Cook.

Krashen, S. D. (1993). *The power of reading: Insights from the research.* Englewood, CO: Libraries Unlimited.

McQuade, F. (1980, October). Examining a grammar course: The rationale and the result. *English Journal, 69,* 26–30.

Rosen, L. M. (1987). Developing correctness in student writing: Alternatives to the error-hunt. *English Journal, 64,* 62–69.

Strong, W. (1986). *Creative approaches to sentence combining.* Urbana, IL: ERIC and the National Council of Teachers of English.

Weaver, C. (1996). *Teaching grammar in context.* Portsmouth, NH: Boynton/Cook.

Prepared for the Michigan English Language Arts Framework project and © 1995 by Constance Weaver. Issued as a SLATE Starter Sheet by the National Council of Teachers of English (1996). In C. Weaver, L. Gillmeister-Krause, & G. Vento-Zogby, *Creating Support for Effective Literacy Education* (Heinemann, 1996). May be copied.

Facts

On the nature of whole language education

Whole language is a perspective on education that is supported by beliefs about learners and learning, teachers and teaching, language and curriculum. . . . Whole language is not a program, package, set of materials, method, practice, or technique; rather, it is a perspective on language and learning that *leads to the acceptance* of certain strategies, methods, materials, and techniques.—Dorothy Watson, 1989

Background

Whole language is a perspective on education, a philosophy of education, a belief system about education. It is an educational theory grounded in research and practice, and practice grounded in theory and research (to paraphrase Harste, 1989). This perspective or educational theory derives from several kinds of research: research demonstrating the psycholinguistic and social nature of the reading process, research demonstrating how children acquire language and how learning to read and write is similar to learning the basic structures of the language as children learn to talk; and research on how humans learn concepts and ideas. In fact, one way of characterizing whole language is to say that it is a "constructivist" view of learning, with particular emphasis on the development of literacy. Derived from research in cognitive psychology, constructivism asserts that human beings develop concepts through their own intellectual interactions with and actions upon their world. Learners and learning are not passive, but active. Forming concepts about language—oral or written—is easier when learners are presented with whole, natural language, not unnatural language patterns like "Nan can fan Dan," not the vastly simplified language of some primers in basal reading programs, and not the bits and pieces of language found in many workbook exercises and skills programs. Hence the term "whole language."

History, in brief

In the United States, the advent of whole language is often traced to the mid-to-late 1970s, when Kenneth Goodman and others' insights into reading as a psycholinguistic process gained increasing recognition, Yetta Goodman's interest in the development of literacy merged with related lines of research, and Dorothy Watson started a teacher support group called Teachers Applying Whole Language (TAWL). Of course, whole language has roots that are historically deeper and intellectually and geographically broader (K. Goodman, 1992; Edelsky, Altwerger, & Flores, 1991; Y. Goodman, 1989; K. Goodman, 1989; Watson, 1989; K. Goodman & Y. Goodman, 1979). But what we think of today as a whole language theory of learning and teaching did not become widely known in the United States until the late 1980s, or even the early 1990s. In Canada, other leaders emerged during approximately this same time period, among them Judith Newman and David Doake. In New Zealand and Australia, where whole language is known as "natural" learning, the best-known researchers and theoreticians are Don Holdaway and Brian Cambourne, respectively.

Some key characteristics of whole language education

- **Acceptance of learners.** This means, in part, that all learners are accepted regardless of their cultural or socio-economic background or other characteristics or labels. But in whole language classrooms, "acceptance of learners" also means that whole language teachers develop the classroom environment and the curriculum for and with the students, to meet their needs and engage them in learning about what interests them, as well as to cover essentials from the curriculum guidelines.

- **Flexibility within structure.** Instead of having children do one brief activity or worksheet after another, whole language teachers organize the day in larger blocks of time, so that children can engage in meaningful pursuits. **Thus they engage in fewer different tasks, but larger and more satisfying projects.** They may have a readers' and writers' workshop, for instance, when the children read books and perhaps use them as models for their own writing. They may study a theme or topic at least part of the day for several days or weeks, using oral and written language and research skills to pursue learning in the realm of social studies and/or science and math, and using language and the arts to demonstrate and share what they have learned. Together and individually, the students have **many choices** as to what they will do and learn, which enables them to take significant **responsibility** for their learning. However, the teacher guides, supports, and structures the children's learning as needed. Flexibility within the larger time blocks offers the **time** that learners need (especially the less proficient) in order to accomplish something meaningful and significant.

- **Supportive classroom community.** Many whole language teachers help children develop skills for interacting with each other, solving interpersonal conflicts and problems, supporting one another in learning, and taking substantial responsibility for their own behavior and learning.

- **Expectations for success as they engage in "real" reading, writing, and learning.** Kids aren't kept doing "readiness" activities, in preparation for later reading and writing; rather, they are given the support they need to read and write whole texts from the very beginning. Whole language teachers have discovered that virtually *all* children can learn to read and write whole texts. This is true also of children who have heretofore been sent to resource rooms because they had difficulty with skills work. Indeed, reading whole texts is often easier for these children than doing the skills work.

- **Skills taught in context.** Instead of being taught in isolation, skills are taught through minilessons and conferences, in the context of students' reading, writing, and learning. For example: phonics is taught mainly through discussion and activities deriving from texts the children have read and reread with the teacher, and through writing the sounds they hear in words. Spelling is mainly taught when children are editing their writing, and grammar is mainly taught as the teacher helps children revise and edit what they've written. Skills like using the index of a book are taught when students need to locate information on a topic they want to research, while using the yellow pages of a phone book is taught when children need to locate resources within the community. In short, skills are taught while students are engaged in real-life tasks.

- **Teacher support for learning: scaffolding and collaboration.** Teachers provide "scaffolding" for learning in many ways. For instance, primary grade teachers read Big Books and charts to and with children again and again, enabling the children to read whole texts before they can read independently. Whole language teachers help children write the sounds they hear in words, thus enabling the children to communicate through writing. They collaborate with children in carrying out research projects and, in the process, they model and explain how to do things that the children could not yet do alone. By collaborating on projects, children provide similar support for each other.

- **Contextualized assessment that emphasizes individuals' growth as well as their accomplishments.** Assessment is based primarily upon what children are doing from day to day as they read, write, do math and science, research topics of interest, and express their learning in various ways. Comprehensive, "portfolio" assessment will include data not only on the products of children's efforts, but on their learning processes. Whole language teachers commonly involve children in assessing their own work and progress, and in setting future goals for learning. Parents and peers may also be involved in assessment. Individual growth and strengths are emphasized, along with progress in meeting agreed-upon goals and predetermined criteria.

REFERENCES AND RESOURCES

Edelsky, C., Altwerger, B., & Flores, B. (1991). *Whole language: What's the difference?* Portsmouth, NH: Heinemann.

Goodman, K. S. (1989). Whole language research: Foundations and development. *The Elementary School Journal, 90,* 208–221.

Goodman, K. S. (1992). I didn't found whole language. *The Reading Teacher, 46,* 188–199.

Goodman, K. S., & Goodman, Y. M. (1979). Learning to read is natural. In L. B. Resnick & P. A. Weaver (Eds.), *Theory and practice of early reading,* Vol. 1 (pp. 137–154). Hillsdale, NJ: Erlbaum.

Goodman, Y. M. (1989). Roots of the whole-language movement. *The Elementary School Journal, 90,* 113–127.

Harste, J. C. (1989). *New policy guidelines for reading: Connecting research and practice.* Urbana, IL: National Council of Teachers of English.

Watson, D. (1989). Defining and describing whole language. *The Elementary School Journal, 90,* 130–141.

Weaver, C. (1990). *Understanding whole language: From principles to practice.* Portsmouth, NH: Heinemann.

Prepared for the Michigan English Language Arts Framework project and © 1995 by Constance Weaver. In C. Weaver, L. Gillmeister-Krause, & G. Vento-Zogby, *Creating Support for Effective Literacy Education* (Heinemann, 1996). May be copied.

Facts

On myths about whole language education

Is whole language really warm and fuzzy?—Susan Church, 1994

Background

There are many myths and misconceptions about whole language education. Several of these are addressed below, followed by myths about learning and teaching that whole language teachers themselves have rejected.

Myths reconsidered

1. **One of the common myths is that whole language teachers don't teach "the basics."** By this, critics usually mean that whole language teachers don't teach the composite skills that allegedly must precede real reading and real writing. This is not true: whole language teachers *do* teach skills. Equally important, however, is the fact that whole language teachers have a different view of what is truly basic. They believe that authentic reading of trade books and authentic writing of texts for a variety of purposes (notes, letters, stories, reports, etc.) are more "basic" than skills work. **Thus, whole language teachers reject the myth that bits and pieces of language and skills must be taught before children can engage in real reading and writing.**

2. **Given this difference in what whole language teachers consider "basic," it is perhaps not surprising that another common myth is that whole language teachers don't teach "skills"—or at least that they don't teach skills directly.** It is certainly true that whole language teachers don't engage in the typical teach/practice, apply, memorize/test syndrome that characterizes traditional teaching. Instead of teaching skills in isolated lessons, according to a scope and sequence chart or the organization of some workbook, whole language teachers typically help children develop skills in the context of their needs and interests. When they teach minilessons on skills within the context of authentic literacy and learning experiences, they do not test to see if children have learned these skills or strategies; they help the children apply them, watch for signs that the children can apply them independently, and keep helping the children as necessary. **Thus, whole language teachers reject the myth that skills must be taught in isolation from, as well as prior to, real reading and writing. They have relinquished the notion that learning consists of paper-and-pencil mastery of isolated skills and facts.**

3. **Another misconception is that a teacher is "doing" whole language if he or she is using trade books rather than basal readers.** Actually, the critical difference is not whether the children read from basal readers or trade books, though whole language teachers much prefer trade books from which children can choose their own reading. Rather, the critical difference is what the teacher has the students do with the literature. Instead of asking students questions to see if they have understood the reading selection, whole language teachers engage them in discussing their reading—in dialogue journals, for instance, and in literature discussion groups. Meanings are constructed and reconstructed through social discourse and collaboration, which promotes a richer understanding of the text and an ability to consider it more thoughtfully and critically. This, of course, promotes critical thinking. **Thus, whole language teachers reject the myth (implicit in traditional programs) that the best way to foster reading comprehension is to ask questions after a selection has been read—or to require children to write answers to so-called comprehension questions.**

4. **Another common misconception is that whole language teachers don't assess students' learning.** It is true that whole language teachers don't have much confidence in the results of standardized tests, because they are aware that such tests typically lack content and construct validity: they don't reflect the content of classrooms where effective learning is taking place, and they don't adequately reflect the real-world skills that schools are trying to develop. Furthermore, whole language teachers know that the primary purpose of standardized tests is to rank order individuals, and they reject this aim. On the other hand, almost everything that occurs in whole language classrooms may become part of assessment and evaluation. For example, assessment may include recorded observations, student self-evaluations, and various kinds of artifacts, such as periodic performance samples, think-alouds, data from conferences and interviews, inventories and questionnaires, dialogue journals and learning logs, and student-kept records of various kinds. By drawing upon such varied

sources for assessment, teachers can focus on students' growth and learning strengths, instead of trying to expose weaknesses. **Thus whole language teachers reject the myth that standardized tests are an appropriate way to assess students' learning. They reject not only the practice of basing assessment on standardized test scores, but also the practice of assessing students by comparison with one another. And they reject the myth that it is reasonable to expect every learner to learn the same things at the same time.**

5. **Another myth is that whole language teaching is appropriate only for unlabeled students or for gifted students—not for students labeled as learning disabled, Attention Deficit Disordered, or "at risk" of school failure.** In fact, whole language teachers have found that special needs students have their best chance of becoming independent readers, writers, and learners in whole language classrooms. More skills work holds them back; what they need is opportunities to engage in reading and writing whole and meaningful texts, along with their peers. Whole language teachers have found that special needs students flourish when given such opportunities and when given the support they need to become genuine readers and writers. Major keys to success are individual choice, ownership, teacher support, and TIME to change old patterns of dependency and failure. **Thus, whole language teachers have relinquished the myth that some children need skills work *instead of* authentic reading and writing because they have been identified as learning disabled, Special Education, Title I, remedial, or "at risk."**

6. **Another misconception is that whole language students do worse on standardized tests, and that whole language learning and teaching are not supported by comparative research.** Actually, the small but growing body of comparative research shows students in whole language classrooms typically scoring as well or better on standardized tests than students in more traditional classrooms. More generally, this emerging body of research (so far, dealing primarily with preschoolers and children in kindergarten, grade 1, and grade 2) has found that children in whole language classrooms typically show slightly greater gains on reading tests; have developed a greater ability to *use* phonics knowledge effectively; have developed vocabulary, spelling, grammar, and punctuation skills as well as or better than children in more traditional classrooms; are more inclined and able to read for meaning rather than just to identify words; have developed more strategies for dealing with problems in reading; have developed greater facility in writing; have developed a stronger sense of themselves as readers and writers; and have developed greater independence as readers and writers. **Thus, whole language teachers reject the myth that students learn better in traditional classrooms.**

7. **Another major misconception is that anyone can be a whole language teacher simply by going to an inservice or two, replacing basal reading programs with trade books, maybe buying some of the newer instructional materials labeled "whole language," and obtaining from conferences or from fellow teachers some clever ideas for turning skills work into a fun activity.** While some of these tactics may help, they usually are not enough to bring about the shift from the typical transmission concept of education to the transactional, constructivist concept that underlies whole language learning and teaching. Teachers need opportunities to read and discuss professional literature with colleagues, to share teaching ideas and get feedback, to visit others' classrooms, to see demonstrations in their own classrooms by effective whole language teachers, and so forth. Perhaps most of all, they need respect and support for their risk-taking, particularly from administrators. **Making the paradigm shift from traditional to whole language teaching leads whole language teachers to reject the myth that whole language can be successfully mandated by administrators, or successfully accomplished in a short period of time.**

REFERENCES AND RESOURCES

Church, S. M. (1994). Is whole language really warm and fuzzy? *The Reading Teacher, 47,* 362–370.
Newman, J. M., & Church, S. M. (1990). Myths of whole language. *The Reading Teacher, 44,* 20–26.
Weaver, C. (1994). *Reading process and practice: From socio-psycholinguistics to whole language (2nd ed.).* Portsmouth, NH: Heinemann. Chapter 8 was the major source for this fact sheet.

Facts

On phonics in whole language classrooms

The truth is that some attention to the relationships between spelling patterns and their pronunciations is characteristic of all types of reading programs, including whole language. . . . The fact is that all students, regardless of the type of instruction they receive, learn about letter-sound correspondences as part of learning to read.—Steven Stahl, 1992

Background

One myth about education is that whole language teachers do not teach phonics. Not true: they simply teach phonics and phonemic awareness (awareness of the "separate" sounds in words) as children read and write authentic texts, rather than in a separate program or separate lessons. Another myth is that phonics is not learned as readily when it is taught in the context of reading and writing, instead of being taught intensively and systematically. Recent research indicates that this also is untrue. As a former advocate of intensive phonics now notes, "The integrated phonics instruction typical of some whole language first-grade classrooms might work as well as the more structured phonics instruction typical of basal reading programs" (Stahl, McKenna, & Pagnucco, 1994, citing Stahl, 1992); and indeed, "there is little evidence that one form of phonics instruction is strongly superior to another" (Stahl, McKenna, & Pagnucco, 1994) for developing phonics skills and phonemic awareness. Furthermore, recent research suggests that students in whole language classrooms learn and use phonics skills as well as or better than children in more traditional classrooms (summarized in Weaver, 1994). And as McIntyre and Freppon (1995) note, although whole language teachers' instruction in phonics is an integral part of daily classroom interactions, it is not necessarily random or eclectic, "but can be carefully planned and well thought through in whole language."

How whole language teachers help children develop phonics knowledge

Whole language teachers have faith in children as learners. Children can and many will develop a grasp of letter/sound relationships with relatively little direct instruction, just as they learned to talk without direct instruction in the grammar of the English language. Most of the following examples, however, illustrate ways that whole language teachers often use in directly helping children develop phonics knowledge and the ability to use it in reading and writing. Since teacher aides and parents may want to use these procedures too, this list is expressed in the imperative, as ways to help children learn phonics and phonemic awareness.

• Read and reread favorite nursery rhymes to reinforce the sound patterns of the language, and enjoy tongue twisters and other forms of language play together.

• Read aloud to children from Big Books or charts large enough for all the children in the group or class to see the print easily. Run a pointer or your hand or finger under the words, to help children make the association between spoken words and written words.

• Part of the time, choose Big Books and/or make charts of stories, poems, and rhymes that make interesting use of alliteration, rhyme, and onomatopoeia.

• When sharing such Big Books or charts, focus children's attention on the beginnings and ends of words. Research shows (summarized in Adams, 1990) that at first, it is much more difficult for children to hear separate sounds in words than to hear the beginning of a syllable (the "onset") as a unit (s- as in sit, but also spl- as in split) and to hear the vowel plus any following consonants (the "rime") as another unit (-it, as in sit and split). Furthermore, even emergent readers process unfamiliar print words in onset and rime chunks, if they already know a fair number of print words (Moustafa, 1996). Therefore, it is helpful to focus first on elements that alliterate and that rhyme, before focusing on individual sounds. It is especially important not to focus on vowels by themselves, but in combination with any consonants that follow the vowel—what are called "rime" patterns (like -ate, -an, -ast, -est, -ing, -ish, -ight, -ound, -old, -ook).

• When discussing the onsets and/or rimes, it often helps to invite children first to share what they have noticed about the sounds, instead of beginning by telling what you have noticed. Ask questions like "What do you notice about the sounds in this poem?" (Mills, O'Keefe, & Stephens, 1992).

• During the discussion of onsets and/or rimes, you and the children can make charts of words with the same sound pattern. For example, "Galoshes," by Rhoda Bacmeister (*Poems Children Will Sit Still For*, edited by Beatrice deRegnier), invites lists of words beginning with s- and sp- and spl-. Children may also enjoy starting lists of words that end in -ishes and -oshes, and in making up other nonsense words that follow these rime patterns. As children read other poems, additional words can be added to the charts (see Jack Prelutsky's "Spaghetti," for instance, in *Noisy Poems*, edited by Jill Bennett, 1987). These lists can be ongoing, with the children adding words in their own approximate spellings.

• Words from the charts can be put on separate strips of paper or cards, and children can be invited to categorize them in different ways, including "words that begin the same" and "words that end the same." The same procedure can be done with pronounceable word parts: common onsets and rimes. Words constructed from these word parts can be listed and categorized together according to the onset and/or the rime. For example, the onset *st-* could be combined with only three of the rime patterns listed above (to make *state, sting,* and *Stan*), but the simpler onset *s-* could combine with several of them. Children will often notice how other words can be made by varying the pattern slightly (for example, *s-* plus *-ant* makes a word if we add *-a: Santa*). For various ideas, see Powell & Hornsby, 1993; Wagstaff, n.d.

• Read alphabet books with children, and make alphabet books together.

• Read with children other books that emphasize sound (books such as *Noisy Poems*, edited by Jill Bennett; *Deep Down Underground*, by Olivier Dunrea; and Dr. Seuss books). Comment on sounds.

• Help children learn the important reading strategy of predicting, by covering all but the onset of a fairly predictable word in a text (Post-Its can be used for this purpose). Invite children to make predictions and then look at the rest of the word to confirm what it actually is. This usually works especially well with rhyming words at the end of a line of text, particularly if the word mostly covered rhymes with a line before it.

• Talk about letters and sounds as you write messages to children and as you help them compose something together, or individually. This is a very important way of helping children begin to hear individual sounds in words as well as to learn to spell some of the words they write.

• Help children notice print in their environment—signs, labels, and so forth.

• When children demonstrate in their attempts at writing that they realize letters represent sounds, help them individually to write the sounds they hear in words (Freppon & Dahl, 1991). At first, they are likely to write only the first sound of words. Next, they commonly write the first and last sounds (especially when these are consonants). Vowels typically come later (McGee & Richgels, 1990).

• Provide tape recordings of many selections for children to listen to, as they follow along with the written text. It helps to provide small copies of the text, not just a Big Book or chart.

REFERENCES AND RESOURCES

Adams, M. J. (1990). *Beginning to read: Thinking and learning about print.* Cambridge, MA: Harvard University Press.

Freppon, P. A., & Dahl, K. L. (1991). Learning about phonics in a whole language classroom. *Language Arts, 68,* 190–197.

Gunning, R. G. (1995). Word building: A strategic approach to the teaching of phonics. *The Reading Teacher, 48,* 484–488.

Kasten, W. C., & Clarke, B. K. (1989). *Reading/writing readiness for preschool and kindergarten children: A whole language approach.* Sanibel: Florida Educational Research and Development Council, ERIC: ED 312 041.

McGee, L. M., & Richgels, D. J. (1990). *Literacy's beginnings: Supporting young readers and writers.* Needham Heights, MA: Allyn & Bacon.

McIntyre, & Freppon, P. A. (1994). A comparison of children's development of alphabetic knowledge in a skills-based and a whole language classroom. *Research in the Teaching of English, 28,* 391–417.

Mills, H., O'Keefe, T., & Stephens, D. (1992). *Looking closely: Exploring the role of phonics in one whole language classroom.* Urbana, IL: National Council of Teachers of English.

Moustafa, M. (1996). *Reconceptualizing phonics instruction in a balanced approch to reading.* Unpublished manuscript. San Jose, CA: San Jose State University.

Powell, D., & Hornsby, D. (1993). *Learning phonics and spelling in a whole language classroom.* New York: Scholastic.

Richgels, D., Poremba, K., & McGee, L. (1996). Kindergartners talk about print: Phonemic awareness in meaningful contexts. *The Reading Teacher, 49,* 632–641.

Routman, R., & Butler, A. (1995). Why talk about phonics? *School Talk, 1* (2). (National Council of Teachers of English.)

Stahl, S. A. (1992). Saying the "p" word: Nine guidelines for exemplary phonics instruction. *The Reading Teacher, 45,* 618–625.

Stahl, S. A., McKenna, M. C., & Pagnucco, J. R. (1994). The effects of whole-language instruction: An update and a reappraisal. *Educational Psychologist, 29,* 175–185.

Wagstaff, J. (n.d.). *Phonics that work! New strategies for the reading/writing classroom.* New York: Scholastic.

Weaver, C. (1994). *Reading process and practice: From socio-psycholinguistics to whole language* (2nd ed.). Portsmouth, NH: Heinemann.

Facts
On research on whole language education

The claim that hard evidence is lacking on the benefits of whole language methods, such as those used in New Zealand, can be rejected in the light of several surveys and empirical studies.
—John W. A. Smith & Warwick B. Elley, 1995

Background

We hear and read in various places that whole language education is not supported by research. However, that is simply untrue, even though research comparing whole language with other approaches is still in its infancy. In fact, whole language teaching and learning is supported by three different kinds of research: research into the reading and writing processes themselves; naturalistic studies of how children learn to speak their language and to read and write it; and research comparing children's learning in whole language classrooms with other, more traditional classrooms. Research in learning theory and in learning styles also supports whole language education. Here, comparative research is the focus, since that is the kind most widely understood.

Children becoming independent readers, writers, and learners

Not all of the comparative research studies include standardized tests. Though such tests are not very good assessments of children's strengths and needs, the results of studies including such tests along with a variety of other measures are generalized here (Foorman et al., forthcoming, does not meet the latter criterion). A much fuller description of most of these research studies can be found in Weaver, 1994. All the located studies involved children in preschool, kindergarten, grade one, or grade two. Three studies involved two grade levels and one involved three grade levels; three of these were longitudinal studies involving children deemed to be at risk of educational failure. So far, these studies suggest the following conclusions:

- **Children in whole language classrooms typically do as well or better on standardized reading tests and subtests (though the differences are seldom statistically significant).** For example, the whole language kindergartners in Ribowsky's study (1985) scored better on all measures of growth and achievement, including the tests of letter recognition and letter/sound knowledge. In the Kasten and Clarke study (1989), the whole language kindergartners performed significantly better than their counterparts on all subtests of the Metropolitan Readiness Test, including tests of beginning consonant sounds, letter/sound correspondences, and sounds and clusters of sounds in initial and final positions of words. In the Manning, Manning, and Long (1989) study, children in the whole language classroom did better on the Stanford Achievement Test's subtest on word parts, even though only the children in the skills classroom had explicitly studied word parts.

- **Children in whole language classrooms seem to develop greater ability to use phonics knowledge effectively than children in more traditional classrooms where skills are practiced in isolation.** For example, in Freppon's study (1988, 1991), the skills group attempted to sound out words more than twice as often as the others, but the literature-based group was more successful in doing so: a 53% success rate compared with a 32% success rate for the skills group. Apparently the literature-based children were more successful because they made better use of phonics in conjunction with other information and cues. (For another relevant study, see also Cunningham, 1990).

- **Children in whole language classrooms seem to develop vocabulary, spelling, grammar, and punctuation skills as well as or better than children in more traditional classrooms.** For example, see Elley's 1991 summary of studies on learning English as a second language; also Clarke, 1988, on spelling; and Stice and Bertrand, 1990, which included spelling. In addition, see Calkins, 1980; Gunderson and Shapiro, 1988; Smith & Elley, 1995. DiStefano and Killion (1984) is also relevant.

- **Children in whole language classrooms seem more inclined and able to read for meaning rather than just to identify words.** For example, when asked "What makes a good reader?", the children in Stice and Bertrand's study (1990) reported that good readers read a great deal and that they can read any book in the room. The children in the traditional classrooms tended to focus on words and surface correctness; they reported that good readers read big words, they know all the words, and they don't miss any words. In the Manning, Manning, and Long (1989) study, children in the whole language classroom were more likely to read for meaning. They also read with greater comprehension *and* with greater accuracy (not counting the errors that resulted in no meaning loss).

- **Children in whole language classrooms seem to develop more strategies for dealing with problems in reading.** For example, the children in the whole language classrooms in Stice and Bertrand's study (1990) typically described six strategies for dealing with problem words, while the children in traditional classrooms described only three.

• **Children in whole language classrooms seem to develop greater facility in writing.** For example, in the Dahl and Freppon study (1992), a considerably larger proportion of the children in the whole language classrooms were writing sentences and stories by the end of first grade. The children in the whole language classrooms in the Kasten and Clarke study (1989) were similarly much more advanced as writers by the end of their kindergarten year.

• **Children in whole language classrooms seem to develop a stronger sense of themselves as readers and writers.** Take, for example, the Stice and Bertrand study (1990): when asked "Who do you know who is a good reader?", 82% of the kindergartners in the whole language classrooms mentioned themselves, but only 5% of the kindergartners in the traditional classrooms said "me." During the first-grade year, when the children were asked directly "Are you a good reader?", 70% of the whole language children said yes, but only 33% of the traditional children said yes.

• **Children in whole language classrooms also seem to develop greater independence as readers and writers.** In the Dahl and Freppon study (1992), for instance, passivity seemed to be the most frequent coping strategy for learners having difficulty in the skills-based classrooms. But in whole language classrooms, those having difficulty tended to draw upon other learners for support: by saying the phrases and sentences that others could read, by copying what they wrote, and so forth. That is, these less proficient literacy learners still attempted to remain engaged in literacy activities with their peers. They did not just give up.

REFERENCES AND RESOURCES

Calkins, L. M. (1980). When children want to punctuate: Basic skills belong in context. *Language Arts, 57,* 567–73.

Clarke, L. K. (1988). Invented versus traditional spelling in first graders' writings: Effects on learning to spell and read. *Research in the Teaching of English, 22,* 281–309.

Cunningham, A. E. (1990). Explicit versus implicit instruction in phonemic awareness. *Journal of Experimental Child Psychology, 50,* 429–444.

Dahl, K. L., and P. A. Freppon. (1992). *Learning to read and write in inner-city schools: A comparison of children's sense-making in skills-based and whole language classrooms.* Final Report to the Office of Educational Research and Improvement. U.S. Department of Education, Grant Award No. R117E00134. Part of the data described here is reported in an article by Dahl & Freppon that is included in the 1991 *Yearbook of the National Reading Conference* (papers from the 1990 conference).

DiStefano, P., & Killion, J. (1984). Assessing writing skills through a process approach. *English Education, (16)* 4, 203–207.

Elley, W. B. (1991). Acquiring literacy in a second language: The effect of book-based programs. *Language Learning, 41*(3), 375–411.

Foorman, B. R., Francis, D. J., Beeler, T., Winikates, D., & Fletcher, J. M. (Forthcoming). Early intervention for children with reading problems: Study designs and preliminary findings. *Learning Disabilities: A Multi-Disciplinary Journal.*

Freppon, P. (1988). *An investigation of children's concepts of the purpose and nature of reading in different instructional settings.* Unpublished doctoral dissertation, University of Cincinnati, Ohio. This study is reported in a 1991 article by Freppon: Children's concepts of the nature and purpose of reading in different instructional settings. *Journal of Reading Behavior, 23*(2), 139–163.

Gunderson, L., & Shapiro, J. (1988). Whole language instruction: Writing in 1st grade. *The Reading Teacher, 41,* 430–437.

Kasten, W. C., and Clarke, B. K. (1989). *Reading/writing readiness for preschool and kindergarten children: A whole language approach.* Sanibel, Florida: Educational Research and Development Council. ERIC: ED 312 041.

Manning, M., Manning, G., & Long, R. (1989). *Effects of a whole language and a skill-oriented program on the literacy development of inner city primary children.* ERIC: ED 324 642.

Ribowsky, H. (1985). *The effects of a code emphasis approach and a whole language approach upon emergent literacy of kindergarten children.* Alexandria, VA: Educational Document Reproduction Service. ERIC: ED 269 720.

Smith, J. W. A., & Elley, W. B. (1995). *Learning to read in New Zealand.* Katonah, NY: Richard C. Owen.

Stahl, S. A., McKenna, M. C., & Pagnucco, J. R. The effects of whole language instruction: An update and a reappraisal. *Educational Psychologist, 29,* 175–188.

Stephens, D. (1991). *Research on whole language: Support for a new curriculum.* Katonah, NY: Richard C. Owen.

Stice, C. F., & Bertrand, N. P. (1990). *Whole language and the emergent literacy of at-risk children: A two-year comparative study.* Nashville: Center of Excellence: Basic Skills, Tennessee State University. ERIC: ED 324 636.

Tunnell, M. O., & Jacobs, J. S. (1989). Using "real" books: Research findings on literature based reading instruction. *The Reading Teacher, 43,* 470–477.

Weaver, C. (1994). *Reading process and practice: From socio-psycholinguistics to whole language (2nd ed.).* Portsmouth, NH: Heinemann.

Facts

On standardized tests and assessment alternatives

Much of the time and money devoted to testing is misspent. . . . Test scores provide little useful information to help improve instruction and students' learning. In pursuit of higher test scores, the curriculum has been narrowed and "dumbed-down" to match the tests. Children learn less.—FairTest

Background

Every year, America's public schools administer more than 100 million standardized exams. These include readiness tests, to determine if a child is ready for the kindergarten program offered by the school; screening tests, to determine if a child will be labeled as learning disabled or, at the other extreme, as gifted and talented; intelligence tests, which are widely but erroneously thought to measure intellectual ability; and achievement tests, which measure a much narrower range of skills and content than what we really want students to learn. Because of these and other concerns about standardized tests, educators have been developing alternative methods of assessment—methods and measures that more accurately reflect the curriculum and what parents and the public want children to learn, know, and be able to do.

Concerns about standardized tests

The following is only a partial list of concerns that have been raised about standardized tests. While such concerns and criticisms apply particularly to multiple-choice tests, many of these observations apply to other large-scale tests as well:

• The primary purpose of many such tests is to rank-order students, their teachers, and their schools: that is, to guarantee that some will be labeled as successes and others as failures, with the vast majority considered mediocre. This is the main function of **norm-referenced tests**. When the distribution of test scores no longer resembles the bell curve, the tests are renormed—typically about every seven years. Criterion-referenced tests are also used to sort and label students, though they are not particularly designed to do so.

• Standardized tests (especially the multiple-choice variety) give a false impression of objectivity and consequently of equal opportunity and fairness. However, "the only objective part of standardized tests is the scoring, which is done by machine. What items to include on the test, the wording and content of the items, what will count as correct answers, how the test is administered, and the uses of the results are all decisions made by subjective human beings" (FairTest, *K–12 Testing Fact Sheet*).

• Standardized tests are biased in favor of those whose culture and upbringing most closely resemble that of the test makers—typically, white middle-class males who live in metropolitan areas. Or in other words, such tests are typically biased against females, children of color, children from lower socio-economic backgrounds, and children who live in rural areas. Efforts to eliminate such bias have only partially succeeded. Indeed, the very nature of such tests is biased in favor of middle-class students.

• Standardized tests tend to narrow the curriculum to what will be tested. Because teachers are pressured by the demand to produce higher test scores, they often spend a lot of time having students practice items like those that will be on the tests. Indeed, the tests not only determine all too much of the curriculum but may virtually become the curriculum. Such heavy emphasis on testing crowds other, more important learning activities out of the curriculum. Thus, standardized tests tend to discourage effective teaching and engaged, meaningful learning.

• For many young children, standardized tests result in "death at an early age" (Jonathan Kozol's book title)—or at least to a life sentence doing remedial practice and drill in special classes or lower "ability" groups or tracks. That is, scores on such tests result in many children's being given an inferior education that virtually ensures that they will not learn what their more advantaged peers will learn. Because so-called readiness tests are used to assign children to different classes and "ability" groups, they and other screening tests condemn many children to relative failure from the primary years onward.

• Standardized tests tend to focus attention on what students do not know and cannot do, in situations unlike daily life. At the same time, they do not tell us what we really need to know in order to foster individual students' learning.

Alternative methods and means of assessment

Two authentic and widely accepted alternatives to standardized tests are known as "performance assessment" and "portfolio assessment." Performance assessment looks at actual student work produced over time, and—potentially, at least—at the processes by which the students produce such work, both individually and collaboratively. "Portfolio assessment" is similar. The term seems to imply that students' work will be collected in an actual portfolio, though in fact other containers may be more practical and, furthermore, the essence of portfolio assessment lies not in the container but in the concept. Like performance assessment, portfolio assessment focuses on students' products and processes of learning, but also on their growth in other areas, such as their interest in reading and writing, their concept of themselves as readers and writers, and their ability to evaluate their own work and set goals for themselves as learners. In reading, for example, authentic assessment might include many of the following kinds of information (Weaver, 1990):

• Tape-recorded samples of students' oral reading, analyzed to determine what strategies the reader uses effectively and what strategies (if any) the teacher might help the reader develop.

• Tape-recorded samples of a retelling and discussion of some selection(s) they have read, with analysis of the reader's strengths in retelling and discussing, plus recommendations for instruction.

• Tape-recordings of students describing their thinking process as they read both fiction and non-fiction texts, along with the teacher's analysis and recommendations for instruction.

• Notes on individual conferences with the reader, including particularly conferences in which the teacher has focused on teaching a reading strategy or developing a particular reading skill.

• Results of interviews undertaken to determine students' understanding of reading; the strategies they are aware of using to deal with problem words and problems in comprehending texts; their evaluation of themselves as readers and their willingness to read independently; and their goals for themselves as readers.

• Records of students' reading interests and lists of what they have been reading during the year.

• Students' responses to what they are reading: responses through art and drama and literature discussions, for example, and responses written in what are often called literature logs or reading journals. Recorded observations of literature discussions and students' written responses are particularly helpful in assessing change and growth in many of the above areas, as well as growth in understanding literary elements and appreciating and critiquing literature.

To generalize: authentic assessment is derived from what students are doing daily in the classroom. At a minimum, it includes samples of students' work, recorded observations of their learning processes, and students' evaluation of their own processes and products, along with teacher evaluation. While authentic assessment information can be summarized numerically for grading, its primary benefit is that it improves teaching and learning. See the guidelines developed by the International Reading Association and the National Council of Teachers of English (1994).

REFERENCES AND RESOURCES

FairTest. (n.d.). *K–12 testing: Fact sheet*. Based on FairTest's comprehensive study, *Fallout from the testing explosion*, by N. Medina and M. Neill. See also *Implementing performance assessments* and other FairTest publications. Write or call the National Center for Fair and Open Testing, 342 Broadway, Cambridge, MA 02139, (617) 864-4810.
IRA/NCTE Joint Task Force on Assessment. (1994). *Standards for the assessment of reading and writing*. Newark, DE: International Reading Association, and Urbana, IL: National Council of Teachers of English.
National Commission on Testing and Public Policy. (1990). *From gatekeeper to gateway: Transforming testing in America*. Chestnut Hill, MA: Boston College.
Weaver, C. (1990). *Understanding whole language: From principles to practice*. Portsmouth, NH: Heinemann.

Facts On student achievement in our public schools

Test scores of representative samples of American youth probably declined during the 1960s and somewhat into the 1970s but overall have not declined and probably have increased over the last 20 years.
—Rand Institute on Education and Training, 1994

Background

Standardized test scores are inadequate measures of our children's learning, and one reason is that they reflect a student's performance on a limited kind of task, on a particular day, in a stressful time-limited situation. Using standardized test scores to measure our students' learning is like using a still photograph rather than a videotape. But since standardized test scores are commonly used to measure and compare students' "achievement," it is important to examine such scores in order to address the widespread myth that our students are not doing as well as they used to. We need to look deeper than the superficial data usually reported in the media.

SAT scores revisited

Overall, the average SAT scores in 1992 were about 5% lower than in 1960. However:

• About half the decline between 1960 and 1990 reflects changes in who is taking the test—and who isn't. The test is now taken by proportionately fewer students from the top 20% of their graduating class and proportionately more students from the lower 60%. Furthermore, the test is now taken by groups that have traditionally scored lower: minority students, students of lower socioeconomic status, and students for whom English is not their native language. The 1995 SAT scores were higher than they have been in years, but the significance of this is uncertain because of a change in scoring procedures.

• The SAT test today is more difficult than it was in 1975, according to the Educational Testing Service, which develops the test items (Berliner, 1992, citing the 1991 draft of the Sandia report).

Comparing SAT scores "then" and "now" is not a good way to measure the successes of our schools—for these and other reasons, including the fact that SAT scores say nothing about how well our educational system is succeeding with students who have not chosen to take the test (e.g., Robinson & Brandon, 1992).

Other standardized tests

Other kinds of standardized tests include so-called intelligence tests and achievement tests, both of which are commonly norm-referenced. That is, the tests are designed so that the scores of a representative sampling of students taking the test will be distributed on a bell curve. These tests are renormed about every seven years, *to ensure that once again half the students taking the test will be, by definition, below average.* Thus any real gains in students' learning over time will in effect be periodically wiped out. It's like resetting the odometer to 0 again and again, or making the high jump higher and higher.

Taking this re-norming into account, "We can estimate that around eighty-five percent of today's public school students score higher on standardized tests of achievement than their average parent did" (Berliner, 1992). In general, today's generation is doing better on the California Achievement Test (CAT), the Iowa Test of Basic Skills (ITBS), the Stanford Achievement Test (SAT), the Metropolitan Achievement Test (MAT), the Comprehensive Tests of Basic Skills, and the College Board Achievement Tests. Students are also doing better on intelligence tests, which measure school achievement more than native ability (Berliner, 1992; Stedman, 1994).

International comparisons

International comparisons can be made on several factors, but they must be made cautiously because of the various factors involved. For example:

• In 1989, the U.S. had the 4th highest high school completion rate of 20 major countries (NCES, 1992). The U.S.'s college graduation rate is also about double that of most other countries. We spend much more than most nations on higher education, but we are about average among industrialized nations in what we spend on K–12 education (Berliner & Biddle, 1995). Furthermore, in real dollars the per-pupil expenditures were about the same in 1990 as in 1976, for regular education instruction (Sandia, 1993). Despite claims to the contrary, the amount of money spent on instruction itself has a major impact upon the quality of education that students receive and upon their educational attainment (Berliner, 1992; Berliner & Biddle, 1995; Bracey, 1994).

• Typically a much larger percentage of our students have taken the tests on which international comparisons have been made. For example, in the first International Assessment of Educational Progress (IAEP), 75% of U.S. students were compared with the top 9% in Germany, the top 13% in the Netherlands, and the top 45% in Sweden (Rotberg, 1990, as reported in Berliner, 1992).

• Rank orderings of countries can be very misleading. For example, in the first IAEP study of reading, U.S. 9-year-olds finished second in the world among 31 nations, while our 14-year-olds finished eighth. However, the actual scores of the 14-year-olds were almost as close to first place as those of the 9-year-olds (Bracey, 1994).

International comparisons of test scores have not typically presented U.S. students in a favorable light, but national differences need to be reinterpreted in light of factors such as these. Furthermore, when the results of our higher educational system are compared with those of other countries, the U.S. looks very good indeed (Berliner, 1992; Sandia, 1993).

NAEP: Criterion-referenced tests

Standardized tests measure our students against each other, while criterion-referenced tests measure our students against the testmakers' concept of what our students "should" know and be able to do. Over the past three decades, National Assessment of Educational Progress (NAEP) scores have generally been level, or nearly so, in reading, writing, and math. However, high school students have fallen below 1970 levels in civics. Our 12-year-olds' performance in science fell considerably from 1970 to the early 1980s, then rose somewhat until 1990. A breakdown and analysis of the data shows a rather small percentage of our students achieving at the higher levels of proficiency on the NAEP assessments (Stedman, 1994).

The good news: How good is it?

So far, traditional instruction has been the norm for most of the students included in the NAEP data, the vast majority of whom are not achieving high proficiency in the school subjects tested. If indeed the NAEP adequately assesses what students ought to be learning, then schools and teachers may need to adopt more effective ways of fostering students' learning. On the other hand, the good news is that, using the scores on large-scale tests as the measure, the quality of education in our schools has not declined in the last two decades; indeed, scores on a variety of these tests seem generally to have increased (Rand, 1994).

REFERENCES

Berliner, D. C. (1992). *Educational reform in an era of disinformation*. Paper presented at the meeting of the American Association of Colleges for Teacher Education, San Antonio, Texas, February. ERIC: ED 348 710.

Berliner, D. C., & Biddle, B. J. (1995). *The manufactured crisis: Myths, fraud, and the attack on America's public schools*. Reading, MA: Addison-Wesley.

Bracey, G. W. (1994). The fourth Bracey report on the condition of public education. *Phi Delta Kappan, 76*, 115–127. Earlier Bracey reports were printed in the October 1993, 1992, and 1991 issues of the *Phi Delta Kappan*.

National Center for Education Statistics. (1992). *Condition of education 1992*. Washington, DC: U.S. Department of Education.

Rand Institute on Education and Training. (1994). *Student achievement and the changing American family*. Santa Monica, CA: Rand. (For more information, call (310) 451–7002).

Rasell, M. E., & Mishel, L. (1990). *Shortchanging education: How U.S. spending on grades K–12 lags behind other industrialized nations*. Washington, DC: Economic Policy Institute.

Robinson, G., & Brandon, D. (1992). *Perceptions about American education: Are they based on facts?* Arlington, VA: Educational Research Service.

Rotberg, I. (1990). I never promised you first place. *Phi Delta Kappan, 72*, 296–303.

Sandia National Laboratories. (1993). Perspectives on education in America [known as the Sandia Report]. *Journal of Educational Research, 86*, 259–310. A 1991 draft of this report has also been widely circulated and cited.

Stedman, L. C. (1994). The Sandia Report and U.S. achievement: An assessment. *Journal of Educational Research, 87*, 133–146.

Facts

On student achievement in our public schools: SAT scores revisited

This study does not support the view that schools of the 1970s and 1980s have deteriorated in significant ways with respect to the schools of the 1950s and 1960s in their instruction in mathematics and verbal/reading skills. Moreover, it suggests that schools have made significant progress in decreasing inequalities between minority and nonminority students.

—Rand Institute on Education and Training, 1994

Background

For more than a decade, the American public has repeatedly been told that our educational system has declined in the quality of education provided to our children. The 1983 report *A Nation at Risk* was especially influential, followed by other reports that have generated a crisis mentality regarding how much and how well our students are learning. However, some recent analyses of the data have concluded that our schools are doing better than ever before in educating our young people—at least, insofar as we can tell from a thoughtful and probing analysis of standardized test scores.

What about the decline in SAT scores?

Perhaps because Scholastic Aptitude Test (SAT) scores are reported yearly and because they affect the lives of students applying for college, the public has been especially concerned about reported declines in SAT scores. Rarely, however, has the media provided enough information to put this decline into perspective. Consider the following:

• The 1995 SAT scores were higher than they have been in years, but the significance of this is uncertain because of a change in scoring procedures.

• Overall, the average SAT scores were about 5% lower in 1992 than in 1960 (The Sandia Report, 1993). The verbal scores and math scores dropped substantially through the 1970s, then rose significantly by 1985. The average mathematics score rose again slightly by 1992, while the average verbal score first declined and then rose to within one point of the 1980 score (Stedman, 1994).

• About half of the decline between 1960 and 1990 can be attributed to the fact that the test is now taken by proportionately fewer students in the top 20% of their graduating class and proportionately more students in the lower 60%; furthermore, it is taken by more minority students, more students of lower socioeconomic status, and more students who are non-U.S.citizens or who report that English is not their primary language—all factors that correlate with lower test scores across a wide spectrum of measures (Sandia Report, 1993; Stedman, 1994). In other words, about half the decline in test scores reflects changes in who is taking the test—and who isn't.

• The gap in scores between white students and students of color has narrowed in the last twenty years, particularly for African-American students (The Sandia Report, 1993).

• In 1941 when the SAT test was normed, 6.68% of the group scored above 650. The proportion of high scorers has increased 65%, despite the fact that a considerably larger proportion of test takers now come from groups that have consistently scored lower than the elite group on which the test was originally normed (Bracey, 1994).

• Educational Testing Service, which develops the test items for the SAT, has admitted that the SAT today is more difficult than it was in 1975 (Berliner, 1992, citing the 1991 draft of the Sandia Report).

• When students taking the SAT in 1975 are matched with a demographically similar sample from 1990, we see a slight gain in test scores from 1975 to 1990. In other words, students who traditionally have taken the

SAT—relatively advantaged and primarily white youth—show a significant gain in scores since 1975, despite the fact that the test is more difficult.

In summary, the SAT test scores declined about 5% between 1960 and 1992, but since 1975 the scores of the scholastically high-ranking, socioeconomically privileged, and racially white students have risen slightly—despite the fact that the SAT test is significantly more difficult than in 1975. Furthermore, the scores of Asian students have risen to slightly top the scores of white students, the scores of African-American students have risen substantially, and the scores of Mexican-American, Puerto Rican, and American Indian students have also risen somewhat. Overall, the 1995 test scores are the highest they've been in years.

How valid are SAT test scores in determining the successes and failures of our public schools?

Not very. This is partly because the SAT scores have bearing, naturally, only on the achievement of students who have chosen to take the test; these scores do not necessarily say anything about how well our schools are succeeding at educating most of our students. Another reason is that the proportion of students reflecting different groups—different class standings, different ethnic groups, different socioeconomic groups in particular—changes from year to year. Thus, comparing SAT averages across the years is like comparing apples and oranges. Furthermore, these scores reflect achievement in only two areas, mathematics and verbal/reading skills. Perhaps most critical of all, the SAT reflects students' ability to disentangle "verbal conundrums and mathematics puzzlers" in a speed endurance test more than it reflects their general mathematics and verbal/reading ability (see sources cited by Stedman, 1994, p. 137). It is noteworthy that over 240 colleges and universities have dropped the SAT as an admissions requirement.

Assessment experts argue, then, that the SAT decline is not worth worrying about (Bracey, 1994 and earlier reports; Stedman, 1994; Sandia Report, 1993; Berliner, 1992). From the other kinds of measures discussed in these studies, including data from the National Assessment of Educational Progress, intelligence tests and other standardized achievement tests, and College Board Achievement tests, we see that "college-bound students have not lost ground academically" (Stedman, 1994, p. 137). During the greatest decline in the SAT scores, 1967 to 1976, "college-bound students improved their performance in English composition, the three high school sciences (biology, chemistry, and physics), and the two major foreign languages (French and Spanish). In the past decade, there have been increases on all the achievement tests. Scores have risen even as the number taking them has gone up" (Stedman, 1994, p. 137). Furthermore, the scores of non college-bound students have generally risen even more than those of college-bound students (Rand Institute on Education and Training, 1994, p. xxxv). Though standardized test scores are not an especially good indication of the quality of education that students have received, at least the overall comparison between 1975 and the early 1990s is encouraging.

However, these gains in test scores should not be taken to mean that there is no room for improvement; indeed, the National Assessment of Educational Progress scores indicate that relatively few students achieve substantial proficiency in the various subjects assessed, while many still struggle with basic concepts and processes in the disciplines. American education can and should be improved—but at least it is not as unsuccessful as we are often led to believe.

REFERENCES

Berliner, D. C. (1992). *Educational reform in an era of disinformation*. Paper presented at the meeting of the American Association of Colleges for Teacher Education, San Antonio, Texas, February. ERIC: ED 348 710.

Berliner, D. C., & Biddle, B. J. (1995). *The manufactured crisis: Myths, fraud, and the attack on America's public schools*. Reading, MA: Addison-Wesley.

Bracey, G. W. (1994). The fourth Bracey report on the condition of public education. *Phi Delta Kappan, 76*, 115–127. Earlier Bracey reports were printed in the October 1993, 1992, and 1991 issues of the *Phi Delta Kappan*.

Rand Institute on Education and Training. (1994). *Student achievement and the changing American family*. Santa Monica, CA: Rand. (For more information, call (310) 451–7002).

Sandia National Laboratories. (1993). Perspectives on education in America [known as the Sandia Report]. *Journal of Educational Research, 86*, 259–310. A 1991 draft of this report has also been widely circulated and cited.

Stedman, L. C. (1994). The Sandia Report and U.S. achievement: An assessment. *Journal of Educational Research, 87*, 133–146.